CW01514023

The 15 L[a]

of *'Successful'* Property

Investment

The <u>Essential Beginners Guide</u>
to Laying 'Solid Foundations'
for Your Property Business

By David Tarn...

Also by David Tarn

The 123 on Property Investing – The Complete No-nonsense Guide to Becoming a UK Property Investor

Available on Hardback, Paperback, Audible, iTunes & Kindle

A Quick Start Guide to Property Investing: in 9 simple lessons

Available on Paperback, Audible, iTunes & Kindle

This book is dedicated to

Clare; My wife, my rock, my patient and unconditionally loving life partner who, without her emotional intelligence, guidance and complete understanding of my vision, none of this journey would have been possible.

To my wonderful and amazingly unique children Isabel, Elliott, Nathan and Kurtis. I love you so much for who you are individually. Thank you for allowing me the time and space to write this book.

To my Dad for ingraining me with what I believe were the sound and fundamental traits to become the businessman I am today. His many lessons in understanding the value of money, doing things as they ought to be done, and helping me to understand patience, have helped pave my path.

CONTENTS

"Believe nothing you hear and only half of what you see"

Edgar Alan Poe 1809-1849

"Be careful whose advice you buy but be patient with those who supply it. Advice is a form of nostalgia; dispensing it is a way of fishing the past from the disposal, wiping it off, painting over the ugly parts and recycling it for more than it's worth"

Mary Schmich

"Rather than love, than money, than fame... give me truth"

Henry David Thoreau 1817-1862

Preface

It is often said that businesses are not built by extraordinary people but rather by ordinary people doing extraordinary things. This is because creating wealth is not credited to how intelligent you are, the industry you find yourself in or how destined for greatness you are, but instead forged through behaviour.

I owe a considerable debt to the property industry. Individually it has created a lifestyle and helped to generate wealth far beyond what I thought possible. It allows me flexibility in my life to pick and choose what I do and when I do it. Crucially it affords me perhaps the most valuable commodity of all, time.

If I am reflecting on my journey, that is a statement I would love to capture, and for the best part, it is an accurate summary. The property industry has given me all of that and much more. However, no single component can be exclusively responsible for such successes.
I am humble enough to accept that I would most likely be nowhere near where I am today without my decision to invest in property. However, I cannot attribute this solely to property investment because, despite what you are led to believe through the countless and somewhat predictable social media videos, no industry can give you this without a significant number of other contributing factors. Some of which, you might argue, carry far more weight than the specific industry or sector within which you are working.

Property has certainly helped generate the wealth I am accustomed to with its many hidden factors discussed throughout this book, but it is how I have played the game that has brought longevity of success. Undoubtedly things could have been different if not for the careful, strategic and dedicated approach I have applied to my property investment journey.

The sole purpose of this book is to give you a thorough, insightful and crucially honest look at how I was able to build a multimillion-pound business from scratch and how you might be able to do the same if you press pause, adjust some of your thinking and beliefs, and implement the lessons taught throughout this book in your own way and at your own pace.

Honesty is at the forefront of everything I do, whether in a business, social or personal environment. An ethical approach and credible experience-based advice is why this book is so different from the crowd. I write this book to engrave it as part of the solution and to aid with an antidote to the irresponsible dream-selling hype that infects this wonderful industry.

Given that property investment can, over time, significantly improve your life in ways beyond recognition, it is frequently exploited by unqualified 'fake it until you make it' Furus (fake Gurus). This dream-selling preys on your vulnerability by exposing your overwhelming desires for wealth and freedom. This book will help bring balance with sound advice and steady 'back down to earth' observations. It is designed to allow you to make considerations for yourself, aiding a more sustainable approach to your investment business and allowing you to build solid foundations rather than shaky skyscrapers.

Introduction

Today's modern world, driven by technology, allows instantaneous communication. As we advance, location is progressively unimportant. Location merely becomes somewhere to rest your laptop, tablet, or phone.

Being able to secure internet access means you are ready to get to work on your business.

The rules of making money via property investment are the same for the people of the UK as for the people of the USA, Australia and many other developed countries. Although the landscape of the property industry changes rapidly as it continually evolves, and there are, of course, many regulatory differences across the different countries, the principal laws of making money largely remain unchanged regardless of your location on the globe.

Idle time is the devil's playground. Productivity thrives in those who live an action-orientated life, much in the same way as monotony fills the lives of those who allow it to obstruct their freedom.

Understanding the formidable power of compounding and, crucially, how this can reverberate through your life with its, as Darren Hardy coined it, 'ripple effect', is a game-changing formula when deciding which path to take.

Investing your capital via property is a reasonably straightforward process. Specific industry-related knowledge is needed for sure, but anyone can do it, and anyone with existing industry experience can show you how to become a property investor.

That said, not many people understand, and even fewer can effectively articulate how to be genuinely 'successful' within property investment.

This book will demonstrate that the fundamentals for successful property investment are more than that of a basic understanding of a simple model, often misconstrued as strategy; but instead, a far more coherent approach is required if you do, in fact, want to be 'successful' with your investments.

Competition within the property industry is high. The number of property investors living or investing here in the UK varies depending on what you read. The most recent government survey, *'The English Private Landlord Survey, 2018' ®,* concludes that there are over 1.5 million landlords living in England alone. The London agency Ludlow Thompson estimated that in 2020 there were over 2.7 million investors throughout the entirety of the UK. It would be fair to suggest that these figures will have risen significantly throughout the coronavirus pandemic as property prices soared beyond expectation and demand outstripped supply during late 2021 and almost all of 2022.

The government's survey, however, raised an interesting and reassuring conclusion. It highlighted that 45% of landlords own just one property and that a further 38% own between two and four properties. Leaving the remaining 17% to own five or more. When we look at these findings, something strikes me as curious. If property investing is so damn easy, so lucrative, such a sideline thing that requires minimal effort yet yields such riches, why do 83% of the estimated 1.5 million property owners in England alone, that is, over 1.2 million of them, only own between one and four properties?

The answer is patently clear. Although investing your capital in a property can be done with relative ease, becoming a property investor is far more challenging. Furthermore, becoming a 'successful' property investor remains elusive to the masses.

The reason for this is easy for me to convey. Most aspiring property investors tend to jump on the proverbial bandwagon. Believing in the hype, being sold the dream far too easily, and focusing too much on their immediate future rather than their education and long-term vision are common mistakes. Worse, many are used carelessly as pawns to fund another's property journey. The reality of creating the fundamentals of a business plan, applying diagnostics to their current situation, laying down a personalised and coherent strategy, and then applying the correct principles, including adopting patience and concentrated effort, is not what most investors signed up for. This is the exact reason the findings should be reassuring for you. If you create the correct foundations within your business and apply a strategic approach, you can capitalise on other investors' failings. Remember, the cream will inevitably rise to the top.

I stand firm by my statement that investing in a property is easy to practice; however, what is easy to do is often just as easy not to do. Many investors who enter this industry are flawed mainly by their assumption that the business of property investment needs little respect, that it is a simple process that prints money as its byproduct as if the two were intrinsically linked somehow. I hasten to estimate that around 95% of the aspiring investors who entered this industry on this false premise will testify that this is, in fact, entirely wrong. Moreover, the worrying reality is that they will usually only arrive at this conclusion once they have spent tens of thousands of pounds of their hard-earned capital.

The good news for those of you who want to understand the truth about property investing, for those who are willing and able to block out the hype, who can concentrate on their own journey, and are prepared to do what's required to succeed within this industry, is that this book will help guide you. Likewise, this book will help you with 'the how', something often neglected in 'success' type self-help books, particularly ones surrounding property.

The principles and considerations taught in this book can be applied universally throughout the industry, but in fact, they are not mutually exclusive to property investing. They can intersect to be employed in most businesses generally. Any business that ingrains these relevant fundamentals to its core is sure to thrive as a result.

Terms such as exponential growth, leverage, compounding, assets, liabilities, due diligence, strategy, communication, service, cashflow, return on investment (ROI), projection, analysis, negotiation, profit, focus and patience are among the most commonly used terms in business regardless of respective fields. Property investing is no different.

To truly thrive as a property investor, you will need to understand these terms more explicitly and relate them to the property industry and, more overtly, to the country where you will invest. But grasping the fundamentals of business will not only elevate your success beyond bricks and mortar but will exponentially increase your growth in terms of size, speed, and diversity within the industry.

As you continue through this book, it will become clear that understanding the basic principles of your business is far more valuable than understanding the specifics of the property industry. Fortunately, I teach both. To be clear, I am in no way lessening the importance of understanding the individual elements of property investment but instead observing that they are, in many cases, secondary elements. I argue that there is a bigger picture to observe and that understanding this principle will promote you further than the 'average' property investor.

It is essential to understand that property investment is fundamentally a business, and like any other business, you must adopt and implement the correct principles appropriately if you are to be successful.

It would be reasonable to suggest that there will be a far greater number of investors who struggle with their portfolios due to their inability to understand and run a business successfully than there will be those who understand the fundamentals of running a business but struggle with their portfolio. Essentially, your overall success and, crucially, the long-term ease of your portfolio is effectively down to which you choose to leverage, business and property knowledge or just property knowledge.

If you comprehend, embrace, and employ the principal lessons taught within this book which are established practices for any successfully run business, you will stand a far greater chance of being successful with your own business, property or otherwise.

Throughout this book, you will hear references from material that have assisted me in gaining what is now a firm yet continually improving appreciation of business academia. I believe these references will help you further understand the enigma of business too. These books, which created proven principles, have bought me a great deal of inspiration, guidance and success over the years. Loosely used and unified along with my own applications and experiences, they form the primary content of this book.

There really is nothing new in what I will discuss over the course of this book. Almost every concept, law or other has been previously discovered, applied and written about. If you learn anything from this book, there is a good chance that it is because I have written something I have learned by reading, listening or applying and then growing from someone else's teachings. This book's power is no more than collating these teachings with what I have learned independently and then relating it to a property investing journey for your convenience.

Similarly to my first book, *'The 123 on Property Investing'*, I intend to walk you through a systematic process from concept to creation, then follow through to application. This approach will allow you to develop the initial concepts, footings, and foundations, which will springboard you into developing as a businessperson or astute property investor in your own right. However, unlike my first book, I intend to focus more on the business side of your property investment journey since profoundly understanding this element is what I feel is needed to achieve real success within this industry.

Explaining the industry in depth whilst demonstrating mathematics and detailing examples will allow you to decide what investment model is suitable for you as an individual. There will be no bias towards any given aspect of property investment, and like it or not, there will be no active encouragement to become a property investor.
The decision to invest your time and capital into property investment is fundamentally your own. It should be based on understanding the truth

and reality of the industry after hearing all the facts and ultimately assessing your position or competence to proceed to the desired level.

I intend to give you the tools to develop solid foundations for yourself since individualism is paramount and perhaps the most necessary factor to your success. The application of what is taught throughout this book lies with you, and this application will always be your most difficult challenge. Just like with everything we do in life, however, the things that come the hardest are the most valuable to us. You should embrace your journey, do not fear it, but rather understand that it will have many challenges. It is how you progress through these challenges which will define you and your business.

"It is a grand thing to rise in the world; the ambition to do so is the very salt of the earth; it is the parent of all enterprise and the cause of all improvement"

Anthony Trollope 1815-1882

I write this book owning and profiting from significant property portfolios. I achieved and surpassed my version of success some years ago. I can now continue to grow these portfolios exponentially without any necessary input. I have no agenda with this book except that of solid education. Although semi-active in education, I have no desire or need to lead you down the proverbial path to further my business interests. As you advance through this book, it will become evident that I have your best interest at heart in everything I detail. My chief aim is to help as many of you succeed with what you want to achieve from your property investment journey.

If you have the patience and dedication to create strong enough foundations, then property investing can help you build whatever future you desire; that is a guarantee.

I want to thank you from the very bottom of my heart for choosing to read the book I have pugnaciously laboured on for the past 12 months, and I 'genuinely' hope it is of great use to you.

David Tarn...

Before we get on with the real reason you are reading this book, I want to answer a few of your initial questions. Principally who am I? What qualifies me to write this book? And how is it so different that it will allow you to pause your continuous self-help journey and apply the lessons within?

Who I am?

Firstly, being a humble, average Joe with pretty much zero ego, *especially after reading and applying the principal lessons from Ryan Holidays' incredible book, 'Ego is the Enemy',* this is the hardest part of the book to write. However, for the sake of edification, here we go.

Effectively, I imagine I am very much like you in many ways. I have, or instead, at one point, at the start of my journey, had the same fears, overwhelming confusion and confidence issues we all have when we start with something new and entirely foreign. Especially something that we do not fully understand or have little experience with. Trust me when I tell you that I have no hidden or unique talents, I was never destined to be a success story, and I am certainly not a product of fate or destiny. All the *'what-ifs', 'that can't happen to me',* and *'am I doing the right thing'* doubts coursed through my veins many years ago just like they will likely course through yours now. These doubts almost prevented me from starting my journey in the same way they will prevent many of you from taking tangible action.

What separates me from some others is not that I have masses of drive, determination, no problem with hard work and a burning desire for wealth and success. I am sure there are many of you reading this book that will undoubtedly equal me on that. The difference is that I have discovered a balance between being patient and taking definitive action.

I think carefully; I talk through my intentions, analyse the situation, plan, or formulate a strategy, and then crucially, I always walk the line I have chosen. These two valuable assets of patience and action have been engrained in me from an early age. This is the main difference, perhaps, in some cases, the only difference between you and me. However, it may be that this is the only difference that matters in some cases, and that is why this book will be the book that helps you become who it is you want to be because, with the words that follow in this book, I intend to ingrain the essential messages and strategies needed to help you fully understand what is required to develop your skills so that you can start on your path to achieving your vision of success.

I am, at the time of editing for release, 42 years of age. I am one of the many people proclaiming to be the proudest Dad on this Earth. I am the husband of an amazingly supportive and incredibly patient wife and the guy who still gets overly excited around the Christmas holidays. My main hobbies include mountain biking or snowboarding as fast as I can down any given mountain. I have a deep-rooted passion for cooking and developing my physical and mental strength. I am genuinely obsessed but very grounded with personal development regarding fitness, well-being, the body, science, general education, psychology, philosophy, and the passing on of knowledge in any way, shape, or form. The latter of which, I feel, is an obligatory feature of humanity, one which has enabled us to reach the remarkable heights we have as a species. I am never without music playing on my various devices, regardless of my environment. I attempt to play the guitar, drums and piano, the latter of which I merely fumble my way around with unremitting disaster, and I am lucky enough to say that I love the industry I work in.

I do owe considerable debt to the property investment industry for what it has given me over the past seventeen years. It has enabled me to live my life on my own terms. It allows me to choose how I live and not settle for the life I was dealt with or potentially destined for, given my less-than-average successes at school and college, the latter of which was never complete. The property industry provided an opportunity for an average, dyslexic gas engineer to become free from constraint, both financially and time-bound. And all it has asked in return was that I showed it the respect it deserves and applied my ambition continually through positive, action-oriented steps.

For the time being, that is all you need to know about who I am as a person. The rest of me, my personality, ethics and intentions, will become apparent as you continue through this book.

What qualifies me to write a book like this?

Back In 2006, having one buy-to-let property to my name, I decided to investigate how property investing could serve as a tool to help me exit the gas industry. Over the next two years, I made it my mission to engulf myself in all the readily available information surrounding property investment and attend a few somewhat outdated training courses. Over the following 18 months, I successfully purchased six properties with careful planning and implementation through the following avenues: Two JV or 'Joint Venture' properties with one of my then friends and now business partners. One JV with a family member and the remaining three were sole acquisitions from profits accrued via my gas engineering business.

These initial investments were the foundation of what is today an incredibly successful and profitable property business. The reason for this brief trip down memory lane is to highlight a critical point at the start of my journey. In 2006 and 2007, we were almost at the peak of the housing boom. This is where I bought six of my first properties. Just as a credit crisis began unfolding in 2007, followed by the global financial crash in early 2008. This means, and this is a crucial point, I have not had the luxury or benefit of any significant 'property boom' to propel my business forward exponentially. I have had to do this myself, without any fortuitous external help. The past 12 months have been the exception, with a small but measurable property boom helping increase the equity within my portfolio. Nothing like the boom in the early noughties and nothing I have needed or taken any real advantage of. Indeed, nothing to elevate my business beyond its current status.

Some authors, gurus and self-proclaimed property experts display their successes in a way that suggests they have been stern businesspeople who have sought out weaknesses in their approach, leaving them to benefit significantly from their actions. However, in some cases, they simply benefited from a property boom, facilitating their growth from a mediocre property business to a sizable portfolio by allowing them to release equity to fund the growth since longevity or, in some cases, timing is their real secret.

Of course, one might argue they showed courage and have unquestionably applied action to capitalise on the fortuitous situation they found themselves in. I am by no means taking anything away from these proactive investors. Instead, I am merely indicating that this is not how my business has grown exponentially over the past seventeen years. What I have achieved throughout my journey is the result of many years of applying the necessary traits to succeed in business. Adopting the essential principles needed to build a solid foundation ready for the inevitable future growth has enabled my business to grow organically to the point where I find it now. I have embedded myself deep into everything I have done to help achieve my success. I have learned to mould the mistakes, continually applying these lessons to mitigate future challenges. I have continued to be progressive in embracing and adapting to the industry's ever-changing trends, but crucially I have implemented the basic principles of making money. This practice of coherent application helps to reduce the element of luck, which is something we all need in business.

The success achieved through the tangible proof of my strategy, which has allowed me to integrate from one industry to another and far surpass what my vision of success was, would alone qualify me to write about my experiences, offering advice or opinion as I see it. However, in addition to this, I spend the best part of my daily life talking with other experienced and inexperienced investors about their successes, difficulties, challenges, and ambitions. The result is a first-hand understanding of what issues they collectively face with their individual journeys, and there are common themes repeatedly running through everyone I meet or speak with.

This book is partly compiled from meeting, speaking, and observing these aspiring and existing investors over the past 5-10 years.

Their struggles and fears are something I shared back in 2006 but subsequently managed to overcome to help me achieve my version of success.

Further to these overt qualifiers, I am also the author of *'The 123 on Property Investing'*, a hugely successful property investment book found on Amazon, Audible & iTunes. This debut book was released initially on paperback in 2017, but since its release in 2019, it has risen to become the 'second' bestselling property investment book on the Audible platform. Damn you, Rob Dix. Incidentally, Rob's books are other 'must-read' books and an excellent source of responsible education for your repertoire.

Over the last ten years, I have gained the relevant experience needed to teach others how I was able to integrate from a small-town gas engineer to become one of the country's leading full-time professional property investors. I have an extensive and diverse portfolio consisting of single-let properties, both turnkey and refurbishment projects, that I hold in a personal portfolio with my wife. I am the director of two independent SPVs or 'special purpose vehicle' limited companies, both of which invest heavily in property. One similarly invests in single-lets but independently from the avenue mentioned above, and the other predominantly in more significant yielding properties, principally HMOs or houses of multiple occupation, as well as small commercial buildings and some standard 'circumstantial' single-lets properties too.

My portfolio comprises all types of properties, from one-bedroom bungalows, two-bedroom townhouses, three-bedroom terrace and semi-detached houses, and four-bedroom detached houses. I have multiple houses where I have multiple houses within that street, houses next door to each other, and HMOs next door to each other. I have multiple numbers, ones, two's, three's, four, and five's; in fact, I have over 30 houses numbered 1-10 alone. My portfolio has been ever-increasing at the rate of about 10-15 properties per year for the last few years and between 5-10 in previous years.

I have bought, refurbished, and sold countless houses during my time as an investor. No doubt you will already be aware that this is called flipping. I have been involved in either wholly or partly refurbishing over two hundred and counting properties for myself and my clients by implementing the BRR model, which is Buy Refurbish and Refinance and will be discussed in greater depth later in Chapter 10 Market Entry.

In 2012 I started a lettings and management business, 'WiseOwl Property', which has since grown to manage hundreds of tenancies for our clients and, of course, my own portfolios collectively. This business is run effectively on a skeleton staff basis since developing productive and efficient systems as well as clever leveraging has been my primary focus.

Further to the investment portfolios, lettings business and property investment books, I run a 'business and property' coaching and mentoring service. I still love to work; I still have a passion and drive that gets me to the office almost daily. Nothing brings me more pleasure than helping others achieve their visions. That said, please do not allow the mention of my training and mentorship business to distract you from this book's content, its principal points, and the gravity of the topics within. The mention of this arm of my business would not have been included if I did not believe it was important enough to mention it at this point since it gives sizable weight to my credibility or qualification to write a book like this.

Finally, I would like to include, for no other reason but to add further strength to my credentials, that by the age of 37, property investment had genuinely made me a millionaire, and by the time I hit 40, I was a multimillionaire in terms of my net worth. It is safe to say I am adequately qualified to demonstrate the ins and outs of the property investment industry.

How this book will help you and why it will make you sit up, apply yourself and <u>take action</u>

Over the past 15 years, I have read many books aimed at business owners and property investors alike. In the earlier days, these were a valuable source of education and enlightenment, then used as development on my journey and then as research for my own material later on. Some of these books are a fantastic asset to your property education; I have already mentioned the books by Rob Dix, which particularly spring to mind here. Some books make excellent points and are filled with tips, as in the books that Rob Moore and Simon Zutshi have written. Then some, as you can imagine, are mere drivel. You will discover some of these for yourself during your research. Remember to keep an open mind and always be conscious of ulterior motives when something sounds too good to be true or gets you so psyched about what lies ahead that you cannot sleep.

Often the thing lacking from even the best books we read is the psychological element behind what we want to achieve. The common theme behind many books seemingly centres around convincing you that the property industry is one that you need to be part of and then setting you off on a journey that generally follows a one size fits all model or, as they incorrectly call it, strategy. Many of these books funnel you to an investment model that has succeeded for the author but inevitably will not fit your needs since it was either market, capital or time-dependent. These books give you a broad description of a particular aspect of the industry's workings but need more clarity for progression and need to be more helpful with what to do as a next step.

This is not a criticism but instead an observation. These books can be hugely beneficial with cultivation since understanding the finer workings of an area within an industry before you take the plunge can be pivotal in your success. It will help you gauge if that part of the industry is right for you. However, this approach only covers one aspect of what it takes to become a property investor. Over recent years, my research has concluded that having a basic understanding of this industry's fundamental 'ins and outs' is not enough to get over 75% of you started with property investment. It serves even less as a tool to help you succeed and, in some cases, can often muddy the water to confuse or overwhelm you to the point of inaction.

Do you really need another book, blog, YouTube video or Facebook post convincing you to become a property investor? Again, that decision should be for you to consider and determine for yourself after conducting thorough research based on gathering information from credible sources. A genuinely educational book with a more concise and methodical approach to becoming a property investor and, more specifically, a successful property investor is what is missing from the market right now.

Unlike other how-to books, my previous book included, I will cover more than the industry's fundamentals. I intend to pull back the curtain on the stages leading up to understanding the industry's initial workings. I will help shed light on what you as the individual need to do to prepare yourself for your property investment business and, ultimately, its long-term success. In essence, this is the big, more mature brother to my '123 book'.

I genuinely believe that anyone who adopts the principles within this book will succeed as a byproduct. If you use this book in its intended way as a guide. If you apply what is taught during the following pages rather than merely reading the book and then moving on to the next one, you have the tools at your disposal to begin successfully building your own property business; that is my guarantee.

This book is designed for those who are serious about achievement. The book should be read or listened to in an environment where you can give it your full attention. It should be completed, and judgement should not be passed until done; many of the ideas and rules are explained later in the book in greater depth to ensure you fully understand their origin. At first, some chapters may seem irrelevant to what you want from a property investment book. But you must trust the process and understand that giving you some basic property-specific teachings will not help you with the success of your business. For those who are using this book to plug the gap between one self-help book and the next, it will not have as much value, which is discussed throughout the book. The lessons in this book need to be applied if you are to achieve your version of success. It is not enough to only hear the lessons spoken. Hearing is involuntary, accidental, and effortless. Nor is it enough to listen to the lessons. Although voluntary, focused, and intentional, listening will not create anything tangible. You must apply the lessons, and if this means you need to press pause on your serial, self-help journey, then so be it. Get off the treadmill; you are ready to run the marathon.

So, before we begin, let me ask you two questions: where are you now, reading or listening to this book? And are you prepared for the lightbulb moments, the parts of the book that bring clarity, inspiration and the highest resonating value?
Simply put, are you somewhere quiet, and do you have a pen and paper, a highlighter pen, or are you familiar with Audibles' clip & bookmark' function? If you are genuinely prepared, let's get going. If not, stop and get prepared; this is your future; treat it with the utmost respect, and you will yield the many dividends.

I encourage you to take notes while reading or listening to this book. Highlighting specific parts of the book is a must for review. This will be more challenging for those who have opted for the audio version. Therefore, my web development team have created a resource page on our website that will demonstrate all the workings and mathematics, as well as any charts or miscellaneous elements that need visual representation or further elaboration. All books, resources and studies mentioned throughout are added with appropriate links.

Furthermore, helpful guides and notes on what to do next should you want to continue your research. Anything mentioned in the book that requires you as the individual to carry out more research will be summarised on this page too. This way, you do not need to and will not be actively encouraged to buy this book's 'paper' or 'hard back' copy. If you have been kind enough to purchase the audio version, this choice will not limit you. For those reading the paperback or hardback version, this webpage will be extremely useful to you, too, since it encompasses a plethora of additional research, as well as useful spreadsheets and tools.

To avoid the constant bombardment of 'head over to my website' and the subsequent inevitable negative reviews, however, I will supply the link to this page and all other relevant information at the very end of this book. Anything included on this resource page will have a small ® next to it for the readers, and for the audible audience, I will ask my narrator to quote the word resource each time something appears. This will give you a general idea of what is included on the free resource page and remove the need for me to mention the web address repeatedly.

The caveat

I am somewhat anxious about repetition from my first book, so I will consciously try to avoid this where I can. However, please understand that we are discussing the same topic from the same point in your journey. This means that there may be some aspects of the book that draw parallels. I believe there is enough difference between the two books for this not to be an issue. Still, please recognise that repetition is not lazy writing but a necessity for your education. The primary difference between my two books is that The 123 on Property Investing is far more what some readers would deem property specific, whereas this book is more business specific. The 123 will give you great insight into the property industry, but this book is the book that will help you create the property business. Both books will be beneficial for your education and should be considered to help with your education.

I must stress that I am not a financial advisor and that anything mentioned in this book requires further investigation. Nothing I cite should be deemed as gospel. This book is made up of some principles. The rest, as Mary Schmich states, is advice based on my own meandering experience.

Once again, I sincerely hope you enjoy this book, and I am genuinely humbled that you have chosen to start or continue your education with me. Let us begin.

Laying Your Foundations

"You can't build a great building on a weak foundation. You must have a solid foundation if you're going to have a strong superstructure. It is not the beauty of a building you should look at; it's the construction of the foundation that will stand the test of time"

Gordon B. Hinckley - 1910-2008

Getting started is always the most challenging part, regardless of how many books you read, the courses you attend, or the support you seek. This is the point when you fear the most about what might become. You feel alone, confused, and often worried or scared. Your knowledge is limited, and application is non-existent. You seek that giant leap forward, the one that will carry you to the destination you desire, yet you ignore the small steps that, as you see them, do not hold any intrinsic value. This is an inherent problem, and where many fail before they begin. Momentum is the key to growth, not giant leaps. These smaller action-oriented steps are what, when combined, create our giant leaps forward. No one heads into this industry equipped for the challenges ahead. Even if you are an experienced and successful businessperson, property investment has many different challenges.

Knowing where to start can be the most confusing part of your journey. However, if we can break this self-imposed macro event into micro components, we can begin to clarify the water. I have developed the following 15-part plan based on my laws of property investing to help you in a step-by-step fashion understand the journey as well as to process what you need to understand about the property industry. The following chapters will enable your journey to gain some of that missing momentum as you begin to take each law further. Working through this plan and answering or implementing each point will provide you with a comprehensive 'to-do' list while increasing your education, reducing your overwhelm, and helping to increase your confidence and clarity.

It is essential that you complete the plan in full, giving each part equal regard and seeking guidance and help with any part of the plan that you do not feel adequately equipped to answer. One might consider these tasks the most important. These are the ones that will raise your confidence as you seek the answers you need to progress through the remainder of the book. I might add that the book has no specific ordering in a 'do not pass go' until you've completed this task type order but rather something as an outline to complete in full.

Perhaps the best reason for concentrating on the foundations of your property business is clarity. If you take the necessary time to fully understand what you are building and, more crucially, at the time you are building it, then there is a greater chance that things will unfold as you intend. Should you not fully understand how return on investment (ROI) works, for example, how would you expect to make your capital work for you? Remember, we are not only talking about the calculations of your ROI. You need to understand the principle of why in addition to how you calculate your ROI. For example, understanding how different models yield different results will elevate you from using the calculation in a somewhat arbitrary manner to a more measured application, in turn yielding greater returns for you and your business.

Foundations are the very building blocks of your business; they allow you the stability to grow taller at the correct pace for you and your portfolio. Ensuring we set solid foundations will prevent a potential catastrophe later in your journey. Remember, cracks do not appear immediately. They take time to manifest. Cracks appear when we have rushed processes that we do not fully understand. There is no substitute for education. Experience will come as you progress, as will the property knowledge specific to your business and its models, but your education needs to be established correctly to create your foundations.

Over the years, I have met many investors who seemed to be progressing far faster than I could fathom, only to find out several years later that they were no longer property investors. They exited the industry, sold up or worse. This is because, regardless of your approach, you will likely succeed in the early stages of your journey, often offering false security as you grow. Still, unless your foundations are set solid, cracks will inevitably appear until we potentially have a house of cards scenario.

I do not offer this opinion to worry you but rather for opposing reasons. Understanding this fact should bring comfort, not concern. We have all heard horror stories and read the newspapers projecting doom. Understanding that there is a common denominator between this brings us solace. Let me be blunt; people fail, not the industry. This industry will never fail you; you will fail it if you do not offer it respect. Almost every horror story you read will have an ill-prepared protagonist at its core. Just because you can, it does not mean you should. To be truly successful within the property industry, you must be a particular person. If you are not that person, you will face more significant challenges unless you become that person. Of course, I am not suggesting there is only one type of person that will be successful and should you not become it, you will fail. That would be a ridiculous notion. However, I am saying that unless you take time to lay your foundations, the challenges you face as you progress will be far more significant than if you did.

By taking time to set your foundations, you are increasing your chances of success simply because you will understand the industry on a deeper level. This deeper understanding will allow you to assess opportunities and risks as and when they arise. You will be able to spot a bum deal over a fantastic opportunity. You can calculate returns better, calculate investment areas, understand renting potential, and avoid the sharks and the money pits. All because you applied the correct footing to your business.

"May your hands always be busy, may your feet always be swift. May you have a strong foundation when the winds of change shift"

Audra Mae

The 15 Laws of Property Investment

Establishing the Correct Foundations for Your Property Business

1 Time

"We all think we have time, you know. It's this miracle substance, and there seems to be so much of it, and then all of a sudden, it's gone"

Eloisa James

The five most dangerous words any new investor can mutter to the question of how much time you have to spend on your property business is "as much as it needs". In most cases, this is an answer smeared in delusion. Time is perhaps the greatest commodity of all. It is time that we all crave to have more of. If the answer as much as it needs is, in fact, true, I will return with the question, "so why are you investing"? Perhaps the most common answer to this question is "for freedom".
But indeed, one has all the freedom they desire if they have as much time as it needs.

Time is something we can rarely alter or fabricate more of. For the best part, our lives are governed by the sheer lack of this precious resource. Correctly assessing your available time constraints is one of the first and, in terms of realistic achievement, one of the most important things you should calculate in the early stages of your development. Realistic achievement means understanding what boundaries or limitations are in your current life to help you determine what is possible with the time left. Calculating your available time will help you be efficient as you continue to identify your next steps.

As with any business, property investment has a time versus reward balance ®. The more time we can afford for our development, the better chance of success we have. Moreover, efficiency will prevail as we begin to realise what models we can and crucially cannot take advantage of with our current, and I stress current, availability.

Wanting to invest using other people's money (OPM), implementing the buy refurbish and refinance (BRR) model to turn a commercial building into a twelve En-suite bedroom, house of multiple occupation (HMO) when you only have three to four hours each week to work on your property business may, at least in the early days, be a stretch too far for most of you. Assessing what is realistic with our available time can save us hours of frustration. However, a secondary, far more damming element in overestimating our available time is what it can do to our mindset.

Incorrectly assessing our availability of time and allocating 30 hours per week to work on our property business, only to carry out ten of those hours, will negatively affect your mindset to the point where the entire business will feel like an uphill struggle. This struggle compounds further since you are most likely still in the learning stage of your journey, meaning your efficiency and direction will be somewhere from where it needs to be. If we couple this with the larger portion of the population's inability to avoid procrastination, we have a recipe for inaction. Since you have 30 hours each week, you have plenty of time later to get to the finer details later, right?

I have seen the outcome countless times before. Feelings of failing, frustration, and overwhelm when reality kicks in. The words "I am not progressing as fast as I thought I would" ring true. That is why the first question I ask after hearing this frustration is my question of time. In 99% of cases, the solution is a simple reassessment of your time.

In opposition, if we accurately assess our time, we see the need for efficiency. We see the need to plan and strategise, often highlighting the need to increase our education in specific areas of interest. Should we have calculated enough to allocate the more realistic ten hours each week to our property business, we know that we may need to understand how precisely we will fill this time in a productive and growth-minded way. This links back to our mindset but for the right reasons this time since achieving this more moderate allocation gives us satisfaction and feelings of progress, especially when we have been more productive with our planning and avoiding the dreaded procrastination. ®

To be clear, I am not saying that ten hours should be your benchmark, nor that 30 hours is overreaching or unrealistic. The hours given in the example are purely there to demonstrate different ends of the spectrum and to highlight my point. In short, being realistic in assessing the time you have available to work on your property business means we can assess what is achievable in that given time. We must remain realistic at the beginning of our journey, but above all else, as you will see later in the book, we need to maintain a healthy mindset.

I can sense your question looming. How many hours do you need to work on your property business each week? Unfortunately, the answer to this question is not so straightforward that I can merely quantify the hours needed to build your portfolio. The answer to the question is simple. However, it may not be the answer you seek. It would help if you used as many of your accurately assessed hours as you can or that you need to achieve your vision or at least to get you on the right course to achieving your vision. Of course, before you can allocate these hours, you need to understand your vision, and we will get to that later in chapter 6 of the 15 laws.

"The best-laid plans of mice and men often go awry"

Robert Burns 1759-1796

Around 16 years ago, my wife and I attended our first anti-natal class, and as part of that class, we were asked to draw a circle representing a 24-hour clock. What followed was the required allocation of sleep, work and any other mandatory element within our life to that clock. We were then asked to add our hobbies, free time and other interests until most of our clock was occupied with one event or another. The sobering question was, given that a child will take up so much of our time, what will we have to give up to ensure our responsibilities are met? At the time, my arrogance helped me block out this reality. A pointless exercise indeed since we would make whatever time was needed. The reality is a little different for anyone who has ever experienced parenthood for the first time will testify. In actual fact, a parallel to my foundations' example can be drawn here because, at first, you tend to manage quite well, in my experience. Of course, it takes almost all of your available time, but this is managed since it is a new exciting experience. Once the monotony of life and, dare I say it, the experience grabs hold of you, however, the cracks in your preparation begin to appear, much like in my example above.

Time forms part of the 'big three' for property investors; therefore, it needs careful assessment and a firm understanding of how much of it you have available to concentrate on your business ®. Remember, life has a habit of getting in the way of your plans.

"Most people overestimate what they can do in one year and underestimate what they can do in ten years"

Bill Gates

2 Education

"One hour per day of study in your chosen field is all it takes. One hour per day of study will put you at the top of your field within three years. Within five years, you'll be a national authority. In seven years, you can be one of the best people in the world at what you do."

Earl Nightingale 1921-1989

Unlike time education is something we have complete control over. This is not a limited commodity. The human brain is capable of absorbing far more than we could ever offer it during our fleeting lifetime; when it comes to our education, our destiny truly lies within our own hands.

One hour of application or study will most likely leave you a long way off from becoming the top property investor in the country. But what Earl Nightingale was referring to with that quote was the power of compounding with your education through consistent effort. Not dipping your toe in once in a while and expecting results. This is now how we use compounding to build a business. If we want tangible results, little and often far outweighs a sporadic approach. We will discuss compounding later in Chapter 4, Understanding Why.

First, let me ask you a question. How many of the following characteristics do you hold right now?

You fear what could happen if you don't invest wisely. You fear you are not adequately equipped to assess where to buy property. You fear you are not adequately equipped to spot a suitable property on Rightmove. You fear you are not adequately equipped to assess a property's suitability regarding the mathematics to understand if it is a sound investment. You fear you are not adequately equipped to assess the property's condition to distinguish if it is a sound investment or a potential money pit. You feel confused because one person advises one model, whereas another suggests an entirely different one. You feel confused because you simply don't know where to start. You feel confused about whether or not you should invest through a Limited company. You feel overwhelmed because of the sizable task ahead. You feel overwhelmed because of the implications of what lies ahead. You have conflicting feelings because you worry you may lose your money. You have a mixture of feelings because you worry about what you would do if you got a bad tenant. You have a mixture of feelings because your property investment journey relies on you releasing equity from your home, and the notion of going against everything you were taught about 'saving for your future' gives you serious cognitive dissonance. You have no idea how to calculate ROI, let alone what represents a good return.

This list could go on and on ®, and I am sure there will be more that you would have added relating specifically to your situation or journey. That said, I would wager that you will have answered 'yes, that is me' to most of those traits. They can be categorised as fear, confidence, overwhelm and confusion. The latter being a lack of clarity. To ease your worries somewhat, let me tell you that these feelings are all very normal. Who does not or did not have these feelings at some point on their journey? The only reason I do not suffer the curse of those feelings anymore is that I am now educated in the art of property investment. I can assure you, there is no question that I felt a large part of that list, especially personally for me, the fear of failure.
To mitigate fear, rationalise worry, create clarity and reduce overwhelm, we need to get better educated. Education will be at the forefront of everything you do from here on in. Before we start, we again need to assess where we are. What limitations do we have, and what do we need to get better educated on then seek that education.

I am not talking about training courses to give us an overall idea of investment. I mean specifics. How do we analyse the mathematics of a property? Let us start with that. Do you know how to calculate return on investment (ROI) or workout yields? Do you know what to include when working out how much capital you need to purchase a property? If not, seek these answers out. Again this is not an isolated area; I am using these as examples. If the confusion is about whether to invest through a Limited company, speak to an accountant. Most accountants will give you a free consultation; if the one you call does not, thank them and call another. As you will see in Chapter 14 of my 15 laws to establishing your foundations, this diagnosis of what we need directly relates to strategy and can be mitigated using the strategic method I discuss. Principally we are at the diagnostic stage of our plan.

I am not telling you this so early in the book for you to press pause on your journey and get educated on things you most likely don't even know you need to know yet. Instead, it is to highlight two things. The first is that, just like with your time availability assessment, you need to assess your current standing regarding your education. It may be that you are a complete novice being a two or three out of ten, or you feel you are far more prepared than that being a six out of ten. If you are serious about this industry, you need to actively work on climbing this scale, but again, this does not have to be instantaneous; we can work on this progressively. Those ten hours we suggested you might have; can we increase this by listening to audiobooks or podcasts during our commute? Can you integrate YouTube videos, blogs and articles into your free time or social media scrolling, ensuring that these are specific to the problem you are trying to solve at that time and not simply filling this time with generic investment videos?

Ensuring this material is relevant and credible will help you avoid procrastination. Your education will increase as a byproduct which leads me nicely to the second point: all of the above traits can be mitigated when you take time to increase your education.

As a quick test, let us run a simple exercise. I would like you to say aloud what you feel your current education level is out of ten. For those who are reading, do not read any further until you have scored yourself. For those who are listening, I will give you a few seconds to consider and score yourself.

The reality is that the vast majority of you will be lower than you scored yourself. If you scored yourself between two and four, then you should deduct at least one number from this. If you scored yourself between five and seven, you should consider taking two points from your score because I can assure you that although you might feel confident in your answer, you have most likely been too generous. Remember, you only know what you think you know and do not know what you do not know yet.

If you scored yourself eight or above, what on earth are you doing reading this book? Please write one of your own, and I will read it with great anticipation and pleasure.

For clarity, I only consider myself to have a score of around 8.5 out of ten; every day is a school day.

Keep this score with you since my aim as you progress through this book is to increase this by one or two points, three if you are currently between one and three. Incidentally, some of the fears we discussed earlier at the start of this chapter will be discussed in greater depth as we progress through the book. Your education will increase as a byproduct of the content of this book. The trick for you is to keep your notes updated. Anything that spurs your interest, concerns you, or you don't quite follow, note it down. This is the second part of the puzzle for you to begin to solve. It offers you direction and focus as it begins to clarify what your next steps are. Remember, many answers to your question are within this book, but the application needs to be within you.

Education is the second of the 'big three' for property investors. To complete the triangle, next comes capital.

3 Capital

You may hesitate to believe this from where you are currently on your journey, but just like education, capital is more within your control than you may think. However, for the time being, we will leave that alone until later in the book during the finance section. All we need to do at this stage of our foundational plan is to calculate how much capital we currently have. Like time and education, we need to accurately assess what we currently have since the outcome of what we try to achieve can differ depending on our starting point. It is equally important that you include all the available capital regardless of where it comes from. You might have liquid capital lying dormant in the bank, but if you already know that you plan to release equity from your home, you should include that too. If you have a well-paid job, meaning you can comfortably add to your working capital on a weekly or monthly basis, then please add this capital too. If you have capital tied up in shares, a pension, or any other assets, you should consider including that too.

The idea is not necessarily to use all of this capital but to be more precise with the viability and to help calculate the potential should you opt to use it. For clarity, this absolutely extends to equity within our home. Remember, there will be no encouragement to access this equity. Instead, I am trying to highlight that once you have a clear picture of your current wealth, you are more equipped to make better-calculated financial decisions.

Let us look at two different hypothetical scenarios to demonstrate the opposing potentials.

The first scenario is Amy, who currently has £30,000 to invest. She is reluctant to invest in anything more than a simple turnkey property at this stage. A turnkey property is, as the name might suggest, a simple investment model whereby we buy ourselves a house that needs little to no attention to get it to a lettable state. Let us also assume that she has done all of her research and that I am not here to help her identify any other avenue for her investment but instead to help her choose the right property to purchase.

We settle on a mid-terrace 3-bedroom property for sale for £100,000, which including all fees, *discussed later in the book,* would cost her £29,750. She spends the remaining £250 on a spring clean and tidying up the garden. She is all in with her £30,000 capital. This property will rent for £695 per calendar month (PCM). Incidentally, Amy decided to purchase this property through her newly formed Limited company since she is a practising psychiatrist with an annual salary placing her well into the higher rate tax bracket of 40%. This will be discussed in more depth in Chapter 7, Control Strategy.

The fixed rate of her interest-only mortgage is 4.39%, meaning she has a monthly liability of £274.38 plus; she has this property externally managed by a local agent who charges 12%, including VAT resulting in a monthly cashflow from the property of £337.23. This outcome gives her a 13.49% ROI with an 8.34% gross yield. These are reasonable figures; no doubt, Amy is satisfied. Furthermore, at the start of year 15, she can buy another house from her profits alone and again at the end of year 20. One more property can be acquired at the midway point of year 24. The result is that at the end of 25 years, she would own a further three properties in addition to her first producing a net, meaning an after-tax yearly profit of just over £13,000. In today's money, her £30,000 invested has grown to around £100,000 due to her subsequent deposits used in her mortgages. Remember, these deposits have come from accrued rent.

Note that this is, of course, under the assumption that the properties remain fully occupied and that there are minimal maintenance issues purely for the good of this example. It also does not factor in any capital growth or inflation. Which again will all be discussed. I am easing you in at this point, avoiding the urge to expound and offer essential detail. All will be revealed in due course.

The opposing scenario is that Amy comes to see me with £30,000 to invest. However, she has asked for my advice and guidance in this instance. When we dig a little deeper into her finances, she informs me that she has £25,000 in her share account, yielding a return of around 3% annually. Furthermore, Amy has hidden away a 'high interest', and I use that term very loosely, cash ISA with a further £15,000 saved for her rainy day fund. She currently gets a 1.75% annual return on this, and I note with satire that this is 'tax-free', remember. Amy's house is valued at £500,000, yet her mortgage is for £180,000 since she has owned this for the past 20 years.

The last piece of the puzzle is that Amy informs me she could comfortably top up her investment pot or 'working capital' by around £1,500 each month. After some expert advice, careful due diligence, and subsequent calculations, she invests the £25,000 from her share account, transfers the £15,000 from her cash Isa and releases £150,000 from the equity within her home. Furthermore, she agrees to set up a monthly standing order for £1,500 to her property business bank account.

The result of this deep dive into financials means Amy now has a little over £220,000 to invest from day one. This change in financial footing is where the example gets thought-provoking or, somewhat more accurately, exciting. Assuming she invests in £100,000 turnkey properties exclusively to draw exacting parallels to the opposing journeys, she can now buy seven properties immediately with her working capital. These seven purchases result in an immediate gross cashflow of £2,360 per calendar month (PCM), equal to £28,320 per annum. To offer a like-for-like comparison to the previous example, this would represent an annual net cashflow, including all associated accountancy fees, of around £23,000 annually.

Calculating from day one of renting her seven purchases, Amy could buy her next property from profits alone around the eighth month of year one. Fourteen years and four months faster than before. Her following two properties can be purchased at the start and end of year two, eighteen years and nine months and twenty-one years and eight months quicker, respectively.

Since Amy can purchase property at a much faster rate and due to the fundamental laws that I will explain shortly in the next chapter, by the end of year 25, it is forecasted that she could own, wait for this, 168 properties. Giving her an annual net profit of around £555,000 in today's money.

Amy would have invested a total of £670,000 in her portfolio since she has increased her working capital at a rate of £1,500 per month for the past 25 years adding to her initial £220,000. However, her total capital within her portfolio stands at around 4.2 million pounds. This is again due to the deposits locked up in the portfolio coming in the form of her accrued profit.

Remember, before we get too excited or throw the book out the window, understandably citing complete nonsense, I would like to state very openly that this would never play out the way as demonstrated. My spreadsheet does not include any voids or maintenance over the 25 years. This example was an ideal scenario ignoring some critical fundamentals for the sake of the comparison. Still, the difference is clearly visible. Calculating your working capital early on in your investment journey to consider all available capital is essential to forward project where you might be in a given timeframe.

I accept that few people working through this book will have £25,000 in shares, £15,000 in a cash ISA, and £1,500 available each month surplus from their salary. But that is not the point I am trying to make here. I want to show you the result of the opposing scenarios by highlighting the differing extremities at each end of the spectrum. I would speculate that a number of you have a degree of the above example, not least equity in your home or a surplus of income or that you have more than £30,000 to invest. It does not matter where the capital comes from; all that matters is that you accurately assess what capital you have to invest to work through your calculations correctly.

You may have underestimated your true wealth, which was not considered fully in Amy's case in the first scenario.

For complete transparency, I am not telling you to invest this money but instead urging you to understand your true wealth entirely. If we can accurately gauge our capital, we can forward plan to our future vision using differing scenarios from differing starting positions. Then and only then can we start investigating the possibility of allocating some of this extra capital.

It is worth a quick sidebar here with anyone who worries that I am suggesting their £30,000 would likely perform so dismally over the next 25 years. This simply isn't the case. If we adopt a clever strategy and take advantage of some of the various property investment models we have at our disposal, we can do wonderful things with our £30,000 or even less. I will discuss this later in Chapter 13, Finance, conveniently using £30,000 as your investment capital.

The overriding factor of the three initial laws is calculating your starting position accurately. Time, capital and education are what I consider to be 'the big three' for property investors. Anyone who talks with me about entering the market will be questioned on them immediately. Unless you can confidently answer and demonstrate effectively, you should return to the drawing board until you reach this point. I am confident that the larger portion of readers now has some work to do.

From here on, the book will become far more expansive as we begin to ramp up your education with examples.

4 Understanding Why

"To paraphrase the philosopher, Nietzsche, he who has a strong enough why can bear almost any how. I've found that 20% of any change is knowing how, but 80% is knowing why. If we gather a strong enough why we can change in a minute something we've failed to change for years"

Tony Robbins

Let me be blunt; being or becoming rich does not warrant nor support your why. It is not enough. No one goes to work or starts a business because they want to be rich, and before you tell me, you do. Let me shed some light on the statement.

I would suggest that, in this instance, if that was your counter, then you have not made the appropriate considerations. We need to contemplate why it is, precisely, we want more money in the first place. Few would want to be rich merely for the extra zeros on their bank statement. Presumably, you want riches, so you have choices in your life. But is this for freedom, to give your family things that were denied to you as a child, to travel, to experience your life in other ways, to get a sports car or a bigger home, to get your time back, or merely to be your own boss?

These are your whys, not being rich, which incidentally is just the byproduct, and if we were to be pedantic, an inaccurate one. But we will get to that in just a moment; firstly, we must look more closely at the question of why and analyse the different interpretations of the question.

Why is not exclusive to you and your desires. We must differentiate between 'your why' and 'the why'. Now, of course, these are not mutually exclusive, but for the purpose of clarification, let us assume they are, at least for now.

If we consider property investment as a tool to create something, we must begin by understanding why we are entering the industry in the first place. And to differentiate myself from the crowd, I intend to have a different approach here. As mentioned earlier in the book, I have no intention of convincing you to become a property investor. This is your decision and a decision you must ultimately conclude yourself. Property investing is certainly not for everyone. Done correctly, initially, it will eat into your time, take serious effort and focus, and even keep you lying awake some nights contemplating its various options and possible outcomes. It is not uncommon to catastrophise in the early days. However, done correctly, it can also make you a very wealthy individual and should you decide that it is, in fact, for you, I will gladly show you the way and demonstrate some of 'the whys', which in turn should help you to determine 'your' why.

Long-lasting established wealth may be one of the greatest incentives for property investment. We create this by the correct and educated use of our capital, specifically by understanding assets and liabilities.

However, to understand the term wealth, firstly, we must define it over its often-flawed similarity to riches. For some reason, the words rich and wealthy are often incorrectly used to describe the same thing.

Wealth is defined as *'a plentiful supply of a particular desirable thing or an abundance of valuable possessions or money'*. Whereas rich is merely *'having money in the bank or an excess supply of money from a source such as a job'*. The critical difference here is that once wealth is established, it is sustainable and self-perpetuating. Your riches should be replenished without any significant effort or exchange.

If we are solely rich and choose to spend some of our earned money, our overall worth decreases as a result. Consider someone who drives a £100,000 Range Rover. If they are wealthy, there is a better-than-average chance that their assets pay for their vehicle. If someone is solely Rich, all we can truly say is that they are either £100,000 poorer or £100,000 more in debt. It is enough to say that being rich is still only one step removed from bankruptcy, albeit it is a giant step, one which the individual may never live long enough to take. Nevertheless, spend at a rate faster than we earn, and it is gone, never to be replaced.

You may be familiar with the story of MC Hammer, an innovator of the pop-rap culture of the late '80s and early '90s. At his peak of stardom, he earned over $50 million, which is around $125,000,000 today adjusted for inflation. Hammer had a $1 million house filled with over 200 staff members, and along with his 17 cars, he had stables housing over 25 racehorses. His entourage alone was estimated to cost him $500,000 per month. However, all these expenses took their toll, and all his spending, *along with several lawsuits,* resulted in Hammer declaring bankruptcy in 1996. He ended up with around $13 million in debt.

It would appear, for those of you who are old enough to remember him, as it turns out...they can touch it!

Wealth is only created with capital when it is invested wisely. In its simplest explanation, a wealthy individual has assets that create riches for him. You are creating wealth if you invest your surplus capital into something that continually replenishes your bank balance.

The secret to determining your why is to determine why it is you want the wealth in the first instance. As you'll see later in the strategy section of this book, diagnostics and analysis are vital to implementing your plan.

What follows are considerations of 'the' why of property investing. Your goal is then to determine 'your' why. A why that must be strong enough to endure the inevitable challenges that you will face, especially at the start of your journey. A strong enough why will help maintain momentum as you progress, which is paramount to your success in the early stages of your investment journey.

Let me use a quick example, this time of a hypothetical individual.

Meet Adam; he is 25 years old. Adam has a small but measurable amount of money in the bank; let us say it is a modest £25,000. Adam inherited this money from his grandmother's estate, so he has not had to endure months of hard work with a strict saving regime to accrue it. As you might well imagine being 23 years old, this money is burning a hole in young Adam's pocket. He wants to spend it as quickly as possible and intends to buy a new car with his recent inheritance.

The car in question is a Volkswagen Golf 1.5 TSI 150 Life, which, incidentally and somewhat fittingly, at the time of writing, has a rather coincidental list price of £24,995.

We might conclude that Adam has two obvious choices here. The first being to buy the car outright with his inheritance. The second is to buy the car using finance and to use his current employment income to pay down the loan over time, keeping his inheritance as a buffer or rainy-day fund. However, herein lies Adam's obvious problem. His lack of financial education is acting as his inhibitor. This lack of financial education is the quickest way to turn riches into rags. There is, of course, a third and obvious choice that presents itself here, and that is the choice an investor would consider.

Should Adam adopt a little patience and create wealth with his inheritance, the car will effectively be driven from the forecourt free of charge. To be clear, we are not talking about delayed gratification here. We are only suggesting a few months. For those who are not already on board, let me explain how Adam can do this using his newfound financial education and implementing the investors 'free purchase model', which, incidentally, while we are on the subject, I have just coined. Trademark pending.

£25,000 would, in fact, buy you lovely new VW Golf Life. However, it also buys you a 2-bedroom, mid-terrace property at the value of £85,000, which, including all associated costs and an external management fee, would leave you with an approximate monthly cash flow of £261. This is demonstrated by using data from my local area.

In comparison, the PCP or Personal Contract Purchase option on the VW Golf Life is £253 per month. Purchasing the property before the car using his grandmother's inheritance will continue to feed his account for at least the next 25 years. Just over three times longer than the term for the car payments. This prudent purchase will pay the finance on the car each month for the entire term leaving some small pocket change for Adam each month.

Furthermore, when the car payments are concluded, the list price of the golf would be somewhere in the region of £8,000. Adam would continue to have the property as an asset earning him a pre-tax profit of around £3,100 per year for the next 16 years. Remember that this asset will appreciate yearly rather than depreciate as cars often do.

In light of this recent epiphany, I think we all know which of Adam's three options is best for him, mathematically at least.

This is an elementary demonstration, but can you imagine how the stakes are raised when you are fortunate enough to have two or three hundred thousand pounds in your current account? If you adopt the basic principles of creating wealth with your riches, then the potential here is unlimited.

Our earlier example of Amy's and now Adam's conundrums naturally lead us to a discussion surrounding the powers of compounding.

The Compound Effect

"Compound interest is the 8th wonder of the world. He who understands it, earns it; he who doesn't, pays it."

Albert Einstein 1879 - 1955

The website Investopedia ® describes compounding as: *The process whereby interest is credited to an existing principal amount as well as to interest already paid.*

Compounding can thus be construed as interest on interest - the effect of which is to magnify returns to interest over time, the so-called "miracle of compounding is born." As demonstrated in the article on Investopedia's website, compounding in its simplest form is *'earning interest on interest.'* The principles of which are explained briefly in the below example.

Suppose you had, as in the example of Adams inheritance, £25,000, but in this instance, we placed the capital into a high-interest savings account. For this demonstration only, we will flout the bank of England's current rate of 3.5% and the more recent dismal but extremely capitalistic rates of interest and instead head back to around 2008 when interest rates were bobbing around the 5% mark and suggest that the bank would apply this interest rate on your savings.

Therefore the £25,000 in Adam's savings account would earn him a handsome 5% interest year on year. At the end of year one, our account shows the initial £25,000 plus the generous 5% interest of £1,250, meaning our balance now shows £26,250; fantastic, right?

Here is where the laws of compounding take effect. During year two, we would still receive 5% interest on the initial £25,000 as we did in year one, but now we also have 5% interest being paid on the £1,250 that was accrued as interest in year one. This result is that at the end of year two, we have £1,312.50, which is an extra £62.50 in year two's interest payments. Our balance at the end of year two would now show £27,562.50, a more significant increase than in year one, but without any extra effort or investment.

Year three then has a similar story. Another 5% is paid on the initial balance of £25,000 as in the two previous years, but now a further 5% is added on top of the £2,562.50 of accrued interest. The interesting note is that the interest amount has now more than doubled from the £1,250 earned in year one. Our balance at the end of year three is £28,940.63.

Again, it is plain to see that compounding powers are measurable even on a modest sum as £25,000. Imagine then how good they would be on two or three hundred thousand pounds.

On £300,000 at the end of year three, we would have accrued £47,287.50 in interest alone, compounding our initial £300k to £347,287.50.

Agreed, even after the recent base rate rises, we are still some way from the banks giving us an interest rate of 5% on our savings, so let us look at what compounding can do when using property investment as a vehicle.

Suppose we are fortunate enough to have £100,000 to invest with. We will adopt the same basic turnkey investment model that Amy chose to leverage in our earlier example to highlight the fundamental powers of compounding. Therefore, as in our previous example used for Adam's inheritance, we will purchase properties at the £85,000 mark. This will leave us out of pocket to the handy sum of £25,000, including SDLT or stamp duty land tax as well as broker and solicitor fees, which will be discussed in detail later in the book during Chapter 13, finance.

Our working capital of £100,000 enables us to buy four properties immediately, each yielding, after fees but before tax, £260 per calendar month (PCM).

£260 x 4, *the number of properties we have secured,* equates to £1,040 per month from our portfolio; incidentally, this is called your 'cashflow' (CF).

This means we yield an annual cashflow of £12,480 in our first year of business.

If for the purpose of continuation and ease of demonstration and because I dedicate an entire chapter to the reality of the associated costs when buying a property later in the book, we use the total value of this accrued capital and avoid any other fees such as reactive or planned maintenance and tax liability for the year. It means we can buy another property at month 24 since that is when the compounding laws start to take effect.

Therefore, twenty-four months after our initial investments, we can add an additional property to our portfolio, yielding another £260 per calendar month. Our annual gross profit has now risen by £3,120 from £12,480 to £15,600. The key point here is that we have added this fifth cash-yielding property solely from the accrued profits from our initial investments. Crucially though, we now have a 'compounding effect' since we are earning profits or cashflow from this additional property.

Remember, we still have a good proportion of the extra capital safe within the five property deposits. Effectively, we have somewhere in the region of £106,250 locked away in the properties, that is *five 25% deposits* from our starting capital of £100,000. Crucially we have a cash-flowing business giving us around £15,600 of annual pre-tax profits. If we continue to repeat this process, the compound effect manifests further as we buy more and more properties from our profits alone, accruing more significant annual cashflows from utilising the laws of compounding, as I demonstrated in the earlier example of Amy's purchases.

The law of compounding becomes much more interesting when we bring its partner in crime, exponential growth, along for the ride.

Exponential Growth

"The greatest shortcoming of the human race is our inability to understand the exponential function"

Albert Allen Bartlett 1923 – 2013

It began with a single cell. That first cell splits to become two. Two become four. Four become eight. Eight becomes sixteen, and so on. After just forty-seven doublings, you have ten thousand trillion cells in your body and are ready to spring forth as a human being.
That number is ten, followed by fifteen zeros or 10,000,000,000,000,000 in just 47 doublings. This visibly highlights the enormous power of exponential growth within nature, but this is something that makes the property industry the most obvious choice when we think of 'the' why.

In essence, exponential growth is a pattern of data that shows greater increases with passing time, creating the curve of an exponential function. A modern-day example of this is the recent Covid 19 outbreak and the use of data represented by the 'R rate'. This was the rate of reproduction of the virus. In simple terms, if the R rate was two, it suggests that one person will infect two others.

At the start of the growth and with the R rate at two, one person is infected and then passes this on to two others who pass it on to another four people, *two each*, those four pass it on to eight, *two each,* who pass it on to 16 and here we have just like in our cell example a doubling every time. So, from the initial case developing at the R rate of two, the daily infection numbers continue with two, four, eight, 16 and 32. These numbers are notably small, to begin with, but not for long. The 10th transmission is around 1,000, and the 20th is around one million. Under these simplified conditions, by means of comparison, almost the entire population of Scotland will have been infected within only 22 days.

If we take some time to fully understand the laws of compounding and then use them to help us with exponential growth in our portfolio, what we are left with is a delicious cocktail to enjoy at our leisure and a proven recipe for wealth AND riches. To highlight the nature of exponential growth within property investment, let us now highlight the figures that we were able to present to Amy to show the potential of her portfolio when we included compounding and exponential growth from our example earlier in the book.

If you remember, Amy had a massive £221,500 to invest with: At the start of her investment journey, she was able to purchase seven properties immediately, with a further one at month eight of the first year. The following two properties were purchased in the second year at the end of the twelve-month period and then again at the start of years three and four. Over the next few years, this continues with a slight increase to around three properties per year. Around the tenth year, the increase is to four properties and again to five in year 13. We move to six properties in year 14 and seven in year 7. In year 18, we are at nine properties. By year 21, however, we are able to buy twelve properties with our accrued profit, and by the end of years 24 through 25, we have the fortune of being able to purchase 16 properties each year. The power of exponential growth can be witnessed first-hand here in our example ®.

Inflation

Until we expand the boundaries of our minds to the broader possibilities with ideas that are shared from a more experienced source, and before we accept that we can genuinely change our belief system and can, in fact, be successful ourselves, we all have two things in common. Namely, we all suffer from fear and confidence issues. As I mentioned earlier, these feelings of insecurity are standard practice. Although you probably think you are the only one with these feelings, this is something I have witnessed hundreds of times over the years, more so in those who have initially cited a broad front of risk tolerance and projected an image of high confidence.
It is one of the biggest impediments to our development and can often be the only difference between action and inaction.

Let me reiterate that these are normal feelings. They occur in one form or another with almost every investor at the beginning of their journey, and, in many cases, albeit significantly reduced, they continue throughout.

We can blame nature if it makes us feel any better. As Homo Sapiens, we are hard-wired to be cautious; it is our brain's natural defence mechanism.

Fear is said to be as old as life on Earth. It is a fundamental, deeply wired reaction. Fear helps to protect all organisms against seeming threats to themselves or their existence. Fear can be a simple twinge of an antenna on a snail that is brushed by a possible threat or as complex as existential anxiety in a human being.

Furthermore, this fear has been continually reinforced throughout our lives by the influence of others, attributed by the press and fuelled by the lack of education by those who echo it through their unqualified opinions. At some point in our life, we have all been told that debt is bad, we need to save rigorously for the future, and we must pay down our mortgages to own our 'greatest asset', our home.

The topic of debt and the association we have with our mortgages is something that I could discuss for the next hour of this book should I feel the need; however, at this point, all I have to say on the subject is this: The mortgage we are supposed to pay down is debt. This debt is said, rightly or wrongly, to give us our 'greatest asset'. Therefore a straightforward equation would be d=a or debt equals asset, right?

I feel an overwhelming obligation to offer clarity here. Debt is, in my opinion, categorically not a bad thing, quite the opposite, in fact. Debt is what makes economies grow and allows individuals to grow wealthy. It will allow every single one of you to become precisely whom you want to be in this industry. Without debt, I would not live the life I live now. I would not have the luxury of writing this book tucked away for ten days in a log cabin on the Scottish coast unplugged from distraction, I would not have just booked two weeks in the Maldives for my entire family, and you certainly would not be researching how to improve your life through the idea of property investment. In fact, the property investment industry would likely not exist.

Good debt is, in fact, a wonderful thing. It is bad debt that is a bad thing.

When we take on debt, we need to understand the difference between good debt, like a mortgage and bad debt, like creating a liability from something we cannot afford.

This fear most of us have bred into us through the misguidance of social heredity becomes preventative since it leads to low confidence manifesting as an inhibitor to our development as if success was meant for someone else, not us.
Only those of you who manage to lessen these fears will be truly ready to succeed with your business. This theory is discussed in more depth throughout the book, but for now, I want to explain why I have chosen to open with a passage on fear and confidence in a sub-section entitled inflation.

One of the biggest challenges we face with overcoming our, or rather more accurately, someone else's engrained philosophy of paying down our mortgage is our decision regarding mortgage types. Chiefly repayment vs interest only. This can be a difficult choice, one that many have conflicting feelings of fear and discomfort at the beginning of their property investment journey. I want to shed some light on this choice for those of you who may be concerned with an interest-only mortgage approach.

A quick caveat before I do:

Principally there are two main types of mortgage payments. Interest-only and repayment. Depending on your long-term vision, financial goals, strategy, and overall objectives, it may be that either one of these suits your approach.

There are many different investment models, types, and strategies to consider when choosing which product to leverage. These will all be discussed in Chapter 10, Market Entry. However, for the best part, one will assume that you are reading this book because you want to own a larger-than-average, cash-flowing portfolio exploiting the aforementioned powers of compounding and exponential growth. Therefore, in this instance, and unless you have a constant replenishment of capital, we would almost certainly adopt to leverage an interest-only product over the standard repayment type. Understanding inflation here is paramount to appeasing your fears or confidence issues. Fundamentally, we need to understand how inflation strips our loan's value over the term of the mortgage, typically 25 years.

Let us revisit our earlier example whereby Adam was purchasing property for around £85,000. The actual figure here is somewhat irrelevant since the demonstration is relative regardless of the purchase price. However, it may be easier for you to digest if I apply consistency with this demonstration.

Should we opt to leverage an interest-only mortgage in this instance, meaning, as the name suggests, the amount owed will not reduce over the 25-year term but instead only pay the interest on the loan, we would need to leverage £63,750, excluding fees, from the lender. This is a 75% loan-to-value (LTV) product, which is the typical deposit-to-loan ratio with most buy-to-let mortgages. Essentially 25% of the property's value is fronted by your contribution, and the rest is leveraged from the bank.

We must fast forward 25 years when the full term of our mortgage is due to expire so we can look at how we would repay the capital since this is perhaps the biggest concern people have when deciding which mortgage model to employ.

For many, finding £63,750 in today's world would come with apparent challenges since £63,750 represents a current value of, well, £63,750 exactly. However, with 25 years of inflation eroding its value, this figure has a significantly lower consequence. So the logical question is, how much will £63,750 be worth in 25 years?

Since we are unable to predict what inflation will average over the next 25 years, we need to use historical data as our guide to navigating this question.
As I edit this chapter, inflation is currently running at around 10.5%, which incidentally is another enormously weighted reason to add to our ever-increasing stack of why we would want to invest in property. However, we will discount this recent abnormality in rates with the assumption or rather hope that by the time some of you read this book, interest rates will have established themselves with a more typical rate. That is not a prediction, of course, but instead, more of a fingers and toes crossed statement.

Over the past 25 years, inflation rates have fluctuated somewhat, but a quick search with the 'Bank of England' shows an average growth of 2.7% per year over the previous 25-year period. Therefore, we will use this figure as our benchmark and, for the purpose of this demonstration, adopt the assumption that history will repeat itself in this instance.
Our £63,750, therefore, equates to a current 2023 value of Circa £32,751 as represented in 2048.
What this means is that in 2048 when our loan of £63,750 is due to mature, it would have a value as represented today of £32,751. The rest of the value has been stripped away by inflation.

Remember, the property we purchased has a current value of £85,000. On its own, this would be a comforting notion for any investor; however, when we factor in the property's capital growth, we are gifted the final piece of the jigsaw. Comparing data from propertydata.com and land-registrydata.gov only proves to reassure further.

The data shows that average UK property prices significantly increased over the previous 25 years, rising from £60,000 in July 1997 to £292,000 in July 2022. That is a modest rise of £232,000 over a 25-year period. The figures adjusted for inflation show £105,000 in 1997 to £292,000 in 2022. That is still a rise of £187,000. This shows that the average UK property has increased over two and a half times over a standard 25-year term. The actual figure here is 2.7 times over the past 25 years.

To draw a comparison for conclusion, property prices in my local area, since this is where our example is based, have, on average, more than trebled across all of the locations researched in the last 25 years. The actual figure here is 3.2 times over the past 25 years.

If we use this as our benchmark for assessing our property's future growth, it would be worth somewhere within the region of £229,500 at 2.7 times and £272,000 when applying a multiple of 3.2.
The key thing to remember here is that we only owe £67,750 when our loan matures; we do not apply any increased adjustment for inflation.

This all means, in simple terms, that selling one of our properties from our portfolio as their mortgages begin to mature would effectively pay down just short of four other mortgages. The remaining properties are now unencumbered from this point on, which for clarity, means you have no mortgage or any other liability on the property. The result could mean our cash flow will increase despite having fewer properties within our portfolio since we have no mortgage payments to offset.

The immense powers of inflation simply cannot be ignored when we look at ways to increase our confidence or mitigate our fear of investing. However, as you are about to discover, as I cited earlier during this demonstration, there is cruel contraposition to inflation. The good news is that we can use this as further motivation since it merely places more leverage on 'why' we invest our capital rather than keep it in our bank account. In fact, this may be the deciding factor that forces many of your hands. The draw of a larger bank balance or the wise investment of that existing balance may be a lingering thought for those working through this book. However, the fear of losing capital is something we all share universally. The following statement should not be ignored since this, especially at the time of writing with current inflation rates, is one of the main catalysts for me and many investors alike.

If your capital is not allocated wisely, inflation will take it; most commonly, this is your hard-earned cash; it will chew it up, devalue it and spit back far less than it took. Let me explain how.

Let us say we have £100,000 nestling in our bank account, and we are looking at what to do with this capital. We read some books, seek advice from friends and family who have a few houses between them, and watch some YouTube videos. Despite these less-than-tangible efforts, our fear and low confidence prevent us from doing anything with it, and our inclination to invest this sum subsides. Our lack of attention to our education, specifically our financial education, our fears and our fixed mindset traits result in a lack of action.

In the same way, inflation strips the loan's value from the lender; it will also strip the value of our £100,000 sitting stagnant in your bank account. With interest rates and inflation running as high as they have been during 2022 and the first part of 2023, our £100,000 would look something like this if we allow it to.

Year one, day one:	**£100,000**
Year one, end of month six:	**C.£95,303**
Year two, day one:	**C.£90,827**
Year two, end of month six:	**C.£86,561**
Year three, day one:	**C.£82,495**
Year three, day 365:	**C.£80,483** *assuming historic rates resume*

If we continue through our example to year twenty-five, yes, you guessed it, the typical term of a buy-to-let mortgage, then our capital is now a floundering C.£46,749. This demonstration uses the current inflation rate at the time of writing for the first two years and then averages the historical rate of 2.5% for the remaining 23 years.

Again, for complete transparency, I am firmly telling you that this devaluation of capital should be your main worry, not the worry of what if. The investment that generates a positive income that leads to wealth should be the exciting part, not the worry. As you will see as you progress through this book, the negative press surrounding property investment is either inaccurate or can be mitigated with education, clever strategy, careful planning, proper due diligence, and the correct application of core principles.

By means of a relative sidestep to the horrifying notion that our capital is devaluing significantly whilst remaining dormant in our bank, we have to consider the Time Value of Money (TVM) ®. This concept is linked to inflation almost always rising at a higher rate than interest received. The principal idea is that your capital is worth more now than the identical sum in the future. The sooner we can utilise this capital, the more beneficial it will be since it prevents inflation from devaluing your capital and allows for quicker compounding results and the subsequent exponential growth to take effect.

I have briefly demonstrated three compelling reasons why I believe property investing is a wise choice for you and your wealth accumulation. However, at risk of distracting too much from the point, we must now switch the focus of our attention to your why. Remember that you can continue your education by researching these topics independently of this book, aiding to increase your confidence and mindset as a result.

In its simplest form, your why is something only you can determine for yourself when considering your future within property investment. Furthermore, it needs to be determined as early into your property journey as possible, which is why it lands at point four within our 15-part foundation plan after the big 3 of 'Time', 'Education' and 'Capital'.

This may not be terribly exciting for you, it may not feel overly productive at this moment, or you may not even see the importance of it just yet. It almost certainly will not feel like a giant step forward. But allowing adequate time to understand your 'why' is essential to your development and, ultimately, the success of your business. It cannot be overstated how important this is at this point. Your why will fuel your business; it will keep you going when faced with challenges, but crucially, it is what you can lean on when inspiration or encouragement is needed to keep you motivated.

Using the principles from the book, 'Start with Why' by Simon Sinek, generally, three factors determine our choices or actions. They are 'What', 'How' and 'Why'. Almost all of us know precisely what we are doing at any given time, whether in our business, working environment, or social life. Some of us will even know how we are doing what we are doing. But Simon suggests far too few of us will ever take the time to understand why we are doing this. Understanding your why is as fundamental as understanding your return on investment or determining your investment location.

We should all start with why and write this down to ingrain it; remember, *If you have a strong enough why you can endure any how*.

My final word on why for now is that you must consider this question as if it were your focusing statement as you progress throughout your entire property journey. Because this question really does resonate throughout your entire journey. I still consider why weekly. Principally the focus has shifted from what we have just covered to the following why's.

Why someone would want to live in this property is a question I still ask when looking at buying any new property. More importantly, why would someone want to move out of this property?

Why would someone want to bring us a property to buy in the case of a direct-to-vendor purchase? Why would someone want to sell us a property? Specifically estate agents, vendors, or in some cases, sourcing companies. Why would someone want to invest or do a joint venture (JV) with us? Why would someone want to lend us capital, the bank, bridging loans or angel financiers? Why do I want to take on this refurbishment right now? Why would I want to take one mortgage product over another? The list goes on and on. In fact, almost every question I have always comes back to why. Many years on from the start of my journey, the question of why resonates throughout everything I consider. If I cannot answer the question I have asked, I ask myself why and conclude from there.

All of this will be discussed later in the book. For now, I think you understand my point.

5 Mindset

"Twenty years from now, you will be more disappointed by the things you did not do than you will be by the things you did do"

Mark Twain 1835 - 1910

You may run out of many things during your life, from frivolities such as a mobile phone charge or a lost internet connection to arguably more counterproductive factors like patience or energy. In some acute cases, we may even run out of fundamentals such as money or security.
But the one thing we share that we will all run out of is, of course, time. Time counts down each day pugnaciously towards its ultimate goal of atom reallocation. Time is something we can rarely alter, as I have demonstrated in a variety of ways already throughout this book. If you're waiting for the right time to come, it won't because it is not the wrong time that is your inhibitor; it is your mindset.

Conversely, and with some minor exceptions, we all share two things we will never run out of. This is the love we have for our children and our many ideas.

Although without action, I would cite that our ideas are useless, you might take that one step further and conclude that they are, in fact, a hindrance. The emotional baggage that reminds our subconscious daily of what we should or could be doing with our limited time on this Earth can cause us anxiety or enable depressing feelings of failure and unworthiness. If these ideas are not implemented or filed accordingly, their effects can have severe ramifications on our mindset and subsequent actions.

Before we delve into this fully, let us take a slight but relevant detour to run a quick thought-provoking exercise.

Suppose your bank kindly deposited £86,400 into your account each day just after the stroke of midnight. Understandably though, there are some rules to this gesture.

Firstly, everything you don't spend that day will be zeroed down, and the balance will return to £86,400 the following morning just after midnight. Secondly, you may only spend this money. You cannot transfer amounts to other accounts or draw out any as cash. Lastly, and crucially, the bank withholds the right to withdraw this grand gesture of goodwill any time it sees fit, without notice and reasoning. It might last one day, one month, one year, or for the rest of your life; there is no way of knowing, and there are no guarantees.

Now, pause for a moment and think about how you would act in this scenario.

Ask yourself some practical questions. What would you do with the money accepting the rules? Would you buy everything you could for yourself, your family and your friends anticipating that it will surely be replaced tomorrow?

At what point, realising this could stop at any time, would you start to use the money to build your future?

Would you attempt to spend every penny each day, knowing the balance is lost at the end of the day? Would you rise each morning at the stroke of midnight to begin the ambitious task of spending the money since it would be a tall order to do this repeatedly each day?

For those of us who were lucky enough to rise this morning, it might surprise you to learn that 86,400 is a gift we are all blessed with. The gift here isn't money, of course. It is time.

Each morning just after the final stroke of midnight, we are blessed with 86,400 seconds to achieve precisely what we want on any given day. As we head off to bed each night, the disused time is not credited to our account but instead lost forever. Each morning it begins again just after midnight, but just like the bank that reserved their right, this luxury can be withdrawn at any point without notice and reasoning.

When you look back to assess what you have been able to achieve over the course of some of the most productive times in your life, consider what you could achieve tomorrow, next month, over the next 12 months, but crucially where you might be in five or ten years. Remember, time is continually counting down; it stops for no one. Scientific studies have shown, time and time again, *excuse the pun*, that the longer we leave a task, idea or thought, the further it slips away from us and the harder or less likely we will achieve our goal of completing it.

Time is a gift, not a given. So, the question to ask yourself is, what will you do with your 86,400s today, tomorrow and the next?

I am by no means intending to preach about living each day as if it was your last or to shame you into becoming any kind of super productive and unstainable monster who never lets a single second of wasted time pass. Instead, my intention is to highlight the finite element of time and life. If not today or tomorrow, when? That is my consideration. Most of us are starkly aware that time is counting down, and we would agree, regardless of age, that it seemingly speeds as we age, yet the vast majority of us live as if time was infinite.

In his New York Times 'best-selling' book, Oliver Burkeman cites that the average life comprises 4,000 weeks. The time management book is not what you might think, however. It centres more on understanding your limitations and how we are programmed than trying to show you how to be uber-streamlined. However, it is one of the most thought-provoking books I have read recently, and I encourage each of you to read it, too [®].

A takeaway from the book and to illustrate the time exercise I just discussed is the prioritisation of your tasks. When you rank your tasks from most to least important and take care of them in accordance with the priority, you are much more likely to finish things. This links to your mindset and the exact opposite of feelings of failure by adding yet another incompletable task to your to-do list.

Many of you will be familiar with the following anecdote since it has been widely published in books, blogs and articles since the supposed event. Some years ago, Mike Flint, Warren Buffets' pilot, asked him how he could achieve the heights of success he desired. Buffet asked Flint to write down his top 25 career goals. It didn't have to be 25 different jobs or 25 different promotions. The 25 goals simply had to be related to him, his career as a pilot or something else. Essentially, what did he want to achieve most professionally?

Buffet then went on to explain that Flint was to review his list and circle his five "favourite" items: These were his Top 5 Goals. Not more and not less than five.

"Take a good look at the twenty goals you didn't circle", Buffet said. "These are your avoid-at-all-cost items. They are what have the most potential to distract you. They eat away your time and energy and prevent you from focusing on what matters. They make you take your eye off the ball and lose track of the game. They prevent you from scoring."

He instructed Flint to take the bottom twenty goals off the list and never look at them again. "Don't put them on hold until the top five are complete; throw them away. If they are not important enough to make your top five, they are not important at all".

We all look for that giant leap that will catapult us to where we want to be as if success was a step. However, asides from a lucky few, we need to appreciate that this is not the way of the world, especially in the business world. The business world rewards effort, it rewards consistency, and it rewards patience.
Instead, we need to grasp that smaller action-orientated steps that together form more significant leaps forward are what get us to where we want to be. Every time you fail to act, you place another brick in the wall, strengthening the connection that inaction is expected. Conversely, every time you take even the most minor action, you take out a brick until the

wall in front of you, which was acting as a blockade, is manageable enough to simply step over.

Simply put, you are breaking down the task into bite-sized portions. In the words of the great Kung Fu Tze, "a man can eat an Elephant, if need be, one bite at a time".

Now imagine breaking these five chosen desires into smaller action-oriented tasks or objectives. Let us assume each desire has three smaller goals, perhaps a small, medium and long-term goal. With each goal would come five smaller actions or objectives. That means in a simpler world, your five desires have 15 tangible actions attached to them. Should we adopt a more focused approach and concentrate on our top five desires, we have 75 actions. Deciding to add a whole bunch of desires without time consideration, let us use 25 as in Buffet's example, and we now have 375 tasks to work through in our available time. This is precisely why we fail to make any dent in the list. This failure has severe ramifications for our mindset. Feelings of failure are far more counter-productive than feelings of progression are productive.

Your property business is the elephant, and the bite is represented with these smaller action-orientated steps that, when combined, create, and I couldn't help myself here, so please excuse the pun. A mammoth task.

Mindset is essentially characterised by the way we think or act about specific topics. Therefore, changing our belief system or consciously nurturing it to develop further is essential for property investors. We have already discussed how education can help alleviate some of the fear and confidence issues we may have, but this on its own is not enough. We must continue to develop if we are to avoid slipping back into our old habits.

But this is a property investing book, not a phycology book, so why will we spend the following 4,556 words discussing mindset? And I hear your question, ''Should we not be getting on to Rightmove by now to see how to spot a decent deal''?

Like it or loath it, my answer is that this is not what successful property investing is about and is definitely not what this book is about. This book has been developed to help you focus on what is needed to become successful with property investment and subsequently build a profitable property investment business. If we consider the topics already discussed with the ones yet to be announced and look at their importance for you on your journey, nothing compares to mindset; nothing even comes close. Master this, and you are in complete control of your destiny. Property or otherwise. However, ignore this fundamental characteristic, and nothing else you do within your property business will matter because should you not have the correct mindset, you will not succeed. No genuinely successful investor or businessperson suffers the curse of a fixed mindset. The one thing we all have in common, above anything else, is our mindset's development and continued growth.

Fundamentally mindset is about strengthening the neurological pathways within your brain. Once we create a thought aimed at a certain point of view, our brain banks this thought for future reference; the more we think these thoughts, the more the brain draws on its experience to shorten the distance between the thought and the action, automatically. These neurological pathways can be of tremendous value when we understand how they work and how we can develop them to our advantage.
The flip side of the coin is that it can be detrimental too, should we subconsciously or worse, consciously strengthen these pathways with negative thoughts. Therefore there is often some reprogramming to do. Furthermore, if all we do is think and never act, these pathways will strengthen to thinking rather than acting.

Although increasing our knowledge of a subject can help with this, we can only truly change this by taking action-orientated steps and not by continually reading self-help books. We have all heard the saying that knowledge is power or that knowledge is the key to success, and I would echo those theories. That said, we must understand that knowledge on its own is, in fact, useless.

Isolated knowledge will not take us anywhere. We must bring along action and mix in a measure of mindset to create momentum or movement.

According to Mathew jones, as far back as 2008, the self-help industry was already valued at 11 billion dollars annually.
That is a mass of books, articles, motivational speeches and YouTube videos that have failed to help the 40 million people living in the US alone suffering from anxiety, the 14.8 million suffering from depression, and the 7.7 million people who have post-traumatic stress disorder.
In 2015, the US spent 446 billion dollars on medication, almost half of the global market.

The obvious thing that backs up my statement is that having just the knowledge does not work for the vast number of us.

Sadly, there has been an all too easy rise of under-qualified authors, opinionated books based on fragmented knowledge or worse, irresponsibly written content for personal gain via a dream selling or unsustainable perfect living hype. In fact, essentially, the industry's growth relies principally on your vulnerabilities. Fundamentally, commercialism manipulates you by appealing to your core weaknesses and ultimate desires.

Furthermore, and crucially, this singular quest for knowledge drives us to linger on what is known as the hedonic treadmill; this metaphor is used to highlight our repeated search for one pleasure after another. This, in turn, creates a culture of obsessive serial 'self-help' readers, meaning we take a book and love its life-changing message and principles, filling us with joy and clarity. Still, just as quickly, we dismiss it and merely move on to the next mind-blowing, attitude-changing, life-altering masterpiece that makes us want to apply everything taught with immediate effect. And so on goes the perpetual cycle of self-help, never really moving us forward except by expanding our knowledge.

So, the obvious issue here is that we never actually implement the lessons taught to us in these mind-blowing books. We stay on the carousel, never affording ourselves time to digest, adapt, apply, learn, grow and ultimately achieve what we wanted when we set out reading the book. Many of us are on an endless journey for answers, the meaning of life, the secret to success, the one lightbulb moment that we can journal in our memoirs as the moment the penny dropped and everything thereafter slotted into a sequential masterpiece, as easy as 123.

Today the world is filled with an easily accessible yet overwhelming expanse of knowledge and wisdom that allows the self-help industry to produce a net worth of an estimated 38 billion USD and is set to grow to a staggering 56 billion USD by 2027. Respectively that is about 27 and 40 billion in real money and, by the current, less than favourable exchange rate. Incidentally and by comparison, the estimated cost to solve the global food crisis stands at a mere 25 billion GBP, but that is a different topic for an entirely different book.

The self-help industry is nothing new, however. It is only the accessibility of the industry in modern times, thanks to technological advancements, chiefly the internet, which is new. We only need to look back a short time through history to draw comparisons with the works of early philosophers such as Confucius, Plato, and Aristotle, who left us with timeless wisdom through their BCE teachings, now often only accessible through paraphrasing or quotations.
A more in-depth look at the stoic works of Marcus Aurelius, who is considered the last of the five good Roman emperors, reveals his 12 books or meditations as diarised during his reign between 161 and 180 AD.
It is perhaps the earliest form of a 'self-help' book available today. However, it is worth noting that these books of medications were never intended to be shared or published but instead kept for personal use and, as such, have no actual title. The adopted 'meditations' title is something that was manufactured before publishing.

The new age or modern-day self-help industry started slightly over 150 years ago as a semi-mutation of Protestant Christian individualism.
The Social and religious 'new thought movement' pioneered by Phineas P.

Quimby peaked in the early twenties leaving the church and faith healers behind as it developed further and became more recognisable in the 1930s. The stream of motivational and positive thinking books and speakers we know today was born. Most famously back then was Napoleon Hill with his ground breaking book 'Think and Grow Rich' published in 1937, which today has sold over 15 million copies worldwide.

The question that presents itself is that if this industry is so old, why does it dictate us now, and why has it grown exponentially over the past 20 years?

The answer to this question is also its problem. As I have just cited, it is in its accessibility. We now have information readily available at the click of a button. We all serial read or listen to self-help books like they are going out of fashion. The result, in a nutshell, is one of overwhelming confusion creating a byproduct of inaction disrupting continuity and prolonging action, all leading to increased strengthening of the wrong type of neurological pathways within our brain. The result of this is a weak mindset centred towards inaction rather than action.

Our brains like repetition because it leads to cognitive ease; it is far too easy to become preoccupied and distracted from the reality of our visions and goals. Anyone who does not yet agree only needs to consider the inexplainable condition of procrastination ®, something we all suffer from to some degree. We jump straight into the next topical book like we binge-watch the newest Netflix series. Often as our 'must-read' or 'watchlist' dwindles, we expel far too much energy and time considering what to watch or read next.
How many of us can honestly say that we allow the message or, more importantly, the finer details of the message of the book we've just rated five stars on audible and told all our friends to read, penetrate before we jump right back in and go again?

The answer is, I am guessing, far too few of us.

It is a well-established theory that the brain cannot differentiate between the reality of action and the thought of acting. Thinking we are doing, the brain is fooled into believing we are doing what we are thinking.

This theory was first cited in a study published in the national library of medicine back in 1995 ®, where volunteers were asked to play a simple sequence of piano notes each day for five consecutive days. Their brains were scanned daily in the region connected to their finger muscles. Another set of volunteers was asked to merely imagine playing the notes instead whilst also having their brains scanned simultaneously.

The brain scan images showed the changes in the brain of those who played the notes and the changes for those who only imagined playing the notes. These images were then compared with the third set of volunteers who neither played nor imagined playing the piano. The results of the three brain scans were irrefutable.

The changes in brain function of those who only imagined playing the piano are the same as those who actually played the piano, yet entirely different for the volunteers who did neither.
The resulting conclusion was that your brain does not distinguish real action from imagined action.
This is evident in anyone who's ever watched a thriller or a horror movie and was frightened or felt afraid. The stress response evolved in humans, allowing us to 'fight or flight' when faced with danger; chemicals, including cortisol and adrenalin, help kick start the body, pushing blood towards the major muscles to give you strength. These chemicals are produced regardless of whether the danger is real or imagined.

What does all this mean for us when we are continually reading self-help books, posting on social media about our intent or talking ambitiously with our family and friends? It means that what you imagine to be happening in your mind is actually happening as far as your brain is concerned. This, as I am sure you will agree, is counterproductive to our success and limits our ability to force action since our brain genuinely believes we are, in fact, acting on our desires and intentions.

To affirm, this constant paradoxical treadmill of self-help reading can effectively be the one thing that inhibits our growth. That said, rather ironically and somewhat leaving myself open to criticism, there is a book you should categorically read on the topic of Mindset, and that is Carol Dweck's book aptly named 'Mindset' ®

It is my hope that this book will help to begin to break down this obstacle through clear and concise education and awareness. For those who are reading or listening to this book, who are genuinely serious about creating the life they want and intend to act on their words to pursue their vision of becoming a property investor, this book can categorically help you should you take the time to apply the lessons taught.

The answers you seek are not found in a single 'lightbulb' type moment waiting to be discovered hidden in the text of the next book you read. The answers are often already within you. You simply have not asked the right questions or adopted the correct mindset to extract them. The answers are an amalgamation of every book you have read and will read throughout your life. It starts simply by following the principles within the books that reached us in the way we sought.

If you were to highlight a small number of your favourite self-help titles and apply the lessons demonstrated within those books, you would be well on your way to becoming as successful as you wanted to be without feeling the urge for further confusion or overwhelm.

My goal is to be that very book. The one that makes you sit up, take notice and then take action. This is a bold claim since it ultimately relies on you rather than me. It is you who will eventually finish this book and decide what to do next. Stay on the treadmill or get off and apply yourself. And this brings us nicely back from our rather long detour and back to the focus of mindset.

Mindset is perhaps the most misunderstood and incorrectly overused term within the self-development industry. Mindset is not positive thinking or positive mental attitude (PMA). It is not repeating daily mantras. Nor is it believing that if you reach for the stars and miss, at least you will land on the moon, and it is categorically not 'The Secret.' These are all useful in small measures, but they do not define what mindset is or give any clue on how they can help you because, on their own, they are only small contributing factors that do not create any real change.

Mindset is, and it needs to be ingrained in everything we do. Everything is in uppercase, underlined and in bold. Mindset should be firmly embedded in your entire belief system, your beliefs about who you are, how you act, what you believe you can achieve, and, more importantly, how you set yourself up to achieve what you believe is possible. As the author, businessman and motivational speaker T. Harv Eker, known for his theories on wealth and motivation, put it, "how you do anything is how you do everything".

As an investor, staying focused and growth based with your mindset when setbacks arise is vital to moving forward and pushing through the challenge since it maintains momentum to keep the business driving forward. This focus, in essence, is the primary difference in whether you will or will not succeed with property investing because challenge and effort are inevitable. Self-doubt or imposter syndrome is inevitable. Feelings of slow growth or development are inevitable. Feelings of confusion, just as you thought things were starting to clear, are inevitable, and feelings of fear and worry are absolutely inevitable. How you deal with these feelings determines how you proceed, or in fact, if you proceed at all.

When we say that mindset is ingrained in everything we do, it primarily governs our two main success-minded traits. How we think and how we act. It is not simply thinking positively, especially in terms of blindsided positivity, but what you genuinely think about yourself. How you think about your core beliefs and your most basic qualities and whether or not you think those qualities are fixed or if they can change.

Let me ask you a simple question. What do you honestly think about your intelligence? Your talents and your personality? Are these qualities simply fixed traits carved in stone, unchangeable, and that is that? Or are they things you can cultivate throughout your life?

Your answer to that simple question will help you understand your current mindset.

It is essential to understand that mindset is not a binary element. It is not merely negative or positive or, as Carol Dweck coined it, 'fixed' or 'growth' based. There is an entire spectrum moving between these two extremities. Moreover, you can have a mindset more on the fixed side with one belief and a more growth-based mindset with another. The trick is to work on being on the growth side of the spectrum more often than not so we can positively benefit from what is known as a recursive process.

This process is a simple idea that affirms our belief system, whether fixed or growth based. Let me explain how:

The principal goal of a fixed mindset individual is to try to look smart, whereas, for the growth-based mindset individual, it is to learn. The fixed mindset person does not hold much regard for effort, whereas those who adopt the growth-based values effort immensely. The reaction to failure for a fixed trait mindset is to give up, whereas the growth-based individual merely increases their effort to work harder the next time to achieve the desired success.

Unsurprisingly, individuals with fixed mindsets are low achievers, while those with growth-based minds achieve elevated levels of success. The recursive process is demonstrated like this:

Let us say you are presented with a challenge, be it physical or mental. It may be that this challenge is to seek out an investment area since investing where you live is simply not feasible due to the rising stock prices. You can look at this challenge through two separate lenses, the first is your growth-based lens, and the second is your fixed mindset lens. Which lens you look through will ultimately determine your future. Should you rightly toss the fixed approach aside and opt to look at this challenge with a growth-based mindset, you will increase your efforts to help you seek the answers you need to determine your investment area. Finding this area will allow you to move to the next part of your plan, consequently putting yourself one step closer to achieving your vision. This decision will only affirm that the growth-based approach was, in fact, the correct approach after all. The next time, this will be far easier since you will have strengthened the neurons within the brain connecting a more direct pathway to acting with a growth-based mindset. And therein, we have the recursive process.

The more you understand, and the more you can apply this logic, the more accessible everything will become to you. Crucially this grows exponentially, improving your mindset equally until you finally accept, as I do, that anything is possible if only you apply yourself. These principles are taught throughout Carol Dweck's book Mindset. I would suggest that you spend as much as 40% of your research for the next few months on mindset alone if success is truly your goal.

So how do you apply mindset to your property business? The obvious answer is to remain open-minded that this is an absolute possibility, and you can achieve your version of success if you genuinely believe. Should you not currently believe that, then you need to press pause and work on your mindset, not exclusively, but predominantly. Remember that education will increase your confidence and reduce your fears and worries. The result is a significant increase in your mindset. However, trying to apply mindset to property may be your mistake. This is the principal reason I have purposely excluded property examples from the majority of this chapter.

Mindset is about you and changing or improving your behaviour and beliefs, not about adopting it temporarily for a property purchase. Suppose you look at the root of the problem and address that, then this will naturally filter through to your property journey. To reaffirm my statement, mindset should be ingrained in everything you do. It is in how you act, how you absorb, what barriers you build as you read on, and how susceptible you are to change. How you read or listen to this book is mindset. For example, when prompted earlier, did you press pause and grab that pen or take five minutes to understand Audible's clip and bookmark function? Or did you press on, thinking that did not apply to you, or do you simply not have time to do that whilst listening to this book on 1.5 so that you can get to the end quicker? If any of that reverberates, then I am specifically talking to you. This is a flaw, albeit a minor flaw in your mindset, but flaws are there and should be worked on. I am sure even by this point in the book, there have been a few things that I mentioned that you wished you had written down. If this is the case, humour me, grab a pen and paper now, and apply from here on in. You will be surprised how helpful it can be. Then you will experience the previously mentioned recursive process first-hand.

Whatever the result of this, it tells us something about your mindset. Maybe you were waiting to see if the book was decent enough to make notes; again, that tells you something. I am not suggesting these are fundamental flaws in your personality but relatively small development indicators. I will never tire of telling you that mindset is ingrained in everything you do.

If you want hard property examples, it is in how you apply the lessons taught in this book. Will you work through our action plan ®, or will you only take time to listen to the advice given and then move on to the next book? How will you continue to educate yourself on the areas you are most weak in, or will that be ignored? Instead, the focus will be given to the areas that spark your interest or with which you are already accomplished.

How will you view a property? Will you have a brief walk around the property looking for anything that jumps out, cross your fingers and hope for the best, or will you strategically approach this with our viewing template and guide®?

Will you carefully analyse the mathematics and returns this selected property gives you whilst accurately gauging the implications of the refurbishment and its associated costs? Or will you plough through to buy this property simply because you have been informed that it is a BRR, and that is what you are supposed to buy, right?

Crucially will you apply patience to your journey, understanding that impatience often clouds our judgement? Will you accept that anything is possible and that just because you have not done this before does not mean you are not adequately equipped to succeed? We might very well be talking about investing in a turnkey property as much as we might be talking about a six-bedroom HMO or a seaside town serviced accommodation (SA).

Lastly, are you looking forward to your journey, or are you filled with dread about the unknown and what might happen if it all goes wrong? These are all mindset traits. This is why mindset is in everything we do. Not merely our thoughts on positivity.

As you might reasonably conclude from this chapter, with its dominance in content so far, mindset is simply more important than any other single factor in our 15 laws. The reason I chose to wait until now for its inclusion is two-fold. The first being 'Time', 'Education' and 'Capital' are what I class as the big three and the fundamental considerations before even considering property investment. These are the first three questions I ask any new aspiring investor whom I speak with. The second reason was, in fact, for reasons of mindset, and by that, I mean your mindset.

My gut feeling was that including such a significant chapter like this early on in the book may have lost a portion of my audience. I wanted first to include some real-world property examples to capture your attention and hopefully make a few of you sit up and take note before I moved into what some would have deemed irrelevant at that point of the book.

I am aware that we are subconsciously moulded by the world in which we live. We all want information now; the inconvenience of a small wait can be all it takes to switch off and refocus on something faster. In 2021 Amazon calculated that a page load slowdown of just one second would potentially cost it **$1.6 billion in sales each year**.

Shortly after, Google announced that by slowing its search results by just four-tenths of a second, they could lose 8 million searches per day – meaning they would serve up many million fewer online adverts each day. Knowing this was the driving force for deciding to put mindset where it now sits within my 15 laws. However, I must stress for clarity that my laws are not weighted one to 15 in terms of relevance or significance but merely as a list to consider when looking at what weaknesses may exist in your education.

Suppose we take a few minutes to consider mindsets predecessors, that of time, education, capital, and understanding why. We can clearly see why mindset sits at the top of this pile. In case you are wondering, the answer is that all the other elements include mindset, fundamentally. The benefits of realistically calculating the big three, as well as identifying your why, are all for the benefit of mindset.

Given a little time to reflect, we could identify a connection with mindset for all the points that follow on our list of laws. Fundamentally everything leads back to mindset. If we consider some significant inhibitors to our development, growth, and progression. Fear, confidence and overwhelm being the three main culprits. I cited that education helps elevate these unwanted traits, and it does, categorically. Once we understand established theory to expand the boundaries of our minds by absorbing material that shows how something we never thought possible can be done, then we can grow.

We grow in conjunction with our knowledge, and the byproduct of that is that your confidence, fear and overwhelm become more manageable. But the real victory with this is that our mindset grows exponentially. This is what takes us to the next level, not our education; it is what your education does for your mindset that carries you forward.

Equally, understanding our why helps us when faced with challenge; if you have a strong enough why you have the strength to continue to push through the challenge, this strength is your mindset. You feel too strongly about your why to give up, so you try harder and ultimately reach your intended goal, and the affirmation of the recursive process cements itself further.

As I mentioned earlier, understanding your limitations, challenges, or advantages when it comes to your time allocation is fundamental to improving your mindset. Suggesting more hours than you physically have available can be catastrophic, not only because you will try to complete the tasks and allocate the time to an already crammed schedule and risk burning out, but because you will feel overwhelmed with what you must do in such little time.

The result? Your mindset will suffer considerably. The same goes for our capital. If we look at what was achieved when we correctly analysed Amy's wealth, what do you think that did to her mindset? Do you think she shrugged and said, ok, I will have a look at that later or do you think she continued her education with an awe-inspiring attitude towards her future?

Conversely, taking time to understand that Capital can be raised from sources other than your personal fortune, no matter how big or small, can significantly increase your mindset towards understanding that this industry is for anyone and not only for the rich or those fortunate to have established working capital. The latter will be discussed in more depth later in Chapter 13, finance. For now, let us park the mindset bus in the agreement that its importance to your success can not be overstated.

6 Identifying Your Vision

"In order to carry out a positive action, we must first develop a positive vision"

The 14th Dalai Lama

Suppose you set off on a mystery journey without having an idea of the final destination. Comfortably seated in your car, you pull off the drive with anticipation. The notion is an energizing prospect; you are thrilled with the endless possibilities; where you might end up is the thought of the day. Admittedly this is an exciting prospect, provided we are adequately equipped. At the very least, we have ample time, knowledge and, of course, money.

We might even know why we are doing this; maybe it is something we have always wanted to do. To be more of an explorer or improve our mindset towards risk. This journey will undoubtedly improve your mindset in many other ways, too, not least in the advantages of taking time for yourself, throwing caution to the wind temporarily and having some real in-the-moment type time.

It would be a commendable journey to take, and I implore you to do it one day; I have done this several times in my life and thoroughly enjoyed it each time. In fact, I spent the best part of six weeks in America with my wife and children a few years ago doing this very thing. But should it form part of your business model? Do you really want the focusing statement of your business to be 'let me see where I end up'? No, of course, you don't.

My question is more 'how do you expect to get there if you do not know where you are going'?

Understanding your vision at this stage in your journey will help you pave the way to that destination. You will be happy to hear that your vision does not need to be final and exact with a logistical plan of attack. It simply needs to be something to work towards. The goalposts will almost certainly move, and rightly so, as you advance with your education and investments.

Your aspirations will grow along with your needs and a general understanding of the possibilities within the industry. No one expects you to fully understand the gravity of these at this stage of your research, so your vision needs not to be definitive.

As you form a firmer understanding of this industry and the plethora of opportunities within, your expectations will increase in parallel. These will shift the business dynamics, and your vision will alter as this manifests. That said, we still need to set, at least for now, a course to follow. By this, I mean we need to understand how you want to play this game, what you want from property investment, and what you want it to give you in general. There are endless possibilities for each of you, but each one will yield an alternate plan; this is why your vision needs to suit you, your aspirations and no one else.

Your job at this stage may be straightforward, but it is necessary in equal measure. This is because identifying your vision is paramount to your success since it helps with momentum, offering clarity once established. Simply put, you must afford yourself the time to clearly identify what you currently see as your future desire from property investment. This is what we will call your vision. The important note is that this must be done as early on in your journey as possible. Identifying your vision is a prime example of a smaller step, often deemed unimportant and therefore ignored by many. However, take a few seconds to consider who you think will have a clearer idea of where to go or what to do next. The individual who has a vision or the individual who has no vision.

Since most of you will be seeking answers on what or where to go next on your journey, it would be foolish to ignore this law. What I am offering by suggesting this law is clarity. Granted, identifying your current vision will not unexpectedly yield consommé, but it will begin the process, and anything that helps is another step forward. Remember, it is the smaller steps that, when combined, create giant leaps. These forward leaps are made up of smaller steps alone. The giant leaps do not exist at this stage. If they are presented, remain cautious since they are built on weak foundations. We will never create momentum if we ignore the smaller steps deeming them too unimportant. The result is counterproductive since we will remain dormant while seeking these out. You can spend year after year looking for that giant leap forward, or you can begin to accumulate them, creating momentum. Fast forward five years and consider which approach will yield the best results.

To clarify, when contemplating your vision, you are not looking for short or medium-term goals. You are not even looking for objectives to achieve your vision at this stage. This will all be discussed when we discuss the 14th law, strategy. We are simply looking at where you want to be so we can begin to pursue options surrounding what property model and type of investment you will adopt to help you achieve this vision. You will agree that this is a far more efficient approach.

People invest for assorted reasons, meaning that their vision is different because of this decision. For example, investing for retirement or a slight income boost to their current employment will yield a different approach to someone who wants to replace their income and beyond. Furthermore, we also all start from different positions, so even if we had the vision, realistically, our journey would be very different. This is before we throw mindset, risk-to-reward threshold, education, time, capital, network, experience, stakeholders, peer pressure, support, age, and why into the mix.

The next time you worry this is how so and so does it, remember they will no doubt have a different vision than you, as well as all the others, plus many more variables just discussed. No two journeys are ever the same; therefore, if so and so does it that way, remember to consider this before you attempt to mimic.

In summary, your vision is not your ultimate fantasy or definitive end goal. It needs to be more tangible than that. Setting a vision that is too far from your grasp may negatively impact your mindset since it has the undesired effect of feeling unattainable due to it being too far into the future. I suggest highlighting something that helps you achieve the first measurable or significant shift within your life rather than the ultimate dream. For instance, if you would like to get some of your time back, what would you need from your property business to get, say, twenty hours of your week back? If you want to replace a portion or even all of your current income, place a monetary figure on this. Attribute that figure to your vision as a starting point. If you can identify this shift in lifestyle, you are far more likely to produce a coherent plan towards achieving it.

Vision may be the shortest law I discuss throughout this book, but please do not let that influence your opinion on the gravity of this law. The principal reason it is not discussed further is that it is discussed further in Chapter 15, strategy. Furthermore, since every one of you will have a different vision, there is no benefit in assigning examples to an arbitrary vision. I will gladly offer clarity if you want to know my vision back then.

Just like most people, I had not considered my vision carefully enough, therefore assuming my vision was to build a measurable business that would make me rich. I was currently earning around £50,000 net from my gas engineering business. Therefore I wanted to match this with property investment. My goal was to supersede my current business income with accrued rental profits; then, I could focus on developing a more passive income. As I started to see the returns from building my portfolio, it became clear that I would be far closer to my vision once I established a measurable income from property investment but with the same lifestyle. This was the moment I realized that I could never walk away from the £50,000 the gas business earned me because that would effectively take me back several steps. It then became clear that I was, in fact, doing things entirely wrong. Working my fingers to the bone to build an income to make me rich was not my vision.

My vision was to exit the Gas industry to afford myself the luxuries of lifestyle. Carefully understanding my vision gave me the clarity that I am sure most of you seek. I knew I needed to transition my businesses rather than aggressively build them simultaneously. It was only at the point of careful consideration towards my vision that I developed a strategy to implement the transition. And the rest is history.

"Every one of us has our limitations. Limited time, limited resources, and limited energy. As such, nobody can have it all in life. In light of our limitations, we each have to make sacrifices and scale back the scope of our ambitions. Seeing our vision early on in our journey clearly helps us to prioritise which opportunities to bypass and which activities deserve our dedication. Clarity of vision creates clarity of priorities"

John C. Maxwell

7 Control Strategy

Before we delve into this chapter, I want to be clear that I am not qualified to give you detailed business advice, nor should the following words be the only advice you take regarding your business structure. You should seek the help of a qualified charted accountant to help you determine what is best for you, your specific needs and your business requirements.

That aside, I want to shed some light on the options and how to begin, at least considering which may be right for you.

Realistically, we have two primary choices when deciding on our control strategy. We can either invest through a sole proprietor-type business meaning the properties will be listed in your 'personal' name, or through a limited company, whereby the houses will be listed in the company's name instead. You will be the director and the main shareholder within that company, of course, but the company owns the property in the eyes of the HMRC.

Which model you choose to leverage will be based on many variables; however, the central deciding factor will undoubtedly be one of the following two things. The first is your long-term business vision, and the second is your current income or tax bracket. We have a few possible scenarios to discuss before we can get into the advantages and disadvantages of both control strategies.

Your control strategy can be extended further to how you choose to run your business. Regardless of whether you choose to invest in your own name or through a limited company, there will be records to keep, paperwork to issue basic or more complex accounts to keep, as well as other minor administrative tasks to complete. Some of these will be mitigated when choosing your company structure and when deciding on the type of investor you want to be, and the latter will be covered in the next chapter.

The first consideration would be whether you are investing alone or is this a joint venture, and by that, I mean with your partner or business partner. Should you be investing alone, there are two further questions to ask. There is a third, but we will put a pin in that one for now and return to it later in the chapter.

The first question is the most important and, in some cases, will render the second question redundant. This is, how much do you earn? Essentially how close are you to the higher rate tax bracket of 40%, or are you already within this bracket from your employment income? The word 'employment' is critical at this stage. If you are investing solely, you are employed and earn over the current rate, which at the time of writing, is £50,270, then the choice is almost certainly taken away from you. After further confirmation from a charted accountant, the most likely outcome is that you will form a limited company to make your investments.

If you currently fall into the lower rate tax bracket, you must assess your situation further before deciding which route to employ. In this instance, the second consideration is your vision; now, thankfully, after following my systematic approach to establishing solid foundations throughout your entire business, you will already have this answer by the time you reach this point. *He says with some trepidation in his voice.*

Should you fall well into the lower rate, you have far more flexibility with your choice than if you were closer to the higher limit. Being closer to the limit would mean that one or two properties may tip you into the higher rate tax bracket, meaning choosing to open a limited company at this point would be the obvious one, especially if your vision is to buy more property as you advance. Should you have far more of a lower rate allowance, and by that, I mean you earn well under £50,270, then you have a little more freedom with your choice, and this is where the vision carries more weight.

Let us say that you earn £30,000, and your vision is to acquire four properties for your retirement. You merely need to calculate, quite easily I might add, with the help of your accountant, if your vision keeps you within the lower rate tax bracket. Should this be the case, it may be your wisest choice to invest in a personal avenue. Even if your vision is to purchase more property after you have used up your lower rate tax bracket, you can still invest through a personal avenue and then, further down the line, open a limited company when the time comes to continue your investing.

Just understand that the properties you have purchased in your personal name will remain in your name and, in most cases, cannot be easily transferred to the company without a sale.
To help with compounding, however, you can transfer the profits from the first few houses invested through the personal avenue into your limited company by what is known as a directors loan. This is an interest-free loan from the director as an individual entity for the company to operate. This capital can be redeemed at any point without any tax liability.

Remember our earlier example with Amy, who chose to transfer £1,500 each month to her property business from her employment salary? In this instance, she would have transferred £18,000 to her property business in the first year alone. Should she decide at the end of that year that she wanted this capital back, she would simply make the transfer. This is providing the funds were not allocated or instead providing they were available at this point. To reiterate, this is done without any tax liability. In short, what goes in from the director can just as quickly come back out.

If you are investing with a long-term partner or spouse, we do the same calculations as above, but instead, we now look at our combined income. We calculate our combined lower rate tax allowance and consider our vision. Should one partner's earnings be in the higher rate tax bracket but the others be well into the lower rate, we can tap into that lower rate tax allowance. Again the same considerations as above would be applicable.

Let us say Philip earns £60,000 per annum, but Pamela's part-time income equates to £18,000. This means that the couple has a lower rate tax allowance of £32,700 that they can use before the need to open a limited company presents itself. The properties would go in Pamela's name only for tax reasons, of course, but effectively, these would be a 50-50 split as common-law partners, as anyone who has ever been divorced can testify.

Should the properties be purchased with a business partner rather than a live-in partner, I would suggest opening a limited company from the beginning to avoid any disputes later on. This advice would extend to opening businesses with family members too.

If we now pull the pin from the third question I mentioned at the beginning of this chapter, there is a slight twist in the puzzle. Suppose you are classed as self-employed and already run a limited company. In that case, there is a good chance that you pay yourself the minimum tax-free allowance to cover your national insurance contributions and then make up the remainder of your pay with dividends. If this is the case, you may have concluded from the above that you are either in the higher rate tax bracket or, as most small, limited business owners often are, conveniently £1 under this threshold.

In this instance, we have a choice. Use this lower rate tax bracket allowance with the profits from our housing business and make up the difference each year with dividends until our housing company produces enough profits to use this allowance alone. Or, as you already concluded, invest immediately via a limited company. The fundamental questions are whom you will invest with and how close you, or are you combined, to paying 40% tax. The rest is finer detail specific to you and your circumstances. Again I would reiterate that you seek professional help from a charted accountant.

Earlier, I used the sentence, the need to open a limited company. Opening a limited company should not be looked at as a secondary option. It has become fashionable and almost a given to open a limited company to invest through. However, it did arrive principally through necessity. Let me explain.

In April 2017, the government's change in regulations stated that landlords would no longer be able to deduct their mortgage interest costs against their taxable profits.

Now, if you are a higher rate taxpayer, this would affect you considerably since you could offset these costs to gain a 40% tax relief prior to this, but the new law changes meant you lost this right altogether. Although You were no longer allowed to offset this interest against your pre-tax profits in the basic rate tax bracket either, there was a caveat for those paying 20% tax. The government introduced something they called a tax reducer. This was a 20% deduction from mortgage interest incurred to both tax bands equally. Since basic rate taxpayers can only offset at 20% anyway, the net result meant there was little change for those landlords. This is, of course, unless the removal of the interest payment deduction pushed your profits into the higher rate band.

If your mortgage is on an interest-only basis, this could be hundreds or thousands of pounds each year, and if you are a higher-rate taxpayer, and have multiple properties, then you can see the implications could be far higher. It means some landlords were paying higher taxes than the profit accrued from their investments. The government did not bring this in immediately but rather incrementally over a four-year period. This meant a loss of 25% of the allowance each year.

In fact, it was not that simple since other calculations are involved here, principally the point at which the 20% tax reducer was applied in the calculations. Remember that this only really affected higher-rate taxpayers. If you are a basic rate taxpayer, this will not affect you unless the gross figure of your investment income pushes you through the threshold.

The $64,000 question is what the higher tax rate will be in five years. At any point, the government could decide to lower this back to the historical rate of around £37,000. This would then negatively impact your business if you chose to invest personally and are employed or self-employed but not with a limited company. Security from this is another principal reason why people choose to invest through a limited company since limited companies are exempt from this and pay all their tax at the current rate of corporation tax which currently stands at 19% as I edit this book in January 2023. This is, however, due to rise to 25% in April of this year but only applied to profits of over £50,000.

There are, of course, advantages and disadvantages of each approach but briefly summarised, they are as follows:

As I have just discussed, there is no tax penalty for the higher rate earners regardless of how low and how often the government change the point at which this applies. Generally, since an accountant will be employed, you have less administrative work to complete regarding tax, companies house submissions and accounting records. Furthermore, tapping into your accountant's expertise and knowledge regarding expanding your portfolio, inheritance planning, and improved tax planning or efficiency will be invaluable.

Freely moving your capital from an already profitable limited company to your property business without a tax liability is a possibility, too, via an op-co, prop-co corporate structure, but this needs further investigation not only from your accountant but also from your broker to ensure that lenders are currently accepting this business set-up before you proceed. As we enter one of the most challenging times in recent years for lenders, it is becoming harder to obtain mortgages since the goalposts of what lenders will accept are continually changing.

The advantages of purchasing your properties through a personal avenue are as follows. Currently, each year you have a capital gains tax allowance of £12,300 or £24,600 if you invest with your partner in a 50/50 named split on the property. However, this is being reduced to £6,000 in April 2023 and then further to £3,00 in April 2024. This means any property you sell in each tax year can benefit from a tax-free allowance specific to the amounts above on the profits. Essentially if you flipped a property with your partner and made a profit of, let us say, £30,000, then the tax you pay would be calculated after the respective allowance, depending on the tax year, was deducted from the total profit made. In actual fact, since the solicitors, broker, and other purchasing costs would be applied at the point of sale, you would pay tax on a sum smaller than this, but that is for your accountant to demonstrate.

Should you want to take some profit for yourself after your tax liability is covered, there is no dividend taxation as there would be through a limited company.

Investing via a personal avenue opens you up to more choices when it comes to mortgage companies too.
For example, if there were 100 lenders whose model was to lend to limited company investors, there may be an additional 50 whose model was to lend to those who chose to invest through the personal avenue. The result is that there is more of a supply than demand imbalance. Therefore rates are generally more favourable.

The mathematics clearly demonstrates the benefits of this approach. If we rewind the clock to before the madness of increasing rates, a typical limited company mortgage rate was around 3.69%. The same product offered to a personal investor was around 2.59%. The difference on a £100,000 property would be £68.75 per month, which equates to £825 each year or £4,125 over the five-year fixed term. Suppose we assume that the difference remained relative. In that case, we could estimate, loosely, that over the 25-year term of the mortgage, we would save £20,625 on every property purchased through a personal avenue.

Further to this measurable saving, your accountancy fees and solicitors fees are less expensive since employing an accountant's services is not necessary to help run your business. Even if you employed one to complete your self-assessment tax return each year, there would still be a saving of around £1200 per year in accountancy fees.

Solicitor fees would be cheaper on each property purchase because the need to sign personal guarantors would be superfluous. Owning a limited company in most businesses is beneficial to the individual since the limited part of the company stands for limited liability, meaning that should the business fail for any reason, your creditors cannot seek payment from the director. Once the business is officially dissolved correctly by the accountant, then the directors are essentially liability-free from any debt.

The mortgage companies know this, and since they intend on lending you considerable sums of money, for example, £75,000 on a £100,000 property at a 75% loan to value (LTV), they require what is known as a personal guarantor to be signed by the borrower. Should this be a joint venture (JV), all partners must sign individual guarantees before the lender will release any funds to your solicitor.

The advice attached to and the witnessing of the signatures for personal guarantors need to be given by an independent solicitor not connected with the sale or purchase of the property. This is to avoid any conflict of interest. The problem is that since personal guarantees have become mandatory, solicitors have attached a hefty price tag to their advice. The average cost of a personal guarantee is around £150-£200+vat, depending on where you are located in the country. Shop around for this, however, as I have had clients cite that they have been quoted upwards of £500 for this per person.

I would conclude that around 95% of you will invest through a limited company. So with that in mind, there are a few things to note:

Firstly things need to be set up systematically. Your company should or instead needs to be set up before you open your business bank account since the bank will want to see evidence of the company's formation. Essentially they will require the articles of association and will run a quick check on companies house to see that the company is listed and registered to you and that the directors and shareholders all corollate.

Your accountant can set up your limited company for you, which will cost you anywhere between £100 and £200 depending on the share structure.

Without wanting to overwhelm you with possibilities, if you invest with your partner and one of you pays tax at the higher rate and the other at the lower rate, and you still choose to open a limited company, you may want to consider alphabet shares ® for the profit distribution. The allocation of ordinary shares or the A shares to one partner and B shares to the other will allow dividends to be awarded to one partner without the need for the other partner to take them. This allocation will help avoid tax liability at the higher rate whilst offering the other partner the benefit of earning a dividend from the company. Your accountant will discuss this with you and advise accordingly.

Setting up your limited company is a relatively painless process and can be done yourself by visiting www.gov.uk/set-up-limited-company®. Here they will walk you through the entire process, including name choice. Just bear in mind that your limited company name needs to be available. The above link will allow you to search the database for availability.

The final word is your SIC which stands for 'Standard Industrial Classification of economic activities'; this is a five-digit classification providing the framework for collecting and presenting a large range of statistical data according to economic activity. But in English, this lets the HMRC see, at a glance, what industry you operate in.

This is important to understand because most mortgage companies require your business to be a special purpose vehicle (SPV).
Several SIC codes are available to allocate depending on your business activities, from 'Buying and selling of own real estate', *SIC code 68100, to* 'Other letting and operating of own or leased real estate', SIC 68209, which is the most popular for investors who choose to invest in buy-to-lets (BTL) for the long term.

Should you choose the wrong SIC code, you may find it harder to obtain mortgages. For instance, choosing 68100, as detailed above, would suggest that your primary function as a business is to flip property. This may reduce the number of lenders available since most mortgage companies rely on long-term investments, not short-term, when looking to lend their capital.

For all advice, however, if in doubt, who you gonna call? That's right, 'Ghostbust... err, a qualified accountant.

8 What Type of Investor will you be

Having already considered your vision, this will purely be an academic task, and therefore, this law will yield another short chapter of my book. That said, these smaller laws still offer momentum and clarity when looking to build your foundations, so its inclusion and consideration, regardless of its length, is essential for you at this stage of your research.

There will be many instances when the type of investor you initially thought you would be will be taken from you. Often this is due to your location to your investments; for example, if you are based in the south but after researching your investment area, you have identified a more northern location. Time is another determining factor when considering the type of investor you will be. If time is your restriction, clever leveraging and outsourcing might be in order. Regardless of why this decision may not be your own understanding this early on, so you can prepare appropriately will move you one step closer to your vision.

There are many factors that will govern how you choose to invest or the type of investor you will be, but for clarification, the types of investors we are considering at this stage are a hands-on versus a hands-off approach to investment. Most of you will likely fall somewhere in between this spectrum, but for now, let us keep this a binary choice. Ultimately which you decide to leverage will depend mostly on your circumstances and how you analyse your position with the big three. Time, Education and Capital. And fundamentally, which of these you chose to leverage primarily.

To help shed some light on this, we must first take a slight but relevant detour to explain the time, cost, quality triangle, otherwise known as the iron or project management triangle.
The basic premise of this triangle is that there are three main factors in all decisions relating to any project and that you can only have or control two factors of the triangle at any time during the project.

For instance, let us assume we are carrying out a refurbishment in one of our properties. We decided that we wanted the project to be completed quickly, which would represent the time side of the triangle, and we would very much like it to be done cheaply, too, representing cost.

In this instance, we must accept that the quality of the finished project will most likely and in most cases, be poor.

Conversely to this, the project can be cheap and of good quality, representing the cost and quality sides of the triangle, respectively. The draw here is that it will not be done quickly, clearly representing time.

Lastly, should we choose the project to be finished on time and we want it to be of good quality, well, unfortunately, this will come at a cost.

The time, cost, quality triangle is an excellent tool or concept to adopt when deciding on any project. The idea of it is to highlight which two are the most important to you on the project and then to remain consistent with that choice throughout. For those of you who decide to adopt the flipping, BRR, developing or conversion models within your business, this will be a handy tool and will save you much time and energy trying to figure out why there always seems to be something you just cannot quite put your finger on with your refurbishments or tradespeople.

The reason we needed to consider the triangle is that this will help you decide what type of investor you would like to be. Should time be your most precious element, then you must accept that only one more corner of the triangle can be factored, cost or quality. Assuming cost or, rather, capital is not a restriction to your business, for this example, one would assume that you would choose to leverage quality. This means things are going to cost a little more. This is most likely because you would then need to leverage help from either a sourcing company or, in most cases, a lettings agent to help forward and run your portfolio, respectively. The result here is that, essentially, you would be considered a more hands-off investor.

Should quality be your most precious element, but this time around, capital was your restriction, then again, the choice seems largely made for you. You will have to be far more prudent with your investments to ensure they stack up. This means that you may need to be more hands-on than hands-off, ensuring that properties get sourced appropriately, project-managed properly, and the right tenant is placed in the property after that. This will all take more effort and require a more hands-on approach. I am not suggesting that you need to do all of this exclusively, however. But it will require more of you, at least in the beginning.

Weather you consider yourself 'hands-on' or 'hands-off' or somewhere in between is purely subjective and somewhat irrelevant as a badge. The important thing is that you understand what the tag you attribute means to you and the way you will run your business, and the limitations, challenges, and advantages it will present as you advance.

A few years ago, just as the coronavirus pandemic was manifesting, I had the pleasure of mentoring an investor from South Africa. Not only was he from South Africa, but he mostly lived there too. Bruce, which is not his real name, but it will be for the purpose of our example, and hopefully, when he reads this, he will get the not so clever word play on his name, would class himself as a very hands-on investor.

The confusion arises when I tell you that I consider him a hands-off investor. In fact, the epitome of a hands-off investor. The difference being even though he spent large portions of his working day focusing on his property business, almost his entire strategy relied on leverage. He, of course, leveraged me as his library of knowledge, tools, and resources. He leveraged sourcing companies to find him off-market or direct-to-vendor deals as well as BRRs, flips and rent-to-serviced accommodation, which will all be explained as we advance.
He leveraged other investors and businesspeople to loan or angel him capital when and where it was needed. He leveraged builders to convert the properties from single lets to HMOs or to carry out refurbishment works to increase the equity within the property. Finally, he leveraged agents to manage the properties for him once completed.
This is all in addition to the standard leveraging most of us do by using brokers, solicitors, and accountants.

The reality is that at each point of leverage, there was a reduction in what he was making from the deal. However, this did not matter to him since there were no other options, no alternative or no other way he could invest. In actual fact, regardless of this, Bruce did very well adopting this model since the deals he secured had enough equity in them to go around. Something I try to get across repeatedly is that if the numbers work for you, then you should not be overly concerned about who else gets paid. He calculated the costs, the deals stacked up both on paper and in real terms, so regardless of whether he decided to apply a hands-off or hands-on tag to his investing, he knew exactly what he had to do to counter the limitations and exploit his advantages. Bruce, in this instance, adopted time and quality from the triangle, fully appreciating that he could not embrace cost as well. This saved him precious time and energy as he built what is today a profitable portfolio.

There are five central factors that will help determine what type of investor you will be. They are as follows:

1) Sourcing - Will you source your own properties, or will you enlist the help of a property sourcer? More on this later. Maybe you will apply both to your strategy.
2) Viewing - Who will view and analyse the properties, regarding their suitability to your business, both structurally and mathematically?
3) Refurbishment - Who will determine and complete any refurbishment works needed, and who will project manage these refurbishments for you?
4) Lettings and Management – Who will find, vet, sign-up, and then manage the ongoing tenancy?
5) Vision – will your properties be your secondary or primary concern? Is it your intention to switch careers to become a professional investor now or at any point in the future?

You must consider where you land with this right now, but also where you might want to be with it in the future. I have spoken with many investors who source, project manage and then self-manage their properties to keep costs down initially. They build their portfolios this way and then hand them over to a management professional once they have learned the ropes or built their business to the point that they had visualised with their profits.

Equally, there are many individuals we have assisted who leverage either property sourcers or project managers and management agents to manage their portfolios while they concentrate on expansion. Then take this over at the point where it becomes more cost-effective for them to step away from their current job and absorb more of their business and its day-to-day running.

Side note: I am not suggesting that others exchange one job for another or even that you must exchange your time to earn money from property investment. In actual fact, property is a semi-passive industry that makes money 365 days of the year, almost regardless of your input, once your portfolio is established, of course. It is a business that can grow contra to input though the powers of compounding.

I am by no means suggesting that no input is required, in fact, the opposite. However, as your business or portfolio grows exponentially, your effort does not need to match this like it would in the everyday business world. Consider any other industry where you would try to increase profits. You would look for new contracts and hire more staff, which means more work for you. As this business grows, so does your input, generally.

Your property investment business, because of its semi-passive nature, often grows without that extra relative effort needed by the individual. Should you choose to become a full-time property investor, you are choosing to work on or within your business. It is not a necessity. The business will need you, from time to time, of course, but with property investing, it knocks on your door when it does. Then it seems to leave you alone for a while until you want to grow it, or it needs you again. The breaks in between these events are what give you your freedom, and this is why I cite its semi-passive nature rather than its passive nature.

To summarise, you need to determine your approach to finding, analysing, refurbishing, letting and managing your portfolio to aid its beginning and development. Consider the big three in Time, Capital and Education, as well as the Time, Cost, Quality triangle.

9 Returns

Please note: For complete transparency, I want you to know that parts of this section will be similar to my previous 123 on property investing book due to their nature. It is challenging to articulate pre-determined equations differently. However, the section is updated, expanded upon, and the numbers used in the calculations differ too.

Understanding precisely what to include to ensure accuracy and then taking the time to calculate your returns on each deal can be the difference between a poor to average investment or a good to fantastic one. Calculating these returns can be exciting, too, especially when viewing favourable outcomes on a specifically designed spreadsheet.

Spreadsheet planning is paramount to the success of the investment you are analysing since it helps you see all the mathematical information, whether that is good or bad, in one place. It really can be the difference between a good and a poor purchase or a good purchase and an excellent one. You have all, well, all the financial information at least, there in front of you before you decide to commit. Setting up an interchangeable data input sheet can save time and help you confirm or dismiss a property's potential in seconds. This quick analysis is something I've done right from the beginning and still do to this day, despite being able to compute a general return rather quickly in my head.

Before considering any property, I run broad brush figures through my 'Quickshot' spreadsheet to determine whether the property is worth viewing. Should I proceed to view the property, my next port of call would be to run more accurate figures through my 'Full Feasibility' spreadsheet. This full feasibility will include that day's mortgage rates, any refurbishment works picked up on the viewing and a more accurate rental charge after running some comparables and speaking with my management team. These updated figures yield more accurate returns, which help me determine the offer to make on the property. If the ROIs and cashflow stack up, then I make an offer. Already knowing, of course, before I viewed the property that the area was investable.

But what exactly are yields, ROIs and cashflow? You will have heard these terms many times before, but you may not understand them completely. So, let me explain each term in its simplest form, then I will get to their importance and, for what it is worth, I will give you my honest opinion on them.

Yields

The term yield can be broken down into two different forms. There is 'Gross Yield' and 'Net Yield.' Yields are always expressed as a percentage and can be summarised as follows:

Gross yield

This is the simplest form of calculating a yield percentage. It is not as accurate a measure as its counterpart net yield. Still, it is far easier to compute, meaning it can be used to calculate speedily without getting into any depth with mathematics.

Generally, when you hear investors, developers, property sourcers or TV presenters talking about their yields, and they don't specify the expressed yield specifically as net, it is safe to assume that they are talking about gross yield. This is especially true if they sound like they are bragging and even more so if they are trying to sell you on something.

A gross yield calculation is always expressed as a higher percentage than a net yield calculation principally because net yield includes running costs. In contrast, gross yield is based on the correlation between the price of the property and the rent only.

Therefore as cited, gross yield is a more straightforward calculation which is expressed as follows ®:

'Annual Rental Income' divided by the 'Property Value', or you can use the 'Purchase Price' if you wish. Then multiply that by 100 *(this expresses it as a percentage)*

A typical gross yield example can be calculated as follows:

Firstly, calculate the amount of rent received in one year; for example, a £650 per month rental charge has an annual rent twelve times that amount; thus, £650 x 12 *(months)* = £7,800 per annum.

Next, divide that figure by the cost of the property. Let us say for ease of calculation that we purchased the property for £100,000.

Therefore, in its simplest form, a £100,000 property having a rental charge of £650 per month or £7,800 per year would have an annual gross yield of 7.8%.

That is **7,800 divided by 100,000** = 0.78, **multiplied by 100** to express it as a percentage, and it equates to a **7.8%** gross yield and is as straight forward as that.

Should you wish to pause now and calculate a gross yield, here is an example to try yourself:

The rent on the property is **£550**, and the cost of the property is **£80,000**.

I will give you the answer at the end of the returns chapter

Net yield

This calculation is a natural continuation of the latter. The inherent difference is that it takes into account costs associated with the running of the property; this includes but is not limited to the mortgage payments, insurance costs, agent's fees, and any planned routine maintenance or certification that may apply. Therefore, investors use the net yield more favourably when deep-diving since it is a more accurate way to appraise the viability of any investment property. Although, as I will explain in a short while, I tend not to use net yield, ever.

However, to aid you and for you to make up your own mind, I will give you a clear example based on the above property from our gross yield calculation, which was a £100,000 property accruing £7,800 of rent per annum.

The net yield calculation is as follows:

'Annual Rental Income' minus 'Associated Running Costs' divided by the 'Property Value' or 'Purchase Price' times by 100 *(to express as a percentage)*

The following example uses a typical buy-to-let (BTL) interest-only mortgage product with a 75% loan-to-value (LTV) using an interest rate of 4.6%.

Glancing at my 'Quickshot' spreadsheet, I see a monthly mortgage payment of £287.50, equating to £3,450 per annum. These yearly mortgage payments will be subtracted from our £7,800 accrued rent. This is leaving us with a balance of £4,350.

However, employing a letting agent costs us conservatively and, more precisely for ease of calculation, conveniently, 10% of the monthly rent, which is another deduction of £780 from our £4,350. This further deduction leaves us with a balance of £3,570.
Continuing with deductions here is subjective; some add insurance, as cited above, and some nominal routine maintenance fees like gas and electric certification. We can add licencing fees in the case of HMOs and even void period percentages should we be inclined to do so. My personal feelings are not to include the latter as it is a hypothetical input, whereas the other deductions are more constant and known.

Our example here shows a net yield of 3.57% which, to demonstrate with clarity, was calculated as follows:

Annual rent **£7800** minus the mortgage and the agent's fees of **£4,350,** leaving **£3,570**. Divide that figure by the cost of the purchase, **£100,000,** and we get **0.357**. Lastly, multiply that figure by 100 to express it as a percentage. This equates to a **3.57%** net yield.

Should you wish to pause now and calculate a net yield, here is an example to try yourself:

The rent on the property is **£600**, with a mortgage payment of **£276**. Let us say that the management charge is **10%**, but remember that 10% comes from the total rent received i.e. 10% of the £600. The cost of the property in this example is **£96,000**.

I will give you the answer at the end of the returns chapter.

Return on Investment ROI

You might argue that return on investment is the most important calculation you need to understand the property's potential. I would certainly be in your corner should you conclude this for yourself.
There are variations of ROI, ROCE being the main culprit. ROCE stands for 'Return on Cash Employed', but in essence, ROI and ROCE are one and the same thing. They both measure how well your money is working for you. I have a tendency to look at them slightly differently, but that is my preference and not a definitive meaning. For clarity, I view ROI as the return I get from the money I initially invested in the deal, whereas I consider ROCE as the return on the cash I have left in the property or the deal.
After re-financing or once the rental profits begin to accrue, it essentially decreases the amount of capital you have left in that particular property meaning your ROCE increases as a result. An example using £25,000 of your working capital to purchase a property. After costs, the property yields a £294 cashflow per month, expressed as £3,528 per annum. This would give an ROI of 14.1%. However, at the end of year one, the cash employed in the deal would now be £21,472.

This is the initial £25,000 minus the £3,528 of cashflow that you have accrued from rental profits. Your ROCE is now 16.4%. This ROCE increases exponentially over the next few years. 19.6%, 24.4%, 32.4%, and 47.9% in years 2,3,4,5 respectively. By the time we end year seven, our ROCE is infinite since we have our entire initial investment back in our account through accrued profits. Of course, this uses an ideal scenario with no voids or maintenance charges. Applying them would slow the ROCE growth, but the principal theory would be applied similarly.

This way of thinking is just my view and is a matter of simple perspective. Depending on how strategic you want to be with your spreadsheet analysis and if, in fact, you see any benefits to this viewpoint, only you can decide if you want to adopt this. The main benefit of ROCE for me is when considering more significant investments.

For instance, I have just had an offer accepted that will require a large sum of capital to be invested into a 56-bedroom student let. When calculating the numbers and the potential profit, I applied a ROCE viewpoint as my broad-brush calculation. This showed that I would have all my invested capital back in my account within four short years. My ROI on the deal would remain the same, whereas my ROCE increases yearly. In this instance, it offers much-needed confidence, especially when dealing with larger investment numbers.

ROI is calculated as follows:

'Annual Rental Income' minus 'Associated Running Costs' divided by the 'The Amount of Capital used to Purchase the Property' times by 100 *(to express as a percentage)*

As with the yield calculations, we start with the rent accrued over one year, so as per our previous examples, we are using £7,800 per annum. Next, we subtract the costs associated with running the property, essentially the mortgage and management fees of £4,350, which leaves £3,570. You will note that up to this point, the calculation so far is the same as the net yield calculation. The difference from this point on is that we do not use the arguably arbitrary figure of the property value or purchase price but instead the more useful figure of our total invested capital.

This figure should include every penny of your working capital used to purchase the property. Including, but not limited to, the 25% deposit contribution, the mortgage valuation and application fees, if applicable. Stamp duty land tax (SDLT) solicitors fees, broker fees, sourcing fees, and other legal or finance costs attached to the purchase.
Let us suppose that these all equate to the modest and conveniently demonstrable sum of £30,000.
The yearly rental income minus the associated running costs is now divided by our £30,000 of capital used for the purchase.

So **£3,570 divided by £30,000**, and just like other times, to express this as a percentage, we must **multiply the figure by 100**. Our ROI in this demonstration is **14.4%.**

I know some investors who don't include their mortgage arrangement, broker or even the solicitor's fees in this mathematical equation. And I suppose It is not essential, so it is up to you what you decide to include or to omit; in the same way, it doesn't matter when calculating the associated costs with the net yield working. All that matters is that you are consistent with your sums each time. My advice, should you want it, however, is to include all of your outgoings so you can see precisely how well your money is working for you. This will allow you to measure your returns against other asset classes or investment avenues

Should you wish to pause now and calculate a return on investment, here is an example to try yourself:

The rent on the property is **£600**, with a mortgage payment of **£258.75**. The management charge is **10%,** and the total money used to purchase the property was **£26,200**.

I will give you the answer at the end of the returns chapter.

Cashflow

This is the simplest of the calculations and represents how much gross profit you will make on your investment once you begin to accrue rent. For clarity, net profit would be calculated at the end of the tax year and would include any other costs incurred, including maintenance charges and the running costs of the business.

Cashflow is calculated as follows:

'Monthly Rent' minus 'Running Costs'

The same running cost as my previous demonstrations will be applied here for continuation. The difference here is that cashflow is usually demonstrated as a monthly figure. So the costs will be applied monthly as a result. Should you want to calculate your annual cashflow, simply multiply the monthly cash flow by 12. Sorry if that sounds condescending; it is not my intention. I just want to be clear for everyone's benefit.

The monthly rent received was £650, but as per the above calculation, we must subtract our running costs. Applying our mortgage payment of £287.50 and a 10% management fee of £65, The monthly costs equate to £352.50.

Monthly rent of £650 minus running costs of £352.50 equals a monthly cashflow of £297.50. Or £3,570 annually.

Being bombarded with a whole host of numbers, calculations and equations, it would be understandable if you were thinking, what just happened? I trust it was not too overwhelming for you, however, you would be forgiven if you didn't quite keep up. In the 123 on property investing, I went on below to demonstrate, specifically for the book's readers, by laying out the calculations. However, this time, we have created downloadable cheat sheets for you as part of this book's free resource pack. Enjoy.

What is the importance of each calculation, and which should you use?

Many investors, successful ones at that, use yield calculations as a way of determining their returns by means of appraising a proposed purchase. Therefore I am sure my following comments will be heavily scrutinised by some, and rightly so. We all have different views and methods, there is no right and wrong here, only what works for you. This is what I have been trying to articulate and will continue to do so throughout the remainder of this book. We all have our own way and should do what works for us.

Fundamentally though, for what it is worth, my opinion is that yield is perhaps the most unnecessarily overused term within the property industry. Watching TV programmes such as 'Homes Under the Hammer', you will find the term is used continuously throughout, often fueling its use with new investors. I can see its use for these types of programmes, but its value in assessing a property's feasibility I don't see.
In fact, if I am brave enough to put this in print for the second time, I have still never, in all my years of investing, calculated a yield on any of my properties, not even merely out of interest.

I honestly could not tell you what any of my properties yield regarding these two calculations. Conversely, each property's return on investment and cashflow are permanently engraved in my thinking and documented on a spreadsheet.

Should you question why these TV shows use gross yield as a measure rather than ROI or even net yield, I can shed some light on this for you. It is for generic and nonspecific demonstration purposes only.

Without digging too deep into the personal side of someone's investment, you can work out their gross yield in a matter of seconds. Simply take their annual rent and divide it by the purchase price and there you have it; this is why these TV shows use gross yield because it is non-intrusive. It would be a little invasive to ask an investor how much of their capital is tied up in that particular investment and what their running costs were on each property. Moreover, it is a much simpler way of demonstrating figures for the audience. Personally, if I hear someone talking about yields concerning their investment, I assume I am talking with someone who doesn't fully understand the point of the property investment game and the fundamental laws of money. Therefore I often try to educate them by questioning their use of yields. To this day, I have never had a response that made me question my heavily weighted opinion of ROI over yield, and until that day comes, I will continue to have this viewpoint.

My advice, however, is to research these terms for yourself to conclude which you will choose to calculate. At that point, you can leave the yield talk to the stock market investors.

I use ROI and cashflow exclusively to assess a property's suitability in gauging precisely how well my money will work for me on a deal-by-deal basis. Furthermore, this lets me see how well my money performs compared to other asset classes. After all, if property investing ever became a poor investment vehicle for me, I would switch to whatever the better option was. For now, at least, I'll stick to property investment.

For the remainder of this chapter, I will only discuss return on investment and cashflow as the driving force for your calculations.
To truly understand these returns, we must first take a deeper look at what they represent.

Suppose we had £25,000 in working capital and wanted to purchase a two-bedroom terrace property for £83,000. In this case, our capital would comfortably allow us this purchase, and by comfortably, I mean we would have about £60 change from the deal, hence the slightly odd purchase price contrary to my other more easily demonstrable purchase prices.
If this property is rented for £575 per calendar month and we self-manage, then our ROI would be 16.2%.
Should we decide to enlist the help of an agent who agreed to a 10% management fee, it would yield a 13.4% ROI.

On the other hand, achieving £550 in rent would yield 14.98% and 12.3%, respectively.

So we have 12.3% rising to 16.2% at the corresponding ends of our potential return spectrum. These returns result in an annual gross cashflow of between £3,076.50 and £4,036.50. The difference is just over £1000 per year on each property you own, assuming they are equally comparable.

I am not building a case for rent maximisation here. Nor is it a case for self-management; we will get to that too. The reason for the highlight is to help you consider how a small variable in your investment can significantly alter your returns. And the reason for pointing that out is to signify how you should not, nay, cannot, use another investor's returns as your benchmark.

We could potentiate this further by saying you should be considerate when comparing future investments against past investments. Let us rewind the clock briefly to the point just before the Bank of England raised the interest rates. Before the first-rate hike in December 2021, it was not uncommon for a buy-to-let, interest-only mortgage product obtained using a limited company to be around 3.4%.

If we apply that change to our spreadsheet using the exact figures we just demonstrated, we have an annual return of between £3,823.50 and £4,783.50. This is a further difference of £747 for each return, resulting in increased ROIs of 15.3% and 19.2%, respectively. Let us suppose you bought ten properties at this rate. Would that mean your ROI benchmark should be 19.2%?

If this is to be your benchmark, how are you to continue investing through this next period? We have already discussed the 'Time Value of Money', the benefits of compounding and how inflation is our biggest enemy whilst offering us a helping hand with the erosion of our debt from the lender.

In short, our ROI expectations need to remain fluid since they are market dependent and, because of this, are somewhat beyond our control. Essentially, ROIs are what I have repeatedly described as a day-one calculation or used as a measure against other asset classes. This has never been more important to clearly understand and apply the logic than in recent times with the uncertainty surrounding the Bank of England's base rates and the resulting payment rates from lenders.

The object of the game is to measure the gain from investing against your loss through inflation, compared to what we can earn in other asset classes or even, depending on how high rates rise, from the bank's products.

As I write this chapter, there is no way of telling where rates will end up, but one thing is for sure, equilibrium will prevail throughout the length of your journey. If we assign your journey to the average term of a mortgage product, 25 years, rates will rise and fall, prices will rise and fall, rents will rise and likely not fall, and uncertainty will creep in periodically and sporadically.

But what is the alternative? And that is not a rhetorical question. Ask yourself, what is the alternative here? Ignoring stocks and shares, since I'm not walking you through that minefield, let me try to articulate this for you mathematically.

Let us return to our comfortable base of £25,000 working capital. Suppose the lower ROIs due to higher interest payments are putting us off investing this capital for the time being. We decide to apply caution and ambiguously watch the market to see where it goes. We now, at the time of writing, have £25,000 devaluing at the current rate of 10.5%, meaning, and assuming it remains at this figure, that by the end of year one of our observing, the £25,000 we had would now be devalued to £22,642.

Alternatively, since we are becoming far more educated than the average Joe, if we apply logic and consciously decide to accept the day-1 ROI, let us look at the counterargument.

What the ROI figure is right now is irrelevant; in fact, representing it here may be counterproductive since I do not want to influence anyone thinking with what their figure should be right now.

What is important is our monthly cashflow of £256.38, or £3,076.50 annually. The options we have are to lose C.£2,252 over the next twelve months through inflation or to make C.£3,076.50 through investment. The difference, by the way, is £5,325.50. In just twelve months. The following year, applying the same rate would equate to £10,454 of potential losses.

As you have come to expect by now, for complete transparency, these figures are gross since there may be some tax to pay on your accrued rent over the first 24 months. The difference would be surmountable, however, and I am sure you get the point I am trying to demonstrate. I have not factored in any potential capital growth nor included any rent increase at the start of year-two or the fact that you would now be starting to benefit from compounded capital. And remember, the earlier you can do this, the better it is for your property business. Which I am sure you will already know since you have no doubt researched compounding, or is that too much of a presumption at this stage of the book?

Previously, I mentioned that equilibrium would prevail.
We consider our ROIs a day-one calculation because they change when the makeup of the deal changes. For example, rent is something that will undoubtedly increase as a byproduct of the recent rate rises. Right now, it is beginning to filter through. As properties become available for re-let, many investors are testing the market to see what rent increase can be applied. Equally, if there has been no rent increase in the past few years, with existing tenancies, then many are looking to increase this now, especially as their fixed rate periods end.

Let us consider what happens to you and your returns in this instance.

At the time of purchase, we have an ROI of 12.43%. However, we have locked in our less-than-favourable, judged by recent times at least, interest rate for the next five years. When our offer was accepted on the property, we calculated the rent at £550 to get our 12.43% ROI and let us assume that we carry through with this. Utterly dismissing that we likely achieve a higher rate due to demand and other investors around us increasing their rents.

So for the first year, you accept a 12.43% ROI. In year two, however, you decide to apply a moderate 4% rental increase. Your rent is now £572, giving you an ROI of 13.05%. The same applies in years three, four and five giving respective ROIs of 13.79%, 14.54% and 15.32%.

If you average these ROIs over the term of your fixed 5-year mortgage product, you would see an ROI of 13.82%. This gives further weight to my claim that ROI is a day-one calculation. There would be a very favourable ROI by the end of the 25-year term. Ignoring what selling the property at the end of the term would do to your ROI at that point and any equity released over this term, reducing your invested cash as a result. Or when you factor in the fact that rates are likely to be far superior in five years when your fixed product ends. Each of these will significantly increase your ROI on their own, but when they compound, you can see the potential.

The latter comment of rates improving in five years is not a prediction or a guarantee but rather a presumption of the fact that lenders rely on a buoyant market to lend their capital and therefore have a vested interest in keeping rates manageable.

So how on earth are you supposed to know what a good ROI is? Firstly let me reiterate that ROI is market-depending. And unfortunately, I cannot morally tell you what a good ROI is for you because, just like your strategy, too many variables determine this for your individual approach.

This is not me avoiding the subject or sweeping it under the rug. I intend to help you work this out for yourself, and I will certainly tell you what I class a good ROI as.

Firstly, I do not care how low the ROI is if I have very little cash employed in the deal and I have not had to apply much effort to obtain the low cash injection. For instance, I have not had to endure a refurbishment to pull capital out because, in that case, I would require a good return for my troubles.

Furthermore, I do not look too heavily at the ROI if the property is in a high capital gain area. For example, investing in London ten years ago might have yielded a low ROI but, in opposition, a high capital gain which offsets the lower ROI entirely. One might argue that as long as the ROI is positive, then it is a good ROI; however, if we are talking a couple of per cent, then we would have to hope that another contributing factor is helping us here, like that of capital growth. If this isn't the case, 2% might be achieved in the bank, in an ISA or in some low-risk shares. So I would look at other avenues for sure should this be the case.

My dismissive nature towards ROI over capital growth comes from hindsight, of course. Although you didn't have to be a genius over the last fifteen years to see that property was booming in London, no one really knows what the next fifteen will hold.

In the example above, we have the first variable determining your ROI. Is the chance of capital gains very possible? If so, you can sit back and relax about your pitiful ROI as long as you are breaking even and you don't have all your money tied up. The counter-demonstration is not to have much capital gain but excellent cash flow. If this is the case, your ROI obviously needs to be much higher to offset the plateauing market in your chosen area. Lastly, we have the happy medium; this is reasonable growth along with reasonable cash flow. This scenario is the dream, but as you might imagine a little hard to achieve.

Due to my investment location, capital gain has never been at the forefront of my investment plan. Albeit, as with most areas of the UK, this increased by around 20% in 2022 alone. Still, historically I have relied on good ROIs rather than capital gains. Since I have had to rely on a solid ROI, my ROIs are generally somewhere in the region of about 16-20%, but the further down the country you go, this would generally reduce in tandem with a rise of capital growth to offset the fall.

Should I think there is a good chance of capital gain and ROI, then I would reduce this percentage in light of the gains, and this is how you should work out your ROI.

I should leave it there since it is down to the individual to work out their own percentage, and given that I do not know what market we will be in when you choose to read this book, it would be challenging for me to demonstrate.

However, to offer some indication, I will summarise for you. Before I do, however, I want to be clear about a few things.

Remember, I am not a financial advisor, nor is this advice in any way meant to be accountable. These are not to be used as a definitive benchmark, and I am talking about investments in their simplest forms. Essentially that means a standard buy-to-let, turnkey property with money in the bank and no necessity to recycle or stretch that capital. They are self-managed properties purchased through a limited company vehicle. ROIs increase as the deal increases, and if a more considerable ROI is necessary, then you need to carefully consider your ROIs and what each one will give you to achieve your vision which is the entire point of determining your ROI. Conversely, ROIs decrease as rates rise. The ROIs below are relative to historical investing and the current market at the time of writing only.

That out the way, I would summarise as follows; Up here in the sunny north, I would suggest aiming for as high an ROI as possible, between 15-18% historically and 11-13% in early 2023, as the base rate has just hit 4%. Suppose you are fortunate enough to have a mixture of both gains and good cash flow. In that case, anywhere between 12% and 16% historically and between 8 and 10 currently should be a good benchmark and so on as the capital gain likelihood increases. Note that if growth slows, not having a contingency can leave you vulnerable and dropping much lower might leave you having to search for other investment classes. This really is a broad-brush demonstration, and with today's investment models of BRR, rent-to-rent, HMOs or serviced accommodation, ROIs are much higher than just demonstrated.

This law aims to understand your returns so you can see if your current thinking can get you on your way to achieving the first measurable change in your lifestyle, which we have previously described as your vision.

For those of you who took the time to try to calculate the returns, here are the answers to the sums I left you with ®

Gross Yield – 8.25%

The rent on the property was £550, and the cost of the property was £80,000.

550 x 12 = 6,600
6,600 / 80,000 = 0.0825
0.0825 x 100 = **8.25%**

Net Yield – 3.3%

The rent on the property was £600, with a mortgage payment of £276. The management charge was 10%, and the cost of the property was £96,000.

600 – 10% = 540
540 – 276 = 264
264 x 12 =3,168
3,168 / 96,000 = 0.033
0.0.33 x 100 = **3.3%**

ROI - 12.88%

The rent on the property was again £600, with a mortgage payment of £258.75. The management charge was 10%, and the total money used to purchase the property was £26,200.

600 – 10% = 540
540 – 258.75 = 281.25
281.25 x 12 = 3,375
3,375 / 26,200 = 0.1288
0.1288 x 100 = **12.88%**

10 Determine Your Market Entry Point

Our preconceptions of the property industry may imagine us as the proud owner of seafront penthouse apartments. We might dream of four-bedroom detached property on an exclusive housing estate or a luxury city flat. We might have friends who are investors themselves who strongly advise investment in mid-terrace style townhouses through to ex-council estate properties. But regardless of what end of the spectrum we invest in and what type of property that would represent, the principles effectively remain the same. Investing in a two-bedroom townhouse to a four-bedroom new estate house has a similar approach in terms of calculations relative to the deal, property due diligence, viewing and subsequent tenant profiling.

Deciding which avenue to pursue is an entirely different thought process, however, and is something that again will relate to your vision. Which, should you decide to go back and use this book and its resource pack as a guide, would be determined by this point on your journey.

The initial decision on where to enter the market can be broken down into a fourfold consideration.

1) **Property Value**: *What 'price bracket' will you invest in?*
2) **Investment Models & Types**: *What 'type' and 'model' of property will you choose to invest in?*
3) **KYCs** or **Know Your Customer**: *What kind of tenant will you look to attract to the property?*
4) **Location**: *Where, precisely, in the country will you invest?*

One question may ultimately conclude another, and you may need to work through the list in an alternative order. However, the one question above all others that ought to be addressed first is: At what price bracket will you enter the market?

10.1 Property Value: What 'price bracket' will you invest in

Pricing your investment should be done with your vision in mind. However, all points in the 15 laws have relative importance to understanding your next steps, where you are heading and concluding what is right for you individually. Taking time to price your investment can be the difference between a modest and a handsome passive income. Understanding what we want property to give us, where we want to be, and in what timeframe are questions we will have considered when we penned our vision. The trick is to take those and determine whether our capital can get us to that point alone or if we need to develop clever strategy and investment models to enable it.

Of course, we all want different things from property investment, and we all have different levels of fear, risk aversion, satisfaction, settlement levels, hassle factor, time and so on, so we will not all necessarily want to purchase as much property as possible with our capital. Naturally, our research would leave us all investing in similar areas of the country should this be true for everyone. Regardless of this, however, one thing I am sure of is that we all want efficiency with our capital. Determining the price bracket of our investment properties with our vision in mind is the variable factor. By this, I mean there is no one price bracket that we will all target since this will be pre-determined by our specific vision.

The best way I can exemplify this is by introducing you to Judy.

Judy is a cautious individual, but she is willing to educate herself to ensure she makes no mistakes. Still, she is dead set on staying within the boundaries of her current comfort zone and completely controlling her portfolio on every level, from sourcing through to management. Judy has £250,000 in working capital. She has some money tied up in her home and has around £500 each month in surplus income. However, she is unwilling to entertain equity release and wants to retain her £500 surplus by employing a buffer to her lifestyle.

Judy has a simple goal which is to make the best use of her £250,000.

Since she wants to control her investments and remain in her comfort zone, she wants to invest no further than 20 minutes from her front door. She still has many options, which doesn't mean she will settle for a couple of easy-going, high-value, low-yielding properties. She wants what we all want from our capital, efficiency. Her local area in the North of England consists of a couple of large towns with a few smaller towns scattered around and a few villages sandwiched between two cities, which she feels are just a little too far away to invest in.

Depending on the town, properties range from £75,000 to around £400,000. She has a good understanding of the area, having lived there for over 25 years, and already knows after careful consideration that her 'vision' with her capital is around £3,000 per month, gross.
This feat might not sound too appealing to you or me, given that the potential with this capital coupled with her equity, surplus cash and the opportunities within this industry is essentially unlimited. But it doesn't matter what we think or what we would do. This is Judy's money; it is her life, her vision and her way of doing things that matter. She has taken time to educate herself and still believes what she is doing is the right choice, meaning it is, regardless of our opinion.

What is important in this instance is that Judy firmly appreciates that her capital is currently devaluing through inflation and that she is being as efficient as she can be within her current boundaries.

On this occasion, what matters and effectively what matters for every model, strategy, or journey is that she prices her investments at the right price to give her what she wants. In this case, and this is the idea of the demonstration, Judy needs to look at her working capital *Vs* the purchase price of the property and its correlation to the rental charge. Let me explain what this means.

A £75,000 property around where Judy lives would rent for around £425 per calendar month. Meaning each property would yield an 11.1% return on investment or ROI. She would be able to purchase around 11 properties with her £250,000 working capital. These figures include SDLT, solicitor, broker and mortgage fees using an interest-only mortgage of 4.6%. The result of these acquisitions would be a gross monthly income of around £2,300, meaning she falls way short of her vision. Furthermore, given Judy's controlling nature and comfort zone requirements, she feels that investing in this price bracket, being the cheapest in the entire area does not suit her.

Judy returns to her spreadsheet and looks at the other end of the spectrum. She knows purchasing property at the £400,000 point will be out of the question, so she looks towards the £275,000 mark to compare results. Properties in this bracket rent for around £1,400 per calendar month. The result here is that she would be able to purchase three properties at this value yielding an 8.8% return on investment. Her monthly gross cashflow would be £1,850, meaning, yet again, she falls well short of her objective.

Judy is beginning to see the significance of fully understanding this area of her business before she moves on to sourcing and viewing property. Realising this would have been a complete stab in the dark and could have cost her valuable time and money. She returns to her spreadsheet and inputs varying purchase values and their correlating rental charges until she settles on a price bracket that gives her the desired outcome.

Judy decides on a purchase value of around £95,000-£105,000, which her research shows an average rental charge of £595-£625 per calendar month. The result is a return on investment of around 13.7%. She would be able to purchase around nine properties giving a gross monthly income of around £2,900. She knows the areas well and feels there is enough of a step up in quality over the lower £75,000 price bracket. She is glad she spent some time establishing this since it was an excellent learning exercise that had efficiency at its core.

Judy can now confidently say that she knows exactly what she is looking for when she fires Rightmove up. Can you?

Regardless of what your vision is with your capital, choosing the right price bracket for your investments should be calculated, as in Judy's demonstration.
Should you have more ambition with your business than Judy, this is fantastic; however, we are now talking about adopting different investment models or investing in different property types.

10.2 Types of Investment & Investment Models

Investment types and their models are often misconstrued as investment strategies. Often you will hear an investor cite that their investment strategy is BRR or maybe HMOs. However, as you will find out later with Law 14, Strategy, there is nothing strategic about naming an investment model or the type of investment you invest in. Strategy is a far deeper topic than attributing an investment type or model label. It has analysis, vision, goals, objectives, and tangible actions attached to its creation.

In some cases, reaching our vision with our current working capital means that certain property investment types and models must be applied within our investment strategy. A typical turnkey, single-let property, an example being a typical two-bedroom house in a 'ready to let' condition, needing a minimum capital investment after purchase of under around £1500, might yield a monthly cashflow of between £250-350, representing an approximate return on investment of 12%. This might form part of an effective strategy if, for instance, capital is in enough supply, education is average, or if time is limited. Of course, this type and investment model is not dependent on all three of the factors just mentioned, and there are many other factors that might determine a turnkey, single-let approach.

My current investment approach is predominantly made up of these types of properties, yet education and time are in plentiful supply for me. The continuation of my portfolio growth and the supply of investment property, coupled with avoiding the small but measurable hassle factor of carrying out refurbishments, is the appeal of turnkey properties at this point on my journey. My strategy and vision do not rely on equity release or stretching of capital anymore. Yes, I still invest in HMOs and adopt the BRR model from time to time, but turnkey is my primary focus at this point in my career.

Conversely, an investment type and model of an HMO carrying out a refurbishment by employing the BRR model could easily yield three or four times the cashflow above, offering a return on investment of anything from around 30% to an infinite ROI in the case of releasing all of your invested capital through the refinancing process.

Of course, this model is far more hands-on and labour-intensive, not only in the refurbishment process but in sourcing the investment as well as the continued operation of the investment. One might throw into the mix that not only are these investments in higher demand they are in shorter supply to boot, making obtaining the right one more challenging for the average investor. This should not put you off this model, of course, since the other side of the coin is that we need far fewer of them to reach our intended vision. The nature of their return makes them an excellent choice for investors who need to recycle their cash or obtain higher-than-average returns. That said, it is essential that you are aware of this challenge and head into your search with your eyes open. At this point, you can assess where you fall with the 'Big three' Time, Education and Capital to decide on your approach.

Typical property investment 'Types' include, but are not limited to:

1. Single Let Property
2. Houses of Multiple Occupation - HMOs
3. Serviced Accommodation - SA
4. Commercial or Mixed-use Property

Each of the above 'types' of investments will yield a different return and therefore need different approaches to source, asses, secure and manage.

Single Let Property

A 'Single Let Property' is a property that requires, usually, a single AST or assured shorthold tenancy agreement. Flats, bungalows, two, three, or four-bedroom properties and so on, whether they are terraced, semi-detached or detached, all fall into this category.

Houses of Multiple Occupation – HMO

An 'HMO' is a house of multiple occupation. This is a property that has been divided up to provide secure living accommodation within a bedroom. Usually, the occupants share either bathrooms and or a kitchen. Often, they have a shared communal living space too. In almost every case, the tenant would pay for the rent on the room only since all bills are usually included in their weekly or monthly rent. Bills include but are not limited to council tax, gas, electric, water rates, broadband, tv licence, any tv streaming platforms like Netflix, and the cleaning of the communal areas. Don't forget that you will also need to include mortgage payments and insurance costs in your calculations. Also, HMOs of five or more bedrooms generally require licensing, so this is an added cost to consider.

Serviced Accommodation – SA

'Serviced Accommodation' or SA is essentially Airbnb. This is a property that has been refurbished or fitted for the purpose of short-term lets. As the name suggests, these properties are serviced either during, in the case of longer lets or as is more common after each stay. As with HMO investing, all bills are usually included; however, as you might imagine, the cleaning charges are significantly higher, as are the expectations with TV streaming and overall standard.

Commercial Property

'Commercial' investment typically accommodates activities intended to make a profit rather than regular residential property. A mixed-use building is one that has the above scenario mixed with residential living. For example, a building that houses an office on the ground floor with flats intended for residential lettings above is a mixed-use building.

Typical property investment 'Models' include, but are not limited to:

1. Buying and Holding
2. Turnkey
3. BRR (Buy, Refurbish & Refinance)
4. Flipping
5. Rent to Rent (R2R)
6. Lease Option

Again, each of the above investment 'models' will yield a different return and need different approaches to source, asses, secure and manage. When we mix these models with the types of investments we have, then there are many variants. For example, we can purchase an HMO that requires a BRR, or we can purchase a Turnkey HMO. We can purchase a single-let property to flip on a rent-to-rent basis or to hold for long-term capital growth. We now have many choices to consider, remembering that all will yield different results. The trick is to determine what will help us achieve what we want from our working capital or in the broader context of our property journey.

Buying and Holding

'Buying and Holing' is the concept of buying a property specifically for capital growth. Think investing in London in the early 2000s. This model relies on having a strong inclination that the property in the chosen area will increase well above the national average. Often ROIs and cashflow are secondary elements when choosing this investment model. Since cashflow is often lower, once your working capital has been fully allocated, subsequent properties need to be purchased via equity release once the property's value has increased measurably.

Turnkey Property

'Turnkey' Properties are ones that yield cashflow almost immediately. The basic principle of a turnkey property is to identify a property that requires minimal investment to let it to a tenant. In essence, you buy a property that you can let immediately after completion. I usually class a turnkey property as one that requires only cosmetic improvements to let. Anything around £1,500 or less qualifies as a turnkey property in my book and should take no longer than a week or two to complete. The idea of a Turnkey property and the model itself is that it requires minimal effort and should be relatively hassle-free. It is an excellent model to pursue when funds are plentiful and, or time is a little more limited. It can be a fast way to build a cash-flowing business since the model relies on little input from the investor once the property is purchased.

No Man's Land

Before we continue to the BRR model, I want to take a few minutes to talk about what I call 'no man's land'. This is the term I use to describe the point between 'Turnkey' investments and the BRR model. 'No man's land' is what many estate agents struggle to understand. Unless they are investors themselves, their preconception of a 'deal' is outdated at best.

The best example I can make here would be through three differing mathematical scenarios. The example features Mr A, the prudent investor. Mr B who is the more aggressive, hands-on investor. And Mrs C, the disastrous investor who has, despite her overwhelming argument to the contrary, very little property education.

Mr A is a steady investor playing the long game of property investment. He wants a somewhat hassle-free life; he has a good amount of working capital behind him and is prepared to wait for the right type of property to come along. He has limited time and a fair amount of property education. Therefore Mr A decides upon a model of turnkey properties.

Mr B is a more aggressive investor prepared for the hustle and bustle of multiple property viewings, deeper analysis regarding refurbishment costs, back and forward negotiations and isn't shy when it comes to getting down and dirty with wallpaper stripping, kitchen removals, and even painting when the time comes. He has a good network of trades around him and has plenty of time on his hands but limited working

129

capital. He aims to stretch that capital as far as possible; consequently, he has invested much time in his property education. Therefore Mr B decides to pursue the BRR model, fully explained in a short while.

Mrs C is a little confused about what property types and models to buy. She has watched countless hours of YouTube, listened to many webinars, and talked with some investors on Facebook. The only thing Mrs C knows for sure is that property investing can make you millions of pounds in a few short months, and you don't really have to apply much effort. As a result, Mrs C is not prepared to go through a thorough 'foundational' building exercise for her property business. Despite her self-belief in her property knowledge, she actually has very little education or the education she does have is drastically outdated.

Mr A buys £100,000 'Turnkey' properties utilising an interest-only mortgage of 4.6%. These properties rent for £625 per calendar month (PCM) and, as the name suggests, require no further investment. Assuming self-management, each property generates a gross monthly income of £337.50, equating to a gross annual income of just over £4,000. The capital required to buy each property, including all fees and taxes, which will be detailed later in Law 13, Finance, would be £29,700, meaning Mr A's return on Investment is just under 14%.

Mr B's model of buying BRR properties is a little more intricate and, as promised, will be discussed in depth soon. In short, he buys a property for £75,000, using the same 4.6% interest-only mortgage. He then invests a further £15,000 in refurbishment costs; however, after this refurbishment, the property would be valued at £105,000. The higher valuation means that Mr B can release equity in the property. At this point, Mr B only has £15,595 of his working capital tied up in his property. Mr B's return on investment based on the same rental charge of £625 per calendar month is 25%.

Mrs C, as explained, has not taken the time to understand how the mathematics work on a property in relation to her working capital. She

has entirely missed the point with 'purchase value Vs investment capital. She decides to buy a £95,000 property as she has deemed it a 'Below Market Value' (BMV) purchase, feeling she is getting herself a little gem of a bargain. The property needs new carpets and painting throughout. There are some minor repairs to carry out too. These are a couple of new doors, some light plumbing work in the bathroom and the kitchen requires new worktops. Together, her various contractors charged her £6,500 to complete the work. The property is ready to let, and Mrs C is happy, and her head is held high as she has just become the very essence of a property investor. Or at least what it was in the '90s, anyway. Like the other two properties, this one would rent for £625. The difference here is that Mrs C has not improved the property enough for a measurable revaluation, meaning her refurbishment costs are tied up in the property. Her capital injection is
£34,200, making her ROI 11.78%, including fees and taxes, yet her property is the same as Mr A's and nowhere near as nice as Mr B's. Remember, Mr A only used £29,700 to purchase his property, £4,500 less than Mrs C, but he has not had the hassle of a refurbishment and has had the convenience of cashflow almost from day one.

Effectively Mrs C has waited longer for her property to begin to generate income, has had the hassle of a refurbishment, used another £4,500 of her capital for a similar property and has a far lower ROI and subsequent cashflow than the other two approaches.

The principle point here is that in most cases, not all, of course, but mostly if you are trying to achieve higher returns on your capital relative to the property type and model that you will pursue, either the property is turnkey or a BRR. In most cases, there is nothing in between except 'no man's land'.

Mrs C has almost £5,000 more tied up than Mr A, more if you include the lost rent or the rent added to Mr A's approach, yet has the same standard of property. An arguably surmountable sum when buying one property, but imagine if Mr A and Mrs C intended to buy ten or even 20 properties continuing with the same model. The result is around £50,000 – £100,000 in capital locked away and therefore not working for Mrs C.

The difference here could represent a further three property purchases, yielding around £12,000 per annum. This extra revenue would help with compounding and, of course, the exponential growth of the portfolio.

BRR

'BRR' stands for Buy Refurbish and Refinance, and as briefly explained above, the principles of the model rely on stretching or, in some cases, completely recycling your working capital. This is an excellent model for investors who either have limited capital or for those who want to see their capital reach as far as possible and are prepared for the refurbishments coupled with the potentially slower growth in terms of numbers to their portfolio.

Since most lenders will not allow a property to be refinanced within the first six months of ownership, buying, refurbishing and then refinancing usually takes around eight months to complete. If you have limited capital, this is hardly a problem since the advantage of pulling a large portion, or in some cases, all of your money back out of the deal, far outweighs this minor drawback.

The potential setback to portfolio growth comes when capital poses an issue. Waiting eight months to get your capital back to start the process over again can be a tedious way to build a sizable portfolio since it inadvertently inhibits growth through the lack of compounding. We can, of course, argue that you would, time depending, be able to carry out multiple BRR projects simultaneously, and the reward of equity release would potentially outstrip the benefits of compounding. However, this multiple purchasing model would rely on the correct marriage of ingredients, principally the big three, time, capital and education. However, this is an investment model that you can run alongside other models. Simultaneously buying turnkey properties means having your cake and eating it. We benefit from compounding and instant cashflow coupled with recycling capital upon equity release. It can be a marriage made in heaven.

So how does BRR model work? ® Fundamentally, the BRR model relies on purchasing a 'below-market-value' property or BMV as it is known. The BMV element typically comes from the property's poor condition at the time of purchase. Essentially you would buy a property that enables you to add value. Most commonly, this is utilising a refurbishment to bring the property back to a decent standard. You can add value in other ways, like through a conversion, for instance, by turning a townhouse into an HMO or serviced accommodation (SA) or by increasing the property's footprint by adding an extension.

The central point is that you will improve the property's value to remortgage at a higher amount to release the equity you've created by improving the property in one of the above ways.

Let us say you buy a property for £80,000, which including fees and taxes, would cost you around £24,000 in working capital. You then inject a further £10,000 into the property through a refurbishment, meaning your total capital outlay is £34,000. After your expert refurbishment and the mandatory six-month ownership has lapsed, you approach the mortgage lender. This can be the same lender if they offer further advances or one that has a far superior product at the point of refinancing.
This lender agrees to lend on the newer improved value of £110,000, meaning at this point, they would advance you £82,500. Part of this capital goes towards paying off your existing loan from the first mortgage, which including fees, was £61,000, 75% of £80,000 plus a £1000 mortgage arrangement fee, leaving you with a surplus of £21,500.
Remember, we initially put £34,000 of our working capital into this project, so with this surplus of £21,500 or 63% of your money back in your account, we only have £12,500 of our money left tied up in this deal.

This would leave us with a return on investment of around 39%, using an interest-only mortgage at around 4.6%.

The BRR model demonstrated above is typical for the types of BRR that I do, so I feel it is a more responsible example of how the model works. However, there are indeed instances, and I have taken full advantage many times of this, where you can release 100% of your invested capital, meaning you have none of your own money left or tied up in the deal at the point of refinancing. Effectively enabling a property for free would give you an infinite ROI at the point of refinancing.

The cherry on the cake for those of you with the correct ingredients and the drive to extend far beyond expected growth is that you can take full advantage of much bigger BRR deals. Commercial to residential or more significant HMO conversions that fall into the sui-generis category can give you 100% of your invested capital back plus profit, meaning, again, you would effectively own the property for free at the point of refinancing. However, this time, you make a tidy sum of money for your troubles.

Sui Generis is a Latin phrase that means "of its or their own kind", "in a class by itself", and therefore "unique" and is the term used to identify any HMO of seven bedrooms or more.

Flipping

'Flipping' is a term that I am sure most of you will be aware of. This is perhaps one of the oldest property investment models. I confidently use the word investment here since my understanding of the term is that investment is something that increases your capital over time. Flipping property certainly does this. Generally speaking, the time element with investments is longer-term; however, this is not mandatory to deem it an investment. By *'investing'* your capital and time over a shorter period, you are not excluding yourself from this categorisation.

Flipping works in an almost identical way to the BRR model. The primary difference is that at the point of refinancing, you simply sell to release the equity instead of keeping the property in your portfolio. It is another excellent way to increase your working capital. Flipping can be a model that is applied to those that have limited but still measurable capital to increase their working capital before investing in longer-term models or running alongside their chosen model. The key advantage of using flipping to stretch your working capital is that it is often faster than the BRR model due to the six-month ownership caveat. In the time it takes to release capital from one BRR, we may have been able to carry out two property flips.

The key to successful property flipping is two-fold. Firstly we need to accurately assess the future sale price, barring any unforeseen circumstances like a market crash. In my experience, this does not happen since markets take time to change significantly and often don't change for the worse out of the blue. When they change for the worse, it is often not unforeseen but rather the result of something that has been on the horizon for some time and, even then, takes time to filter.

Secondly, we must accurately assess the refurbishment costs to ensure our capital injection does not exceed our expectations. Every penny run over budget is a penny taken from our profit when we sell the property. If we can determine these two values effectively and accurately, then we can make calculated decisions on the viability of the deal.

Remember to include any mortgage redemption and sale fees, mainly agent and solicitor costs. It may be worth mentioning to the agent when viewing these types of properties that you intend to quickly turn the property around for re-sale to see if they would be happy to reduce their standard sale fee in return for the repeat business. Each time my company flips a property, and unless it is a direct-to-vendor purchase, we use the same agent we bought the property through to sell it for us. It is a great way to build and maintain relationships with local agents.

Rent to rent (R2R)

'Rent to Rent' (R2R) and 'Lease Option' can be jointly demonstrated since they are fundamentally the same model. This model, though not always, can benefit from what has come to be known as the 'No Money Down'

(NMD) approach. There are other ways we can invest with NMD, which will be explained as we progress through the book.

In 2013, a former student from the London School of Economics stumbled on an ingenious way to make money: he looked for rental properties where landlords hadn't maximised their income, rented them, and then sub-let them to various tenants. This was the start of what we know today as the 'rent-to-rent' (R2R) and the 'lease option' models.

These models primarily focus on making money from someone else's property or situation. The basic principle is identifying the opportunity in the property or portfolio. Either the owner is struggling with their investment and needs a rent guarantee, or they have not recognised the potential of the investment. In some cases, it is simply due to the fact that not every landlord wants to rule the world or work on their property business. Many landlords of yesteryear solely want hassle-free property investments, and if someone comes along and offers a rent guarantee, then you must appreciate that to them, this is worth its weight in gold.

We can capitalise in these cases by offering the security or guarantee of rental income, often negotiating a discount in return for this, and then increasing the returns on the property or portfolio and benefiting from the extra revenue ourselves. In short, you are subletting the property from the owner, potentially for a discount, but then increasing the rent through various means and methods.

Typically you would identify a property that you can increase your income on. For instance, turning a sizeable Victorian-style townhouse into a five or six-bedroom HMO. Although R2R is not always a no-money-down approach, I want to be clear that this would not be a true NMD deal. However, it would be far cheaper than purchasing the property since the only capital required would be in the form of minor alterations to the property. All furniture can be leased and added as a running cost of the business should it be necessary to keep start-up costs low.

This naturally brings us to 'Serviced Accommodation' (SA). Identifying a property in an advantageous location and offering the current landlord the guarantee of rent, then furnishing the property with leased furniture can be done by employing the exciting NMD approach.

Let us say that a two-bedroom property is marketed to let in a small coastal town for £725 Per calendar month (PCM). You have identified its potential as a serviced accommodation since the area is in demand all year round. Renting the property for £160 per night returns £4,866.66 monthly. Here we can see the advantages. Taken from this sum are our rent and running costs which may include our leased furniture pack. We must also attribute a realistic occupancy rate for the property. Once we do have these calculations, however, we can make a calculated decision. Let us say that our running costs equated to £2,000pcm, plus the £725 rent and attributing an 80% occupancy rate.

Therefore £2,725 taken from 80% of £4,866.66, which is £3,893.32, still makes us £1,168.32pcm or just over £14,000 per year. Remember, in this instance, the property model would be a true NMD.

Should you not be confident in finding these deals, there are companies online who specialise in R2SA or 'rent to serviced accommodation, often only charging £3,000 for bringing you the deal. It is worth a special mention here since if capital is a limiting factor and your ambition is at the other end of the spectrum, then this can yield excellent results. To continue through our demonstration employing a £30,000 starting capital. We would be able to buy ten of these deals earning us somewhere in the region of £11,683.20 per month or just over £140,000 per year gross profit.

I am not one of the companies that source these deals, in case anyone thought I was touting my services with a too-good-to-be-true deal. The numbers in my example, although typical, are entirely made up and do not represent a deal I have done or assessed. They are simply there to highlight how it works and demonstrate how you would calculate it yourself.

R2R and Lease Option

The principal difference between 'Rent to Rent' and 'Lease Option' is that the latter has the opportunity to purchase the property at a pre-determined value input into the contractual agreement. It is a lease with an option, hence the name.

For instance, if you employed the R2R model with a five-year contract, at the end of month 60, the property either gets returned to the landlord or the contract is renewed. Employing the lease option model, you have the right to buy the property. The thing that makes this appealing is that the right to purchase the property is not fixed to the end of the contract term. You have the right to do so at any point during the contract term if you wish to purchase the property at the pre-determined value. The result is that if the market increases measurably at any point during the contract term, you can opt to purchase the property, meaning that you can own the property using a lower deposit amount than you would if you were buying it at the current market value. Alternatively, suppose you discovered the model worked far better than you anticipated. In that case, you may want to secure the property to ensure this is a continued business. Further to this, owning the property means that you would now begin to benefit from the capital appreciation on the property.

An example of a lease option with an agreed-upon purchase of £150,000, when the market has increased to the point whereby the property is now valued at £180,000, is as follows:

The costs to purchase the property at the agreed price of £150,000, including fees and taxes, would be around £43,500. However, purchasing a comparable property at full market value, in this case, £180,000, would set you back £52,600. This is a reduction of £9,100, which is a significant saving. However, should the value of the property remain £180,000 at the end of the mandatory six-month ownership period, we could revalue this property at the higher amount, releasing almost 50% of our equity, 49.32% or £21,505 by my calculations. The result is that we own a £180,000 fully operational, serviced accommodation property for just under £23,000. Furthermore, our overheads have been reduced by £207.50 due to rental and mortgage differences.

For reference, this calculation was also done using an interest-only mortgage of 4.6%.

10.3 Know Your Customer (KYC)

For any company to succeed, it needs to understand its customers' needs. What it is that they want, what is missing in their customers' lives or current user experience and how to plug that gap effectively. Amazon, McDonald's, and Netflix are all excellent examples of companies that have understood this basic principle to become industry leaders in their respective marketplace. Amazon brings to the market convenience, McDonald's brings speed and consistency, and Netflix flourishes through its diversity and extensive choice in relation to its subscription fee.

Property investment isn't quite so complex, but a firm understanding of your customer is hugely beneficial yet often overlooked at this stage of the journey. Identifying who your prospective clients are will enable you to identify what they may want from a property, allowing you to seek these ideals out when conducting your search. It is beneficial to evaluate at this stage to avoid being stuck with a particular property or properties in locations that simply do not suit your personality or your objectives with your property business.

For example, should we want to attract a working professional, we may opt for a location that is close to a hospital, university, town centre, train or bus station. This could be either a flat, a small apartment or a two-bedroom property. Parking may not be necessary if we are close to good transport links. Conversely, should we want to attract a small family, we may opt to look for a property with a garden and a driveway closer to schools in a more rural area.

Equally, if we plan on employing a property investment model such as HMOs, then we need to determine our ideal customer before we begin our property search. To attract working professionals, we may need to identify large enough properties to house En-suite bathrooms in each room. Conversely, as you can imagine, squeezing as many bedrooms as possible into an average-sized townhouse may leave us with a different client base despite our desires.

This is why it is essential to assess this now. Of course, this does not have to pigeonhole your choices, and we do not need to place a blanket 'client' category across our search. We can identify our customers individually as we look at different property types and models.

Each time our management company receives a new instruction to let a property, they, at that stage, profile the property. This usually starts by enquiring with the owner about their thoughts and desires with their 'ideal' tenant. Nine times out of ten, we get the same response despite these properties' apparent location, size, condition, and price bracket differences. The consideration of their ideal customers was never contemplated when searching for their property.
The property manager's job is more challenging at this stage since they have to assess the property and profile it to suit the property rather than the tenant. Often, needing to educate the investor on the reality of their property. Identifying your clients before searching for your next property is a more logical, efficient and, therefore, successful step.

Something I like to tell other investors is to remember that the property picks the tenant, not the other way around. If you have a run-down property in a poor location, then you will have to choose your tenant from a much smaller, often poorer-quality pool of applicants.

For complete transparency, I am not suggesting this is necessarily a poor investment decision, especially regarding mathematics. These properties are numerous in supply and sought after by a particular type of tenant and can yield significantly higher returns than their counterparts. I know many investors who swear by this model and do very well with it.

However, I am almost sure that not many of you envisage these types of properties or investment models when considering your property investment journey. You wouldn't be reading this book if you were.

Your customer is your profit, and you do not have a business without them. Identify whom you will target and let that guide you when searching for the products to give them.

10.4 Location

Location, location, location. At this point, we are not generically talking about the classic, near local schools, good transportation links, universities, town centres and hospitals. We are looking at the country as one big opportunity.

In 2017 when I wrote *'The 123 on Property Investing'*, my advice was to buy locally from where you live. Citing that, on average, about a fifteen-minute radius from one's front door is the best thing we can do. I still echo this sentiment, if possible, but possible is the operative word here. This decision is often taken out of our control, so the need to look elsewhere is a growing problem.

The difference six years on from my first book is accessibility. There has been continued development in education, networking, and infrastructure to allow us to invest almost anywhere in the country, all from the comfort of our armchairs. The industry is far more geared up to the concept of remote investing these days. Perhaps the most significant paradigm shift has been with estate agents. Since the coronavirus pandemic, they are simply more susceptible to remote investing and, more specifically, to remote viewings.

To compound this, we now have agents who will view property for buyers, for a fee, of course, and we have an increased number of property sourcing companies. Networks have increased tenfold, meaning the information that is attainable from the likes of Facebook and LinkedIn has increased dramatically too.

Choosing where to invest, if not in our local area, has never been easier than it is right now. That is not to say that this is now an easy task; attached to this assignment is a considerable time commitment.
It is merely easier than it was six years ago. Investing in our local area has become increasingly difficult for large parts of the country. Not only are many priced out of the market, but availability recently has been a big issue for many investors.

At least one aspect of this, principally availability, will balance at some point, but many will still face pricing as their biggest hurdle even when it does. This is why we need to consider our investment area carefully. Even if our area is accessible with pricing, supply or availability may be the inhibitor.

Due to availability, my local area has become increasingly difficult for many local investors over the last three years. Pricing has remained accessible, and supply has not wavered, but demand has increased significantly, meaning that availability has become a challenge. Luckily, I have direct links and close relationships with a couple of agents, and my direct-to-vendor campaigns are running successfully, so my supply has been maintained. However, I know many local investors who have started looking elsewhere due to availability. You must continue to compound and grow your portfolio if you are to maintain success; therefore, if availability is an issue, you need to roll with the punches, adapt and move on.

Investing locally has apparent advantages, though it may not always be the best option if our chief aim is 'return on investment' or cashflow.
In the previous sub-chapter, we discussed 'pricing your investment', and should maths be your primary goal with your investment, the decision to invest locally may be taken out of your hands. However, even if your local area yields acceptable returns, alternative areas are always worth

considering, not only for future investments but to gauge how well your capital might perform if you were to consider an alternative location.

If investing locally is not viable, then the natural question is, 'how do you identify your investment area.'

The answer to the question is relatively simple to demonstrate, although the process and execution is far more time-consuming. The good news for you is that when done right, this task will increase your education, bolster your confidence, and increase your clarity, all as a byproduct.

In essence, since we have now established the purchase price of our investments, we merely need to find where in the country has a decent enough supply of these properties.

At the time of publishing, the most expansive search we can perform on Rightmove is a countywide search. Meaning we need to trawl the 48 counties in England, the 22 in Wales and or the 33 in Scotland to find our investment area. At first glance, this might sound like a daunting task; however, when you consider that, in most cases, you will be investing in one of the three abovementioned countries, this initial filter reduces the list significantly. Furthermore, you will almost certainly be familiar with many of the more affluent and subsequently 'out-of-reach' counties within your chosen country. This leaves you with significantly fewer counties to investigate.

It may be worth highlighting here that there is no one true way to determine your investment location. The following process is merely what we teach clients to implement to determine their chosen location or locations. Remember, you may be investing remotely; you do not need to intentionally restrict yourself to one 'goldmine' location. If we can find multiple areas that give us what we want, there is no reason we cannot take full advantage of this to ensure quality and supply are maintained.

Determining Your Investment Location Guide ®

1) Head to Rightmove (finally) and type your first county ® of choice into the search box.
    I. Let us assume we plan to investigate Herefordshire.
    II. Click 'For Sale'

2) We next set our pre-determined parameters.
    I. **Search Radius** this should be set to 'This area only'
    II. **Price range** (£) in this example, we have set the 'Minimum Value' to £100,000 and the 'Maximum' to £120,000
    III. The **Number of Bedrooms** is set from two bedrooms to four-bedrooms
    IV. We next set **Property Type** to 'Houses' unless, of course, you want to look for alternatives
    V. The **Added to site** selection is left at '**Anytime**'
    VI. The **Include Under Offer, Sold STC** box should be checked to include at this stage
    VII. Click '**Find properties**'

The search we have just run, and this is a genuine search at the time of writing, yields 13 properties, seven of which are sold subject to terms and conditions (STC). Even if we expand our search to include flats and bungalows in our search, it still only returns 15 available properties. Two of which are retirement properties only available to those over 55. There is a wooden lodge on a holiday park, a building plot, even though this search was not selected, and a 'public notice offer', which essentially means the property is sold unless you offer more on the property than the notice.

Side note: this 'public notice' is common practice for repossessed properties, generally going to public notice for seven days or, in some cases, until contracts are exchanged.

I think it is safe to say that I have saved a number of you a job and that according to my parameters and desires, Herefordshire, although I am sure a lovely place to live and visit, it is not the best investment location for what I was trying to achieve from the parameters in this example. Those familiar with Herefordshire or living in and around the area might tell me that my search parameters would never yield much in the way of investment property. However, I picked Herefordshire randomly from my counties list and applied a search similar to what I use as my current investment model. I did not know the outcome of my search before selecting, but I do now, and all it took was 57 seconds to confidently strike it from my list. Yes, I did time it.

If we keep the same search parameters but change the county search to Merseyside, we yield 920 results, including sold STC, with 308 available properties. These results tell me a couple of things. One, I have found a county that may be of interest to me, and two, the market is buoyant in Merseyside. There is apparent movement in the market since 612 of the 920 available properties are sold STC. What I would not do at this stage is carry on investigating Merseyside. I would merely place a tick against the county, note the number of properties available, move it to the maybe pile and move on to the next county from my list.

Repeating this process for the remaining counties would leave you with several counties in the 'Maybe' column and the rest in the 'No' column. Simply discard the no column and move on to the next stage of your analysis.

Starting with the county that yielded the largest number of available properties, it is time to look for comparable properties that suit your investment model. An example of this is, should you be searching for turnkey properties primarily, you need to ensure enough supply within the county. Some counties may have just managed to make your list, which could be because the properties are all in a state of disrepair. This may be good news if your model is 'Buy Refurbish and Refinance' BRR, but bad news if you want ready to let Turnkey properties. Remember, this search is for you and you alone. Nothing else matters at this stage, only what you need to reach your goals. This process will again naturally filter counties as we narrow our search further.

Let us assume we now have four or five counties shortlisted. The next process is to highlight towns within each county. As you search through the county for properties comparable to your investment model, certain towns will keep presenting themselves. At this stage, you should begin to note these towns, potentially listing the most abundant three or four from the county search. These will be the towns with the greatest number of available properties, ensuring availability does not hinder our progress.

It may be good hypothetically to find an area we are happy with, but it is a somewhat pointless exercise if the availability is low. Once we have specific towns highlighted as potentials, we move on to the next county from our shortlist and repeat the process.

After this is concluded for each county, we will have a more extensive list of towns within our top four or five counties. Our job now is to compare the towns against each other. At this stage in our filtering, we must delve deeper into our research. At this point, we will potentially have between 16 and 24 towns highlighted, so understanding these areas on a deeper level is imperative to determine their viability. No longer are we merely looking for availability. Our job now is to start to organise the towns in terms of suitability for investment. Researching demographics, crime rates, infrastructure, employment, capital growth opportunities, and cross-referencing the differing returns on investment and cashflows, each area will give you relative to your working capital are all starting considerations.

This is by far the slowest part of the process. Equally, though, it is the one that will educate you the most, so there is a silver lining to your time input. After you have finished this part of your research, you should have filtered to a shortlist of suitable towns. All we need to do now is to decide which town or towns to pursue further.

My advice is to continue with three or four of these towns until you have a better idea of their availability and you can fully assess your success in securing viewings within each town.

Side note: If you have shortlisted two or three towns within one county, there is no real need to micro-filter these to one specific town. Since you will most likely be employing an agent to manage these houses, there is a good chance that there will be a company with branches in each shortlisted town or they will cover the entire county.

The process of finding your investment location should remain fluid, and adaptions are welcome to suit your model or strategy. It may be that you included your area research at an earlier stage than highlighted above. The idea of the process, as demonstrated, is to show how we are taking an enormous task and simply filtering at various stages to bite-size, more manageable tasks until we are left with a natural conclusion. Essentially, we are taking breaking a macro task into microelements.

11 Sourcing Property

As the country cycled between national lockdowns, social distancing and furlough schemes during the coronavirus pandemic, not many would have predicted what would come from the housing market. As it continued to grow well above inflation, contrary to all predictions and reasonable comprehension, the biggest challenge to investors became the availability of properties. Sourcing and securing properties became a race many would fail to finish. As I write this chapter, securing property deals has become easier but is still nowhere near pre-pandemic levels.

Although more challenging than usual, we managed to source and secure a constant supply of properties during this unfamiliar time. We attribute that to our more profound understanding of sourcing property coupled with a clever strategy. As I have previously mentioned, the property industry moves fast, so adapting is paramount to your success. Understanding the many avenues to source property can help you even when others around you are struggling.

I will discuss some of the most common avenues to source property, offering plentiful advice with areas of consideration. Still, before I do, I must inform you that due to the nature of the list, it has a similar layout to the list I demonstrated in the *123 on Property Investing*. I have, however, changed large parts of the subtext and layout to fit the premise of this book. Indeed, enough for it to be beneficial for you to read again should you have read my previous book.

In essence, when considering property sourcing, there are two primary categories which can divide further into subcategories. These are:

1) Who will source the properties for you?
   a. Yourself
   b. An outside source

2) From whom will you source the properties?
   a. Public domain
   b. The Vendor (aka the seller)

Let us first discuss sourcing ourselves and searching for property already in the public domain. That is 1a and 2a from our list above. These are primarily sourced from *estate agents* and *the internet, Sites like Rightmove, Zoopla, On the Market or Prime Location, as well as property auctions*.

Estate Agents

Like them or loathe them, they are integral to your plans. Estate agents are perhaps the most valuable tool for locating property.

If there is one thing that the technology age deprives us of, it is one-to-one interaction. The personal touch and service central to many businesses and relationships have become a thing of the past. Personal one-to-one and face-to-face interaction still play a massive part in this industry.

I would encourage every one of you to pick up the phone, introduce yourself, explain your position and intentions then, where possible, enquire about the agent's availability so that you can request a face-to-face discussion with their property manager. Not only will this show how serious you are, but it will give you an opportunity to firm up your needs and criteria with your properties.

Developing personal relationships with local agents took me too long to establish since I never understood or appreciated the benefits or their inherent value to my business. I suppose I was not running a business back then in the sense that I am now. I viewed agents as unreliable, false in their intent, lacking in respect and, amongst all else, poor-quality advisers.

Now, depending on your experience, you will either find this a harsh or a true statement since they can be challenging to work with, and it is clear they do not quite fully understand the business of mathematics. However, as I sit here editing this book, I am contemplating how I could exemplify the number of properties I have been involved in buying through my local estate agents. A large number of which never even made it to Rightmove, let alone had a for-sale board erected. In fact, I would estimate that I receive around 20 messages each month to my personal mobile from local agents indicating property that I can, should they interest me, secure before they reach other investors and the general public through Rightmove.

This is because I have, over the years, since realising their value, made my position and intent very clear to the selected few I wish to work with regularly. They know my property criteria, preference, and immediate position. They even surprise me sometimes with properties outside this criterion.

These personalised text messages create a significant advantage for me as a professional investor but collectively have a mutually beneficial arrangement for us. I get to know about specific properties before they hit the mainstream, and the agent can tell the vendor that they may already have someone interested in their property, securing them the instruction to act and giving me a head start in the research department.

At this point in your relationship, persistence is crucial to its development. Agents get inundated with aspiring investors informing them of their intent, an intent that may not always be acted upon. Once they realise that you are serious with your intent and in a position to proceed immediately, however, they will see your value, and you will make the cut to be one of their first ports of call soon enough.

The internet - Sites like Rightmove, Zoopla, On the Market and Prime Location. Otherwise expressed as online portals

These online portals are the most successful avenue for sourcing property from the public domain. Where else can you see almost the entire market all in one place? You can look at comparable, sold history, the internals of the property and book viewings, all without leaving the comfort of your living room.

Rightmove may be the Google of the housing sales world, but once you have determined your investment area speak with the local estate agents to find out what their preferred portals are. The preferred portal can and often does, change from one town to the next. For example, my two local investment areas predominantly use Rightmove, yet ten miles over, they favour On the Market.
Generally, you'll find that the less affluent an area is, the more they will use other sites like on-the-market or Zoopla. This is a result of their cheaper monthly tariffs.

Rightmove is the one that pretty much every other investor I know and I predominantly use. In fact, for complete transparency, my searches are carried out exclusively on Rightmove when searching for a property for sale within the public domain. The site boasts an abundance of features to which you can tailor your search quite specifically to meet your individual criteria.

The more you use the site, the more features you will discover, but if you are new to Rightmove, check out their own guides on how to use the platform. There are some helpful Youtube videos on this, too ®.

There are a couple of useful online tools to work alongside RightmoveGoogles' property tracker and property log for chrome are two of the more used ones; Tracker is currently free, and property log is a couple of pounds a month at the minute. These are plugins that, once downloaded, attach to your browser's toolbar automatically. The benefit of these plugins is that they show how long each property has been advertised on Rightmove - showing its initial entry and every price or entry change thereafter.

Should you use an alternative browser like *Firefox*, then you may want to consider switching when viewing Rightmove to take advantage of these plugins. You can easily uncheck the default setting when downloading

Chrome so that it doesn't become your default browser, subsequently only opening when you search Rightmove.

Firefox used to have its version in 'property bee .com'; however, this was taken down several years ago, and as I understand it, there are no plans to reinstate it.

I have failed to find an alternative for use with the *Firefox* browser. There are a couple about PaTMa being one which does show listing history and has a go at giving you other features like ROIs and rental estimates, but currently, their algorithm for this information is sub-standard at best. Keep an eye on this and decide for yourself, as I am sure it will improve as time passes. This is precisely what happened with Zoopla's property value estimate feature. It used to be poor, but now, providing the confidence rating for their valuation is 'high', it is excellent.

Once you are up and running on Rightmove, you can use one of my all-time favourite time-saving features: their last 24 hours, 3, 7 or 14-day search. This feature is invaluable when we consider efficiency relating to time-saving. Once your initial search is concluded within your chosen area, simply replicate and save this search to access it anytime in 'my Rightmove' but this time change, within the preferences, to last 24 hours, 3, 7 or 14-days depending on the last time, you viewed the platform. This way, you only need to search every few days to see if anything new is added to the market that meets your criteria.

Be sure to keep the original search saved to keep an eye on the ones struggling to sell. These properties can be picked up below your budget and the current market value, or somewhat more accurately, at the right price. Rightmove also lets you save individual properties into your preference library by simply highlighting the love heart symbol next to the property; this is a great way, along with your plugins, to observe any activity with that chosen property in real-time. Similarly, it allows you to compare various selected 'favourite' properties to narrow your search.

Perhaps the most significant time-saving and valuable feature on Rightmove, however, must be the instant notification alert.
By selecting the instant alert feature on your saved search, you will be notified each time a property is uploaded that meets your search parameters. You can set up multiple searches, meaning you can be quite specific, tailoring them as needed.

We get around 30-40 emails each month from Rightmove with properties that meet my pre-determined location, bedroom and pricing criteria. This leaves my team with the effortless task of filtering these into the rubbish or potential file using their gained knowledge by following the methods discussed in the next chapter.

Property auctions

Since the initial airing of TV programs such as 'Homes Under the Hammer' back in 2003, auction houses across the UK have notably increased in numbers. As a result, more properties are sold at auction today than at any point in history. This trend is growing fast, and not only with repossessed or beaten-up houses but with what you and I would call a typical property.
I do not envisage this slowing down at any point in the near future.

I am of the opinion that this medium for selling property is not particularly good news for professional investors like myself or aspiring investors like you. In my local investment area, in the North East of England, properties that need a good overhaul or an entire renovation make up around 85% of the stock sold through this medium.

While this can prove to be helpful in sourcing property, especially ones that you can add significant value to employing the BRR or flipping models, it does come with its drawbacks. Depending on your investment model, objectives, and, of course, budget, it can hinder your growth or even leave you with a property that simply isn't right for you as an investor. You should tread carefully when it comes to certain auctions and be very aware of the implications and legalities involved.

The main auction house here is the 'Great North Property Auction', and I do sometimes attend their night from time to time, but I have to admit, I have never bought, nor do I intend to buy a property at auction anytime soon. My investment strategy will differ from yours, but I'm not too fond of the initial capital outlay, associated fees and timescales involved with auction properties. Specifically with the 'Great North Property Auction' or 'I am Sold'

Your overall strategy, visions, objectives and investment models will be very different from mine, and as I've just touched on, these auctions can be an excellent avenue for securing below-current-market value properties. However, as their popularity has grown so much in recent years, so has their footfall. And herein, for me at least, lies their problem.

The type of investor who now attends auctions may not necessarily understand the industry like you and I. Mostly auctions attract individuals looking for a real bargain or a below-market value property, commonly referred to as a BMV. This is to be expected, and generally, there is no harm with this. We are all entitled to dream. The problem for you and me here is that the supply and demand balance tips in favour of the vendor - the opposite direction for us as professional investors. Typically there will be too many inexperienced investors bidding for one BMV property, resulting in an overpriced purchase for a potential headache of a property and certainly not a BMV.

There are certain costs involved when buying at auction, and they tend to tie more money up in a deal than I would usually like, at least initially.

I will demonstrate a quick example of the costs involved in buying at our local auction house but would note for ease that this example is not considering SDLT. The demonstrated fees relate to the 'Great North Property Auction' and may not necessarily be the same in your chosen area, so always do your due diligence.

Let us say the hammer falls in your favour, and you secure a property for £50,000. Assuming that this is a genuine BMV purchase, since the other investors didn't realise its potential, or they could not attend the auction for reasons we need not consider. It is a safe assumption that this property will require some renovation once contracts are exchanged, and the property is completed. However, before that time comes, staying present, the hammer has just fallen, so you will now be expected to immediately pay a *'reservation fee'* of £5,000 + VAT, which is £6,000 once added.

This fee does not come off the property's value but instead is added to the purchase value, and I will clarify here that landlords cannot claim the VAT back. Since rent is VAT exempt, there is no call for investors to register for VAT.

You must be aware of these fees when considering bidding for any property at auction. Fees will differ from area to area and between auction houses, so it is imperative that you find this out well in advance of the auction since it will alter your returns significantly. For example, £6,000 on a £50,000 purchase is a 12% increase in the purchase price, meaning that your ROI will differ considerably too.

Assuming you have already secured a 75% loan-to-value (LTV) principle agreement from your preferred lender, which is the usual procedure before you bid on the property, you will soon have to pay your 25% contribution. Otherwise known as the 'deposit'.

Based on our example, this would be £12,500. At this point, you have invested £18,500 into a property worth, in its present state, £50,000, and you now have to renovate it.

Based on an average property at this value and on my experience, the cost of this would be in the region of £15,000. Meaning your invested capital has risen to £33,500, and you have had the renovation challenge. Your property has been empty during this process, which could be expressed as 'lost rent', Mortgage payments, council tax bills, energy and water costs all need paying during this period, and remember we did not include SDLT on the initial purchase. The solicitor's fees, broker and finance fees and other associated costs are also added. Again, all of these will be further explained in more depth later in the book.

I understand that this property will have adopted the BRR model; however, with the £6,000 added to the purchase price, the capital pulled from the deal will have significantly reduced.

Specifically commenting on my own investment area, I do not think there are many bargains at auctions anymore due to the high level of interest they incur from part-time investors and builders who have clear advantages when looking at properties needing renovation. Furthermore, I don't particularly like buying property at an auction because of the high costs and timescales involved in completion. I find the cash employed in the deal and the renovation hassle too time-consuming, slow, and costly. Of course, this is just my opinion and should not be concluded as your opinion until you have researched this much further. The auction house close to you or your investment area may differ entirely.

My knowledge and experience are somewhat limited in this area due to my opinions of what is available at the auction house near to me and my investment area. However, before attending any auction, it is imperative that you take the time to note all of the terms and conditions of the contract. These usually state that any property purchased has to be completed within a predetermined timeframe; generally, this is within 28 days of the hammer falling.

In most instances, this is not enough time to secure a mortgage for the property, especially if purchasing through the more modern method of limited company acquisitions. Therefore, you often need to pursue other funding avenues like bridging loans or inject a more significant capital input initially ready for refinancing later. For instance, using cash to fund the initial purchase.

Your deposit may be lost if the deal is not completed within the given timeframe, so be careful and always read the contract or terms of business before you attend an auction.

Direct-to-vendor sourcing (D2V)

Direct-to-vendor sourcing is a way of approaching potential vendors, also known as the property owner. These are either homeowners, landlords or beneficiaries of properties looking to sell. As the name suggests, you are going directly to the vendor to secure the sale of the property, essentially cutting out the middleman, the agent. This method for securing property deals has become increasingly popular with the rise of the 'we buy any house.com' type companies, but with it has come scrutiny and stigma. These companies are often judged as untrustworthy and for good cause. The horror stories of drastically undervalued offers and deceptive sales tricks have given the industry a bad name. Therefore an alternative approach is needed to counteract this.

Sourcing property directly from the vendor can be done in many ways, but the most common avenues are:

1) Your Network and its Reach
2) Targeted Flyer Distribution
3) Online Advertising
4) Landlord Associations
5) Advertising Boards

1 Your Network

Your network can extend far and wide, but to narrow this here, we are specifically talking about your friends, family, work colleagues, and your social media audience, whether they are friends, foes, or mere associates. Although each can be exclusive in their own right, this is all about one thing and one thing only. Informing every man and his dog of your intentions and position, then waiting for vendors and their properties to find you.

Don't expect this to be an overnight success, of course, and certainly don't rely on this as your only route to purchase but rather run this in tandem with your more productive avenues. This will take time to build momentum and generate successful leads, but if you remain persistent and consistent with your approach, eventually, you will yield results. Social media posting about viewing, offering, securing, or anything property will vastly increase your chances of someone seeing that you are serious and approaching you directly. Real-world 'word of mouth' might yield a good handful of close friends, family, or work colleagues, but social media elevates your reach into the hundreds and thousands. Posting on social media regularly will build your audience exponentially, no doubt. Everyone on social media loves to be seen as the person who connects or helps another.

The leg work from many years of building awareness with my network has left me in a great position to purchase property directly. In fact, as I sit here editing this section whilst sipping a small glass of XO *(those who know, know),* I am trying to tally the number of 'Direct to Vendor' purchases I am currently involved with. The answer is two for me. Four more for myself and my business partner, Steven. Three for two separate mentees and one for a close friend. Incidentally, I have another three viewings next week with properties that I am 95% sure I will end up purchasing.

These are two separate one-bedroom apartments from a retiring landlady and a two-bedroom property from a young man who inherited the property after his father, a single property landlord who suddenly died. The latter was brought to my attention by his next-door neighbour, who has now linked me to three property sales in the last two years. This lady worked on the fish counter at Tesco and used to talk with me regularly after seeing how enthused my children were when squid was freshly available on her counter.

I happened to mention that I was an investor and handed her a card, and for around 18 months, I heard nothing until I got a random call, and her name was mentioned. Initially, I had no idea whom he referred to until he called her the fish lady; then, I knew.

The power of spreading the word may not necessarily be evident immediately, but trust me, it grows exponentially, and the deals come from the shadows when they are least expected. The more you discuss your intentions with as many people as you can, the more chance you have of finding a deal like this; it is simple mathematics, it is the law of probability, the more people you tell, the more chance they will know someone and so the connections are made.

A secondary benefit of building your network in this way is that it helps significantly grow your growth-based and action-based mindset. Since you continually reaffirm your intentions to your subconscious, your perception of who you are and what you do grows in equal measure. Eventually, this will take precedence, and you will become more active as a result.

'A man will become what he perceives himself to be'

Mahatma Gandhi

2 Flyer Distribution

Flyer distribution, although one of my favourite advertising methods back when I opened my gas engineering business in 2003, is something that I had often criticised when it came to 'Direct to Vendor' advertising.
For the gas company, it worked well, but the jury was out for a long time when it came to finding a property via flyer advertising. That was until I discovered that everyone was going about this the wrong way.
I have already highlighted the stigma around firms like 'We Will Buy Your House.com'. If we couple that with the cowboy, local landlord approach of handwritten notes or yellow bandit boards around town, then you have a sour-tasting cocktail and an expensive one at that. One that takes too much effort to make and one that no one will drink. The efficiency rating equates to one... out of a million.

To seek a solution, we must think and behave like a vendor looking to sell their property. The problem is that the general population is misinformed about selling their property. In most cases, there is a preconception that, just like a solicitor, an agent is a legal requirement to sell their property. How else do they sell their property? They call an agent, have a valuation, give them the instruction to advertise, the agent brings you a buyer, a solicitor is then contacted, and some weeks later, the seller gets their money or a new bigger home and a smaller bank balance. That is the common consensus for 99% of the population, and standard practice or common consensus has a way of establishing itself as the only way.

The failure to break this mould or to succumb to it is where most flyer advertising comes up short. With flyer advertising, you generally struggle to convey your message correctly to the homeowner. A few short lines of text must be powerful enough to amplify your entire model and business to the prospective client. Phone calls and face-to-face meets don't have this problem, but unlike your network, flyers often don't get you to first base. This is the primary reason I always viewed flyers as a waste of time and energy. I still stand by that thinking. But that is when they are used in the wrong way.

As it turns out, flyer advertising can be a powerful medium for securing direct-to-vendor properties. You simply need to adopt the mindset of 'if you can't beat them, join them'.
Over the past two years, I have had excellent success with my newfound knowledge and approach. If the consensus is that an agent is required to sell their property, then why not become that agent? Or at least on the surface? Let the assumption be that you are an agent.
Without question, I am not advising anyone of you to lie to the vendor or to continue this assumption once you have their attention. This smokescreen is required to get noticed and to prevent your flyer from being tossed out with the rest of the rubbish.

Your flyer must give the impression of a local estate agent without actually suggesting that you are one. Remember, there is to be no monetary exchange between yourself and the vendor, so the offer on your flyer is essential to spark their interest. Essentially your message should convey that you are offering to sell their house for free as some kind of promotion within your business.

Our flyers sound something like this ®.

FREE SALE, Sell your House but Pay NO FEES. *Wise Owl Property LTD was established in the local area over 12 years ago, and we are now expanding our business with this fantastic 'limited time only' offer.*

The flyer houses *(excuse the pun)* images of a house being sold or a happy couple receiving a key. We then have more information detailing what properties qualify for the free, 'limited time only' sale. These flyers enclose our contact details as well as point the potential client to a small one-page website ® where they can find further information, and we can increase credibility.

By adopting this approach, we increased our results from flyer distribution from zero leads from around ten flyer drops to around ten properties from our first two drops. Currently, we average three purchases from every 5,000 flyers we drop. It is necessary to mention here that we focus our flyer drops on selecting specific areas of interest where we know the market and the property well.

For reiteration, apply caution when choosing the words for these flyers and be honest with the vendor about who you are and your intentions at your first available opportunity. We simply inform them that we will visit the property, take around 20 minutes of their time, go away and carry out some due diligence and then return to them with an offer via phone call within 48 hours of our initial visit.

Our approach here, which is conveyed to the vendor, is to make the process appear hassle-free and to distance ourselves from the pushy sales approach they may have expected. We have around an 80% success rate with purchasing their property once verbal contact is established.

3 Online Advertising

This is the medium we have had the most success with recently, but it does come at a considerable cost. Although online advertising can be expensive, the yield is effectively infinite. For us, it was also a necessity for a short while. As demand for property grew during 2022, supply started to dry up and securing a property, even to view, let alone secure, became the commodity. We counteracted this with an extensive online advertising campaign which we have since paused, but its effect still yields results months on.

Our chosen platform was Facebook and their paid advertising. However, Google AdWords is another option we considered, and there are options for paid adverts on other platforms such as LinkedIn, Reddit, Pinterest, YouTube, TikTok and so forth. Should you merely want to purchase the odd property for yourself, then online advertising may be something you opt out of unless money is less of an object. Still, for those of you who are looking to build a sizeable business more rapidly due to having a more considerable working capital standing. Or, for those of you looking to build a side income as a property sourcer, it is certainly worth considering.

It can be a complicated process with split testing, campaign building, pixel placing and so forth, but as I have just mentioned, it can yield huge returns long after the advert has finished. There are many external companies who will handle these advertising campaigns for you if you are not prepared to dig into real depth with this yourself - word of caution. You need to either fully commit to this or employ an outside source since dipping your toe into this will only lose you money. Boosting adverts is a waste of money. You must invest in your education with this and look at building structured campaigns with sales funnels and targeted and retargeted adverts ®.

In short, this method is for the serious investor with enough capital to split test approaches or for those who intend to incorporate property sourcing into their business. The average cost will be around £1,500 per month, representing £1000 for your advertising budget and £500 for your campaign manager.

However, if you are securing properties for your sourcing business for around £3,000 each, this cost is surmountable in the broader scheme of your business.

4 Landlord Associations

In essence, landlord associations could have fallen into the networking category; however, I have had so much success with this over the years to the point that my family home was bought from a member of my local landlord association. Furthermore, I paid £50,000 under its market value at the time, so the need or rather desire to set aside this topic from the pack is clear.

Landlords do not particularly like dealing with estate agents and often want quick, hassle-free sales for their properties. Deals are often stacked according to the situation with retiring landlords, as often, they are selling a property with a sitting tenant, or they are selling multiple properties at once. I would urge everyone reading this book to join at least one local landlord association. This would be either the association closest to them or the area in which they will invest. Should they be one and the same, great, but if not, consider both. Taking this to the extreme, should you choose to invest throughout the UK, consider joining the local associations in any or all of your chosen areas.

Not only are they a valuable source of reliable information, but they are excellent for property purchases too. Make your position to the group known, affirm periodically at meetings or via email, and build your network here for excellent results.

The fastest house I have ever secured came from an email from my local landlord association here in Darlington. The generic 'looking to sell my rental' email landed on my phone, ending with the usual 'anyone interested call me on this number' message. I was playing golf at the time, only noticing the email whilst waiting to tee off stuck behind a four-ball on the sixteenth tee.

I Googled the area as it was unfamiliar to me at the time because it only has six houses in the street, so it is not a big memorable street by any stretch. Initially, I thought it was a low asking price for such a big property. Therefore I was not expecting a pretty picture. But, since the size naturally lent itself to an HMO conversion, the less desirable interior or decor would be of little concern since this model usually requires more extensive refurbishments.

Within twenty minutes of the email being sent, I had spoken with my business partner in the HMO JV company, and I was on the phone with Richard from the landlord association. Being at the property whilst he sent the email to the association members, Richard invited us to view the property. Two hours later, Richard called us back after our viewing to ask if we would increase our offer to £66,000 from £65,000 or pay his solicitor fees. The deal was secured, and the refurbishment took three months at a cost of £25,000.

Four months after the conversion, the six-bedroom HMO was revalued at £120,000, meaning we only had £4,000 of our capital left in the deal. This property makes us around £20,000 after costs and yields a return on investment of around 566%. The deal was secured within two and a half hours of Richard's email. To date, I have been involved in purchasing around 25-30 properties from my local landlord association.

5 Advertising Boards

Advertising boards can come in many shapes and forms. Perhaps the most commonly advised for success, from what I have researched, has to be yellow bandit boards. This is a concept brought over to the UK by our neighbours over the pond in the USA. They are printed signs that investors often use as a way of marketing their property buying power and can often be seen on street corners with verbiage such as 'we buy houses for cash' or ' we will buy your house'. Essentially, they are small variations of the American-type billboards. Their usefulness is directly correlated to the strategic placement of each sign, as they are intended to act as the initial point of contact for investors to potential sellers. Strapped to lampposts or placed on walls, these displays are meant to catch the attention of motorists and pedestrians as they pass by. However, since most towns and cities have regulations governing the installation of these signs on public property, industry jargon has coined the term "bandit boards." Many investors use something called burner phones to promote their buying prowess.

These numbers are sim cards that can be regularly updated, and the old number thrown away to prevent them from being caught placing these signs. In my opinion, it is a colossal waste of time and resources. The only variation I don't mind, and of course, you should make your own mind up with this, are lookalike lettings or sale boards.

Instead of a for sale or to let board, opt to place a board up at the property you have just purchased with the words 'Another House Bought by… Insert Company Name Here' each time you buy a property. You can leave this board up while you refurbish the property or place it in the window whilst looking for your tenant. I have adopted this approach over the years, but its effectiveness is questionable at best; these days, I rarely bother, albeit with the amount of property we own, manage and refurbish. I do question this as I write this. That is about as much as I wish to discuss advertising boards for now. For the purpose of this book and your education, you are now aware of this medium. Whether you choose to pursue it is now down to you and the conclusion from your research. These boards may work better in some areas than others, and I am not suggesting that this should not be used, but rather just as another feather to your bow rather than your chosen model.

In summary, should you decide to source property for yourself, the avenues mentioned above, individually and collectively, will all prove to be valuable in your search to one degree or another.

Suppose you decide to enlist the help of a property sourcing company to help find your investments. In this case, you must tread carefully and remember that just like in every industry, there are the good, the not-so-good and the damn right criminal. These are all waiting to take your business and money, so carry out your due diligence.

Property Sourcing

Property sourcing companies are a relatively new addition to the industry but have risen to the point of saturation over the past five or so years. They comb the property market daily, looking for suitable rentable properties with good scope to increase in value either through a below-market value purchase (BMV), capital growth opportunity or by using renovation and development as the tool.

The properties that are presented to their clients are not simply on-market properties that they might have found on Rightmove themselves, although these properties are often highlighted too. In most cases, sourcing companies present 'off-market' properties. Typically these are the direct-to-vendor properties we have just discussed.

Property sourcing companies invest heavily in the avenues mentioned above to source directly to the vendor, so they can be an excellent source for finding a property you would usually not have had the opportunity to find. Their books are filled with landlords, homeowners and private investors looking for quick sales with safe bet investors like you and me.

Often deals are packaged showing most costs involved to complete on the property along with comparable properties and broad-brush returns of yields, cashflows and ROIs. The deals are sent out to investors through avenues such as Facebook, LinkedIn, email contacts or a post on their website until someone picks up the deal and secures the sourcing fee, essentially taking the off-market property off the market.

Fees tend to range from area to area, deal to deal and company to company, but as a general rule of thumb, for a typical deal, fees are usually in the region of around £3,000. However, for larger yielding deals, the fee often reflects its potential. For example, a standard single-let property that requires a small renovation to increase its value, making it attractive for refinancing purposes, may be packaged at around £3,000. But a large Victorian or Georgian-style property that can be changed into an even larger HMO may be packaged between £5000 and £10,000, depending on the refinancing opportunity, of course.

The larger the deal's cashflow and the smaller the capital left in after refinancing, the larger the sourcing fee potential. And if this is the case, then what does it matter, really? If you recycle most of your capital, does it matter what someone else is getting from the deal?
I have seen sourcing fees upwards of £30,000 for large commercial to residential developments. All that matters is that the numbers stack up when the fees are included. For example, if I was presented a deal by a sourcing company for extensive development but the sourcing fee was £2,000,000, fictitious, I know. Still, after refinancing, I could release all of my equity. Then what does it matter what the company is making from the deal? If I was releasing all my equity from this fictitious deal, then it is simply irrelevant what anyone else's cut is. The main thing for me is that I am doing well from the deal. To reiterate, the important part is ensuring that the maths stack up when the sourcing fee is included, regardless of the amount they are charging.

Many businesses and investors are offering property sourcing across the country, and I don't favour any particular company against another. Similar to property auctions, I see their value regarding an introduction to the property industry, especially If location is your challenge. Perhaps you are overseas or based further south and wish to invest up north since the returns can be better as a general rule of thumb.

Maybe you are an investor who is short on time or education and wishes to leverage someone else's time and education. In this case, this avenue can prove valuable, and you can be successful, providing you carry out the same due diligence you would should you have located the property for yourself.

Overall, and for what it is worth, I have never employed a sourcing company to find me deals. I think the experience of many of these companies and their agenda has to be scrutinised, especially with the rise of paid training for novices to become overnight £300,000 per month property sourcers. Something to be clear, we DO NOT offer training on.

If you are investing in an area you don't know and have minimal experience in, or your overall property knowledge is low, as in my example above, I advise getting reasonably educated before contemplating implementing any strategy that relies on another source. Enlisting the help of a property sourcer can be advantageous to the growth of your property business. However, automatically assuming they have done their homework because they are a sourcing company, so they must know what they are doing is a naïve and potentially costly mistake to make.

For those who are familiar with the title 'The Richest Man in Babylon', incidentally one of my favourite books, remember that you must always adhere to the five laws of gold, particularly the 4th law. It reads as a refresher or introduction to this law.

Gold slippeth away from the man who invests it in businesses or purposes with which he is not familiar or which are not approved by those who are skilled in its keep.

My particular concern with the sourcing industry is that it is another overpopulated area of the property investment industry; it has risen in popularity over the last few years. Now, as it seems, every man and his dog has jumped onto the bandwagon. Most of these so-called expert sources are small-time investors or, in fact, have no property at all and are using the funds from their deals to accrue working capital for their own property investment business; this poses a serious ethical issue for me. Where is the accountability and trust?

How some of these sourcing companies feel they are in a position to advise on something they either have no or minimal experience with is beyond my fathoming. Furthermore, what is their real agenda? Is it to ensure you get a quality product? One in which you can turn your hard-earned cash into a sound, predominantly hassle-free investment. Or is it to bank your £3,000 to further their own investment business or grow their bank balance, regardless of the consequence?

There are, of course, many reputable firms out there vying for your business. My advice is merely to tread carefully and apply caution when your relationship with these firms is in its infancy. Remember, with the property industry, trust should not be given out universally. It must be earned by the individual regardless of your initial impression or nature. Many of these deals are generic and only tick the financial box, but that simply isn't good enough. There is much more to the property investment industry than purchasing a property below market value or at a price that meets a particular yield or ROI. One which has usually been set by the source's own mandate or their clever manipulation of the mathematics, I might add.

My lettings business manages many properties, some for smaller investors, with their entire portfolio sourced by an external company. Usually, having met only at a networking event or online. Not always, but it is often the case that these properties are in the towns' poorer, more run-down areas since it helps the mathematics appear far more attractive when presenting a deal to the inexperienced investor.
Consider buying a property for £50,000 and renting it for £450. As you might well imagine, getting a solid ROI on those numbers is not too hard. Generally, however, I would not have touched these properties with a barge pole, *a very long one,* yet this is someone's portfolio, their business, their future and quite possibly their retirement.

Upon researching content for this subsection in my first book, I came across a forum discussing the topic of property sourcing. The content below is an exact extract taken from the forum that summed up in bullet points, exactly what I wanted to articulate. My views and conclusion have not altered from the first time this was published, so including this again is beneficial to you all.

Here is what was written.

- *For inexperienced/hands-off/non-full-time investors, then it can be advantageous to have someone else sourcing properties for you. They will (most likely) know more than you and have better contacts, etc.*

- *A property sourcer should be thoroughly researched, however.*

- *The due diligence that they do for an opportunity is in no way a substitute for your own - always conduct thorough due diligence for yourself.*

- *If you don't understand the opportunity, don't get involved. No matter what you are told. Be naturally sceptical.*

- *If the opportunity requires a hard sell, then it is clearly not great - it should be able to sell itself.*

- *It is almost irrelevant what the sourcing fee is; add the sourcing fee to the purchase price, then run the numbers. If, with the sourcing fee, the opportunity is still good and makes sense with your overall strategy, then great. So, the actual costs of the property sourcer and the merit of their use are entirely down to the actual opportunity itself.*

- *There is no dark art form of magic to property sourcing - anyone can do it - perhaps not as good as a professional, though. Like anything, in fact!*

- *There are lots and lots of great books, magazines, forums, podcasts, etc., that you can educate yourself - so you can make informed decisions based on various sources rather than relying on single sources of info.*

I agree entirely with the author's summarisation; He perfectly explains his points. It is no-nonsense, straight to the point, and clearly points out the major pros and cons. In essence, there is no replacement for your own research, but just as he mentioned above and adhering to the 4th law of gold, your own research may entail researching the sourcer and listening to the expert.

This should only be done after you are sure they will be as wise with your money as they would be with their own.

This comes down to your investment model and overall strategy, whether you plan to invest in your local area or use an expert in your chosen location. As always, research is the step you need to take. This research forms the smaller step that will carry you to that giant leap forward. Furthermore, the weight it carries is immense since it has the potential to save you thousands of pounds and many hours of hassle.

12 Analysis - property specific

As we approach the business end of the book, we should be appeased that the bulk of our analysis is concluded. At this point, we have already carefully analysed the big three 'Time, Education and Capital'. We have assessed our returns concerning yields, ROIs and cashflows, and our investment location has been established or at least considered in depth. That this stage of your journey concludes these areas is essential since it will allow us to avoid distractions enabling us to focus our efforts to ascertain how we will assess individual properties as they arise, regardless of who sourced them.

Specific to the property, we can break the analysis into three primary components: diligence, viewing, and mathematics. If we can ensure that we are up to speed with this process, then our investment success will be far more likely.

Time is perhaps your greatest commodity, so being efficient with it is paramount to your success. The more time you free up by having the ability to assess a property quickly, avoiding the need to view and potentially buy the wrong one, the more time you will have to ensure that the properties you do view and subsequently purchase are from better stock.

Wasting time on properties that simply do not fit your remit is something you cannot wholly irradicate since a large part of this comes with experience. However, following a systematic approach to analysis can speed the process up.

I must reiterate something I have repeatedly passed comments on, but it is essential for you to understand. Property investment, or more accurately, successful property investment, is not only about mathematics. Your returns are not the entire picture. The investment must stack up on paper and in its tangible form equally.

Area, size, finish, parking, location relative to transportation, schools, shops, main roads, and estates, as well as future expenditure and the implications of that expenditure. Capital growth and the potential of the investment as well as your customer, are just a few things that need to be considered when looking to purchase an investment property.

Further to these considerations, we have far more hoops to navigate today if we are to comply fully with our properties. You will discover this as we progress through analysis.

Diligence

Our diligence starts as we navigate Rightmove looking for properties that fit our chosen model. The term diligence should resonate through each of my laws of property investing and the following components of analysis. For the purpose of this component, however, it more widely refers to our pre-viewing diligence.

So much can be discovered about a property without ever having to leave the comfort of your home. Taking the time to understand how to analyse a property systematically is something that you should study well before you are at the point of looking for your first investment. As you continue to investigate the possibilities of becoming a property investor, you can, especially since it is the fun part, begin to look at and analyse mock properties that take your fancy. The following process is by no means comprehensive but can be used to form part of your own systematic analysis.

Since April 1st, 2020, landlords have had to ensure that their property has an 'Energy Efficiency' of E or above. This was hardly an issue since most properties fell within this range, and ones that had a rating of F or G were easily improved by the installation of a new boiler or the addition of loft insulation, the prior of which will have no doubt been well past its sell-by date, therefore needing to be replaced at some point in the near future, regardless. The latter was merely covered for free by one of the numerous available energy company grants available at the time.

The issue we face as investors is that as part of an aim to reduce carbon emissions from buildings, achieve net carbon zero and improve the energy efficiency of homes, from 2025, all newly rented properties will be required to have an energy rating of C or above. Existing tenancies will have until 2028 to comply with the new regulation changes.

When advertising a property for sale, the current regulations state that the seller must commission an 'Energy Performance Certificate (EPC) for the property should one not already exist. For those with a valid EPC, the certificate must be attainable for the prospective buyer. This means that when carrying out your due diligence, you have access to the current EPC and, more importantly, the 'Energy Efficiency Rating' (EER).
Because these changes for new tenancies are somewhat imminent in the broader scheme of things, my first port of call when considering any property is to check the EER of the property.

This is a simple process that is sometimes made that little bit harder by the agent. Often there is a link on the listing to the energy performance certificate held on the .gov website ®, but sometimes the agent will only place an image of the rating instead. This means you must take a quick detour to check the .gov register yourself. For you to do this, you will need the door number and the postcode of the property. This can be obtained from the agent or is often visible on the property listing.

It goes something like this "Hi, I am interested in the property you have available in fake street, fake town. Could you tell me what number property it is so that I can begin my research?" Then simply head over to *www.gov.uk/find-energy-certificate* and follow the onscreen instructions, selecting a domestic property, inputting the postcode and then selecting the door number of the property. The results will highlight a few things. One is the rating from A to G. A being the most efficient and G being the least efficient. Remember, as mentioned EPCs need to be C or above by 2025. This is us safeguarding for the future. The second thing this shows, and the thing that we need to focus on, specifically, should the rating not already be C or above, is the EER or the energy efficiency rating. Here we have a score from 1-92+ broken down as follows. 1-20, rating of G. 21-38, F. 39-54, E. 55-68, is a D. 69-80 a C. 81-91 is B and 92+ is an A.

The important thing to note here is that each letter has a spectrum from a low score for the letter to a high score for the letter. For instance, a D might at first glance look great as a screenshot of the rating on Rightmove since we only need to be a C; however, if it is a low D, say 55, then we have a fair way to go to make this up to everyone's favourite number, 69 or a C rating. Whereas a high D, say 68, might only need a couple of energy-saving lightbulbs to push the rating to the required C.

Conversely, a rating of an E might fill you with dread, but if it is a high E, say 54, then it might as well be a D; therefore, improving its rating might not be as daunting as it first appeared. The principal reason we need to determine this at this early stage is that if the rating is below a C, we need to calculate how much capital we will need to further invest into the property before 2025 to improve its rating.

Conveniently for us, the EPC register has a breakdown of the property's energy performance. Here we can see things like cavity wall insulation, roof insulation, windows, heating, hot water controls, lighting, and so on. Each of these elements is rated as very poor, poor, average, good or very good. This is the best indicator we have to see where we might be able to improve the overall rating of the property. Further, to add even more value to this part of our initial due diligence, if we scroll a little further down the page, we have some broad-brush estimations of the recommended improvement costs. These Indicate how it will increase the overall score of the rating and at what cost.

Viewing the .gov EPC register should be the very first port of call for any investor looking at carrying out some due diligence on a given property. I can quickly dismiss a property without doing anything else but scan the register. Let me explain how specifically.

In the late 19th century, cavity wall construction was introduced in the United Kingdom. It gained widespread use in the 1920s. In some early examples, stones were used to tie the two skins together, while in the 20th century, metal ties came into use. Initially, cavity widths were narrow and were primarily implemented to reduce the passage of moisture into the interior of the building via capillary action. The introduction of insulation into the cavity became standard in the 1970s and compulsory in the 1990s. The relevance of a cavity is essential when considering the potential energy performance improvements on a property.

As you check the EPC register, you will read one of the following statements next to where it details walls and its rating of poor to very good. 'Cavity wall, as built' followed by something like 'filled cavity' or 'no insulation' generally followed by (assumed) in brackets. Or it will read 'Solid brick, as built', 'no insulation' and again generally followed by (assumed) in brackets.

Whether the cavity is non-existent, present, and unfilled or present and filled will be reflected in the EER score. As you might \reasonably conclude, insulating a property without a cavity wall is far more challenging than one with a cavity. Essentially you would need to clad the external wall at a rough cost, and according to the EPC register, of somewhere between £8,000-£1,400. Here is where it gets specific. Should the property you are considering have a rating of a D and have no cavity, all is not lost.

The spectrum of the rating, in this instance, D being 55-68, is essential. We must assess how close we are to that magical number of 69 and see what other more minor changes to our property we could make to hit the target.

It may be that the rating is a high D, say 66, so replacing the thermostat and time clock on the boiler for a more modern programable room thermostat and adding some thermostatic radiator valves might get us to where we need to be. It could be that we need to replace the boiler or add some loft insulation and exchange the lightbulbs for more energy-efficient bulbs. Each of these will be far cheaper than external insulation. The counter is that the property is a low D, say 55, and the boiler is already a high-efficiency combination boiler.

We might look at the certificate and note that the only route to improving its score dramatically is the wall insulation, rendering this a short but incredibly useful exercise.

There is one final thing to note before we leave the .gov register, and that is the footprint of the property. Just under the big blue box detailing the property's Energy Rating and certificate number, we can find two useful pieces of information. One is the 'property type', i.e. mid-terrace, semi-detached and so on, and the other is the 'total floor area'. At this point, before we close the certificate, we should note down the floor area, and we will return to this later during the comparable search demonstration.

Help with Energy Efficiency

At the beginning of December 2022, the government announced a £1 billion grant to improve the energy efficiency of homes with an EPC of D or below via participating energy companies. The good news with this announcement is that landlords are to be eligible for the grant too. Initially, this is to be rolled out during the spring of 2023. I am confident, however, that this will be extended as we approach 2025 and beyond. Still, there is no guarantee that the grant will cover external insulation, so check the EER of every property you consider.

When the guidance for minimum energy efficiency standard was first published on the 1st of October 2017, it stated, and I quote, "you will never be required to spend more than £3,500 (including VAT) on energy efficiency improvements. If you cannot improve your property to EPC E for £3,500 or less, you should make all the improvements which can be made up to that amount, then register an 'all improvements made' exemption". This meant that, as investors, we would not have any significant or catastrophic costs imposed upon us. However, as I write this, there is no official confirmation, I understand that the plans are to increase this to a maximum of £10,000. I am confident that at this point in the book, I don't need to highlight the detrimental effect this will have on your return on investment.

For the next part of your due diligence, we need to talk about Zoopla and its continually improving algorithm.

When I started training in 2017, I used Zoopla's valuations as a 'watch this space' type of demonstration. Indicating that the algorithm was okay at best and could potentially be used loosely, I added, along with other avenues, to gain a better understanding of a property's value. This was then and still is particularly useful when considering below-market value offers on a property, buying a property that has been sourced to you, or direct-to-vendor purchasing, whereby you need to make an offer on the property without the usual benchmark of the agent's valuation. As the years have passed, I have progressed from using the term 'okay' to it is 'getting better' to 'pretty good', and more recently, since they introduced their low, medium, and high confidence ratings, 'very good'. The caveat when using Zoopla as your valuation is that their estimation does need to be backed up with the words 'high confidence' underneath it. Medium and low confidence should both be taken with a pinch of salt. But the high confidence ratings are generally very good and can be used as a benchmark for you to use.

When a property is listed on Rightmove, it is a safe bet to assume that it is usually priced at or around the correct, current market value. But Zoopla should be your next port of call for the avenues mentioned above, such as sourcing and direct-to-vendor purchasing. You are around three or four minutes into our initial due diligence on a property, and you already know the EPC rating of the property, the implications and cost approximation to improve its rating, if necessary, and you have a valuation of the property with a low, medium, or high confidence rating. This means that within a few minutes, we can decide whether to move on to the next or continue our research on this chosen property.

Zoopla is not exclusive to off-market properties as it can be used in conjunction with Rightmove listings when searching for property. If you recall from our previous demonstration when discussing the BRR model, we advised that one of the essential elements to assessing the suitability of the deal was to accurately assess the 'Done up Value' (DUV) of the property.

Zoopla does not discriminate against poor standard properties and does not assess each property's condition before offering its confidence rating and valuation. Instead, it offers the valuation of a property in good condition. Therefore, if Zoopla had a high confidence valuation of, say, £100,000, but the property is on Rightmove for £75,000, there is a good chance that the property will be a BRR type. Its low valuation is due to the work required to bring the property up to standard. The benefit we have here, which relies on a 'high rating' from Zoopla, is that we can corroborate the agent's estimation of the done-up value (DUV). Furthermore, when considering purchasing a BRR-type property through the avenues mentioned above, we can corroborate the sourcing companies' done-up valuation on the property, or we have something to work with when approaching the mathematics of a direct-to-vendor purchase.

With our pre-viewing due diligence and naturally assuming that before we searched the EPC register and cross-referenced Zoopla, we briefly browsed the images to confirm suitability, the next thing to do is to go back to the pictures to review them in more depth. You would be surprised how lazy some estate agents are and, as a result, what can be established from their images on Rightmove. I have seen images with dehumidifiers and electric heaters in each room, indicating possible issues with dampness or moisture, images with bottles of mould spray left on the basin in the bathroom, as well as images of the garden clearly showing next doors garden, which had a burnt-out sofa in the middle of the grass as well as scrap metal and overgrown weeds.

Aside from the glaringly obvious, you can use these pictures to begin assessing the property's requirements. Should this be a ready-to-let 'turnkey' type property, how old are the kitchen and the bathroom, and how would you rate the tiling in each room with regards to a neutral, modern look? Can you see any carpets that clearly need replacing? Is there ghastly wallpaper that would scare off any normal human being? Do the windows and doors look modern? Are they double-glazed UPVC? Often external images of the property's front and back show fencing, driveways, and gardens; are the fences of solid construction? Are the drive and patio areas level and presentable? Does the garden have a mass of grass bordered with 20-foot-high conifers that will need yearly attention?

These are all factors that will determine your capital input and the suitability of this property to your model. This information is generally attainable from the Rightmove listing in a matter of minutes. Remember, the property is not turnkey if it requires a large capital injection after purchase; you do not want to stumble your way into 'No Man's Land'.

Even if we are looking for a BRR or property to flip, we can still begin to gauge the costings from these images. To reiterate, efficiency is key here. Although physically viewing property is essential in the early days for experience, not all are blessed with time, so accurate assessment is crucial to efficiency.

Considering a BRR or a property to flip, should the property be for sale on the open market, we will have an asking price. We can quickly obtain the agent's estimation of the done-up-value of the property and can corroborate this with our high-confidence Zoopla valuation. Naturally, now we need to establish the refurbishment cost.

Looking through the images of a Rightmove listing while writing, I have found a three-bedroom mid-terrace property for sale for £60,000. This is clearly a repossessed property, evident by the presence of blue tape over the gas and water outlets in the property. This is 'Do Not Use – Appliance Decommissioned' warning tape. The tape is used after the water and gas have been turned off and drained in the property, which lenders generally do when repossessing a property. The next 'tell-tale' sign that this is a repossessed property is the public notice offer of £58,750.

When a property that the lender has repossessed is sold, it is standard practice to place a public notice of the offer on the listing for around seven days.

Walking you through the images of this listing, I can note the following:

Picture 1, which shows the property's exterior, shows me double glazing of the usual standard as judged against the two neighbouring properties. However, the main entrance door is wooden and will need replacing since it is old and cracked. I can also see a perimeter fence that has been patched in many places; it is anything but vertical and has clear signs of rotting on the base of many of the panels. The entire fence will need replacing. The garden has several large bushes almost twice the height of the fence, and the patio leading to the front door will need levelling. As a rough estimate of this image, we have a door at £650, a fence at £750, shrub removal and garden work at £200, and the patio levelling standing at £250. The first picture shows me that an investment of around £1,850 is required for remedial work.

Picture 2 shows me a dual-aspect living room *(one with a window at both ends of the room) that needs* stripping since the wallpaper has begun to peel off sporadically. There is no carpet in the room, only a concrete floor. The internal doors are old-style plain white sheet doors with old stainless steel ventilation grids installed. There is a dado rail at around one meter in height around the room, and the skirting board is patched in and damaged. The ceiling is covered in aertex, and one ceiling pendant hangs loose. Excluding painting and carpeting, which every room will require, as a minimum, this room will need the following:

1. Stripping £150
2. Plastering including ceiling £350
3. Fully skirting, two new doors and architrave £500
4. Sockets, switches & ceiling pendants replacing £200

TOTAL £1,200

Picture 3 shows me the kitchen, which I am sure you guessed by now will need a complete replacement. This small kitchen is nestled into the corner of the property showing me two double-base units and three single-base units. We have exactly the same up high, along with a hob, oven, and extractor unit. There is a tiled wall three tiles high above the worktop on two walls, and the floor again is bare, showing only the concrete. The back door leading to the garden is again wooden and will need replacing. I am unable to see many electrical fittings nor the ceiling, or internal doors, so these will need investigating should I decide to pursue a viewing of the property.

1. Removal of the kitchen, the tiles, and their disposal - £250
2. Supply & fit a small kitchen, including appliances - £2,750
3. New back door - £650
4. Supply & fitting of tiling - £300

TOTAL £3950

Picture 4 shows a bathroom that is in desperate need of replacement. It is a relatively small bathroom, but the entire room is tiled from floor to ceiling. I can see that there is no extraction in the room, and the ceiling is again artexed and covered with black mould in the corner. The door is the same plain white council-style sheet door.

1. Removal of the bathroom, all the tiles and disposal - £500
2. Plastering of the walls - £250
3. Installation of an extractor unit - £120
4. Supply & fit of a standard three-piece bathroom suite - £750
5. Walls to be clad around bath and ceiling to be clad - £450

6. Replacement of the light - £60
7. Door and Architrave - £120

TOTAL £2,250

Picture 5 shows the main bedroom, which is not actually that bad. The walls are covered in pink paint, but they look okay. There is a built-in wardrobe that will need removing, and I assume that the walls will need repairing. The ceiling is not aertex, but the radiator is old and yellow. Painted yellow, not discoloured.

1. Stripping of walls and assuming okay underneath - £100
2. Replacement of radiator and valves - £200
3. Removal and disposal of built-in wardrobes - £100
4. Make good walls - £100

TOTAL £500

That, unfortunately, is the extent of the images. There are no images of the other two bedrooms or the rear garden. There is a floorplan, however, which shows the addition of a good-sized entrance and the layout of the bedrooms. My estimations so far come to £9,750, excluding painting and carpeting, which I would estimate a cost of around £3,000 for a property of this size. This is installing better grade, longer lasting, washable carpets. This addition takes my running estimation to **£12,750**.

The next thing I do from here is to make some presumptions about the rest of the property based on what I have seen so far. I will assume that bedrooms two and three are in a similar condition to bed one and apply a blanket cost of £1,000 for the pair, which takes me to £13,750.

I now need to do a few things. One considers the boiler and electrical system, and given the state of the property and its lack of investment of due care concerning the aesthetics, I would feel confident with the assumption that all the remaining radiators would need replacing along with the boiler. If there has been such little investment in the property over the years with the aesthetic elements, then I'm not expecting a high-efficiency boiler. To clarify this, I head over to the EPC, which has an expiration date of 2029; therefore, since they expire after ten years, it was only carried out a few years ago, in 2019. Under the heading boiler, the rating is average, leading me to conclude that my assumption was correct.

Consequently, I add another £3,000 for a new boiler and the remaining unaccounted-for radiators. I am now running at around £16,750 and have not visited the property yet. I must bear in mind that I cannot see the condition of the door frames, the ceilings in some of the rooms, and the walls will all need closer inspection, as well as the remaining doors. At this stage, I would work out a worst-case scenario for the property to include the above as well as a complete new rewire. Then and only then can I run the numbers on the property to see if there is anything in the property for either a BRR or a flip.

When pricing any refurbishment works, you need to account for the following:

1) Who will remove it? The bathroom, kitchen, carpets, built-in wardrobe and so on.
2) Who will take away and dispose of what has been removed?
3) Who will plan it, specifically kitchens, bathrooms, radiator locations and paint schemes?
4) Who will supply it, again more specifically with kitchens, bathrooms, tiling, flooring, paint and so on?
5) Who will deliver or collect it from the merchants?
6) Who will install it?
7) Who will remove any rubbish once finished?
8) Who will clean the property after each installation?

There is a good chance that you will find a tradesperson to carry out several of the above. However, it is doubtful that you will, in every case, find a tradesperson that will cover all eight points on the list. You must understand that as the tradespeople carry out more of the list, their prices increase in parallel.

Getting back to our calculations, I have now added another £6,000 onto the refurbishment to include the rewire and the other jobs assumed. We have a total of £22,750. After speaking with the local agent via Whatsapp to continue with this section, he tells me that properties in good condition in that area are to expect an asking price of £100,000.

This means that regardless of the investment needed and the usual hassle factor that comes with any refurbishment, the property does, in fact, stack up on paper, at least at this pre-viewing stage. I had already been on Zoopla's website to check the valuation of the property, which was £102,250, high confidence. Despite only firing Rightmove up for this demonstration, I am now beginning to consider this property for myself, so thanks, everyone. I owe you all a drink.

Now, before I rush off and book a viewing on this property, I want to walk you through the subsequent stages of my pre-viewing due diligence, and then I will break down the mathematics in full, so you can see how I arrived at my conclusion. I would point out before I continue that this process is very straightforward for me and comes naturally due to repetition. There is no need for a pen and paper; arriving at my conclusion usually only takes me a few minutes. Therefore, I preach the need to begin to practice this.

One can do many things to improve efficiency, increase knowledge and gain experience. This might take you twenty minutes at first but practise it, and you will begin to establish patterns, decreasing your time spent on each property.

To recap, we have browsed the images to determine if the property generally looks like it suits our investment model. In this instance, we chose a BRR-type property. We have checked the EPC of the property, which shows an EER of 61. We visited Zoopla and checked the valuation of the property and noted that it was high confidence. I have been through the images to take a much closer look to gauge a general idea of the refurbishment costs, and I contacted my trusted agent, on a Sunday, by the way, to further confirm the done-up-value (DUV) of the property.

Side note: Should Zoopla's website have shown a medium of worse, low confidence rating and the agent I spoke with was not a trusted one, the next thing I would have done would be to look at comparable sales or comps for short. Assessing comps on Rightmove is a relatively straightforward process. Scrolling down the listing just under the property map, you will find some helpful information detailing local train stations, schools, broadband speed, the property sale history, and the nearby recent sold and under-offer properties. The latter of which is what we need here.

The property sale history does have its uses, particularly in determining how much you think the debt is on the property. In a direct-to-vendor purchase, you can gauge how much they have left to pay on the property by looking at the purchase price and subtracting 10%, which in most cases would have been the typical deposit amount. This is a broad estimate and carries the assumption that they have not revalued the property at any point, but it can be calculated as follows:

Firstly factor in how long the property has been owned. For instance, if it was last sold ten years ago, you would subtract this from 25 and then divide the loan amount by 25 and then times by that number. An example is a purchase price of £50,000 less 10% equals £45,000. If the property was purchased ten years ago, we would subtract ten from 25, leaving the owner with 15 years of his mortgage left to pay. Therefore we divide £45,000 by 25 and then times that by 15. In this instance, and again it is a rough estimate, provided we have our deposit amount correct and that the owner has not remortgaged over the last ten years, they would have around £27,000 left to pay on their mortgage.

However, what we are really interested in at this point is the comps on properties that are recently sold or sold subject to terms and conditions (STC). Clicking the 'recent sold and under offer' link on Rightmove, I can see that there was a property sold in the same street in February last year for £109,950. On closer inspection of the previous listing images, however, I can see a spacious, well-presented conservatory attached to the living room. This property is extremely well-kept, with modern decor running throughout. The good news is that this is not too dissimilar to what we will achieve should we refurbish.

Back in July 2021, a property sold for £89,000, 0.1 miles away. The property is in average condition throughout and, in my opinion, would need a facelift. This, again, is encouraging on three fronts. First, I know property prices in this area have risen considerably since July 2021, and I note that it sold for almost £90,000 in its current average condition. Our refurbished property will be far superior. Finally, I can see this property has a footprint of 86 square meters; however, the one we are working through for this example is 97 square meters. This was the information we grabbed from the EPC in my demonstration earlier, the one I asked you to hold on to until a little later.

Considering the property's footprint is essential when locating comparables. It is not a true comparable if one property is 100 sqm and the other is 75 sqm.

I am now appeased, without further research, that this property, once refurbished, will achieve somewhere around £105,000.

Before we conclude, however, we need to calculate the rental charge of the property and, should this not already have been considered when carrying out our location analysis, the rental demand. Again this is a simple process, and we have a couple of tools at our disposal. The first and most obvious route would be to speak with a couple of local agents. Simply picking up the phone and speaking to two or three local agents will take a small amount of our day and yield reasonably accurate results. I tend to stay clear of the agent selling the property unless I have a good relationship with them, as they will no doubt simply tell you what you want to hear to sell the property.

Ensure that the agents you speak with are letting agents, not just estate agents; otherwise, they will not be as helpful since there is no value in the conversation for them. Simply call two or three letting agents in the area and tell them that you are either considering buying the property or that you already own it, and you want to gauge how much you could rent it for and what the current demand is for that type of property. We can calculate an average letting cost by calling two or three agents.

We can corroborate our findings or begin our research with Rightmove too. This time we are looking for rental comparables instead of sold comparables. Selecting 'To Rent' instead of 'For Sale' and continuing through the selection fields, inputting a comparable search to the property we are trying to understand will show us our competition and rental charge comparisons.

Searching the property's postcode in our example yields zero results, but widening the search to ¼ of a mile shows four properties. Only two of these are comparable, which is key here.

The other two have driveways and larger gardens, and one has a large porch built on the front. They have been built using completely different bricks, as is evident from the images; they are clearly in a better area than the one we are assessing. They are not comparable, so we can discount them. I now have two solid comparable properties to work with.

Both are mid-terrace properties and in good condition throughout. They are both advertised for £650 per calendar month (PCM). Furthermore, if I locate and select the 'filters' field at the top right of the page, I can place a tick in the 'include let agreed' box. This now yields 11 results, five of which are comparable properties. These 11 results are made up of the four that are to let and a further seven that are 'let agreed'. This shows me two things. Firstly, there is not much competition for that postcode, and two, the market is buoyant. From the five comparable properties, three were advertised at £625 and two at £650. For my calculations, I will use the comparable property indicated as having a let agreed upon and input £625 into my spreadsheet.

With that in mind, my next port of call would be my 'Quickshot' spreadsheet, but before I enter the figures, I need to confirm the mortgage interest rates and, in fact, if mortgages are available for properties valued at £60,000. Allow me to explain this more recent addition to my due diligence process.

Before the madness brought on by Kwasi Kwarteng's disastrous mini-budget in September 2022, rates and mortgages, although already showing signs of change, were a relatively predictable product. For the previous 10-15 years, I could go weeks without speaking with my broker, only approaching her when I needed a product switch, revaluation or a decision in principle for a new mortgage. Incidentally, the correct terminology here is an agreement in principle. However, almost everyone still calls it a decision in principle, presumably because of the easier-to-digest acronym, DIP.

Before this, I relied on the steadiness of the rates, knowing what values and properties mortgage companies would lend on. For instance, some lenders used to enter the market at £75,000, some at £90,000. Then we have companies like 'Together Mortgages' who would quite literally lend a 75% LTV on the neglected shed rotting away at the bottom of your garden, valued at around £137.

The difference is that mortgage products seem to change weekly, sometimes daily, as we continue with more economic uncertainty. Rates fluctuate, variable and fixed rates are up and down daily, irrespective of the Bank of England base rate. Equally, minimum loan values for a property fluctuate almost daily. That means I now need to consult my broker to enquire about available rates and minimum purchase values for this property and for anything I asses in the immediate future. I will discuss this in more depth in the next chapter when we cover financing deals. For now, we will assume that I have contacted my broker, who has confirmed the availability of a tracker mortgage, incidentally with Together mortgages, at a rate of 4.6%.

The calculations I need to run ® do not need to be exact at this stage, primarily because they are somewhat estimated due to the full extent of the refurbishment still being unknown. They are as follows:

Deposit required *(25% of purchase price, £60,000)* - £15,000
SDLT *(3% above standard rate)* - £1,800
Legal fees & broker - £1,300
Refurbishment costs *(estimated)* - £22,750
Total capital outlay - £40,850

If this were a turnkey property, we would input a £1,000 refurbishment cost in place of the £22,750 above, move straight onto the rental charge and conclude our numbers. However, in this instance, we must input the revaluation to calculate the equity release after the property is refurbished. Therefore:

The 'Done up Value' *(DUV)* - £105,000
75% LTV of the DUV £78,750
Mortgage redemption, excluding early redemption penalties - £45,000
Capital back in the bank - £33,750
Capital left invested or 'tied up' in the property - £7,100

Now is the time to move on to our returns. After our equity release, we have a large portion of our capital back in our bank. In fact, we are leaving only £7,100 of our initial investment in the deal, meaning that 82.62% of our capital is safely back with us, ready to use again, which to affirm further is the point of the BRR model. This £7,100 is the amount we need to use to calculate our return on investment.

The rental charge on the property is £625 PCM, meaning that if we self-manage, we would have a monthly cashflow of £323.13, which is £3,877.50 annually. Therefore our return on investment is 54.61% which is an impressive number, as I am sure you would agree.

This property aside and back in your world, let us imagine you are doing this for multiple properties to compare. In this instance, you should have a separate tap on the spreadsheet that details the primary numbers of your findings.

That means the tab should have the following headings:

1. Property address
2. Purchase price
3. Refurbishment cost
4. Full working capital required
5. Return on investment
6. Cashflow

You can then have a further four headings for your BRR deals:

1. Capital back in the bank
2. Capital left in the deal
3. Return on investment after refinance
4. Cashflow after refinance

You will note that in the case of a BRR deal, your cashflow and return on investment will change significantly after refinancing, so they only need to be considered at this point.

At the end of your analysis session, you will have several properties on your list. Your job now is to highlight the best ones and place them at the top of your priority pile.

Viewing a property

When looking to establish a property's suitability, there is a lot to consider, and you should be diligent at this stage and do your research thoroughly. In general, you are looking specifically at the implications of how much investment is needed, be it immediate or in the future, for a given property.

What follows is a makeshift generic checklist ® and tips on what you should look for and consider when viewing a property in the flesh. Regardless of your approach, strategy, and long-term plan, which in turn will determine what model and type of property you buy, the following list should be considered at a minimum. If you intend to buy a turnkey property or fully renovate throughout, you should be aware of and budget for either way, so take note of the points below.

Externally

i. It would help if you aimed to arrive 15-20 minutes early to your appointment so that you can briefly assess the area. You might be surprised by what you can determine in as little as 15 minutes of observing from the side lines.

ii. Take note of the roofline; this should be straight with no dips or raised areas. The ridge tiles should look solid, and the mortar should be intact. Observe the guttering and downcomers, including all Joints. The Fascia and soffits should be secure and appear in good condition. Note the material of the external windows and doors. Are they double-glazed, and what is your estimation of their age? Consider the drive, front garden, yard, and anything else visible during this time.

iii. Note other boards, To-Let and For-Sale. This can highlight any supply and demand imbalance in the area as well as the competition.

iv. Score the curb appeal out of 10 and then score what you believe its potential is next to that score but make sure that the potential is realistic and falls within your budget. If we replace windows, roof, guttering soffits and fascia's, repoint the brickwork and erect a new fence, we will undoubtedly increase the property's curb appeal, but at what cost? I suggest spending only a few hundred pounds for a turnkey property. Bear in mind, though, that a complete refurbishment may bring this up as a by-product, so you can be less concerned if replacing windows, doors, or roofs as part of your BRR refurbishment.

v.   Next, note the curb appeal of the few houses on either side; this is something you will be unable to change, but it will give you a clearer indication of how the neighbours live and of the area itself.

vi. Parking can be a concern and is becoming increasingly important as the number of vehicles on the road hits an all-time high, so note the presence of driveways, parking bays, permit zones, yellow lines or free for all parking.

vii. Note the external walls of the property, especially in the case of a house that is covered in render. But also, and in case you haven't already looked on the EPC register, you can, providing you can see the brickwork on the property, determine if it has a cavity ®.

viii. Look out for garages, as these can be expensive when brought up to standard. A garage roof, including new boarding, can cost around £2,500-£3,000 and a new door from £500. Many have side doors which can be £200-300, yet none of this will have any discernible effect on the done-up value of the property.

Much of this detail will already be obtained from your Rightmove search or if you have taken advantage of Googles street view when considering the property. However, nothing can replace the tangibility of the actual viewing. Often things will stand out like a sore thumb that was missed with your initial pre-viewing diligence.

Internally

As the agent arrives five minutes before the viewing, and unless they seek you out to greet you, allow them to enter the property before you approach. Punctuality is essential since the agent will have factored in the viewing timing and will want to arrive a few minutes early to light and maybe even heat the property. Some agents like to show you around the property room by room; however, if possible, request that you briefly walk through the property on your own. It is a good idea to walk through the property briefly before you get into the crooks of the viewing. Trust your gut here. It is the best measure you can have of a property's suitability. If you like the overall feel of the property, continue to be more thorough with your assessment; if not, you can wrap up your viewing relatively quickly from here, informing the agent that this property is not one you will pursue. They will appreciate your honesty and time. After a brief five-minute property scan, your primary focus is the points below.

i. As you walk around the property, note the look, condition, feel and operation of all the doors and windows in each room, not forgetting back doors and any patio doors to the garden.

ii. Further to this note is the condition of the flooring, carpets, laminate, tiling or vinyl in bathrooms and kitchens and the presence of underlay. Underlay is inexpensive and can make a difference when showing a prospective tenant the property.

iii. Note the walls and ceilings and their coverings – aertex, woodchip, wallpapered, rough and ready in need of repairs or smooth and well plastered. Apart from the latter, each one carries a different cost implication.

iv. The condition, standard and age of the kitchen and tiling should be considered in both the cases of a turnkey and BRR. Remember that every penny saved on a refurbishment is a penny back in your account. Perhaps more importantly, you should assess the implications of replacing the kitchen and your best guess as to when that would be necessary and at what cost. It is important to note that a small kitchen placed in the corner of a room with a few tiles as a splashback, as in my example of the £60,000 I found on Rightmove, is far easier to replace than a kitchen that has boxing above the cornice, has twice as many cupboards including built-in appliances and is tiled floor to ceiling. The cost of which can be more than twice its predecessor.

v. The same as above applies to the bathroom.

vi. Now that you are at the property, you will be able to assess the overall size and layout of the bedrooms, particularly the smallest. You cannot change this, but it is hugely important when considering your tenant search. How likely is it that the tenant you are searching for will need this size bedroom? If this is a three-bedroom house, is the third bedroom sizable enough for a growing child, or will this become the turnover area of the property. "we love this house, but we need a bigger bedroom for Katie now she has grown"

vii. How old is the central heating system installed? Can you identify the type of system from a combination boiler to a system boiler to an older style back boiler? Note down the make and model of the appliance for further research and ask the agent how old it is and if there is any paperwork for it. From the 1st of April 2005, Part L1 of the Building Regulations required gas boilers installed in new and existing dwellings to be condensing types of models. Furthermore, every installation must be covered by a building regulation certificate. This means if the boiler at the property you are viewing does not have a certificate, there is a good chance that it was installed pre-2005 meaning that it is fast approaching the end of its life.

viii. The age and type of consumer unit installed. Look for more modern metal consumer units or fuse boxes, as they are commonly referred to. Look for a larger number of single RCBOs or 'trip switches' protected by an RCD which are the larger-looking trip switches; these are around twice the width of a standard trip switch. Some consumer units have identification as to when they were installed or last inspected. It is rare for a homeowner to get their electrics checked, so should you proceed with a purchase, it is essential to get them checked during the conveyancing process. For now, we need to make our best guess as to its age and condition. Asking the agent may give an indication but do not rely on it. If in doubt, you can always take an image of the unit and show it to your electrical contractor for advice.

ix. Look for any signs of dampness or mould and take time to identify the difference between penetrating dampness, rising dampness and mould caused by living conditions or internal moisture. I would advise educating yourself on this and purchasing a moisture meter. These can be found on Amazon for around £20®

The Garden

If the property you are viewing has a garden, then there are a few points to consider during the viewing, such as how much sun it will get, who owns the fence at which side and what it contains. Whilst viewing the garden, here's a checklist to consider:

i.   Is there a front or back garden? Perhaps both?
ii. Is the garden private or shared?
iii. Where are the boundaries, and whose responsibility are they? This is particularly important when viewing a garden that has a substandard fence or wall divider
iv. Is the garden north or south facing? It may not prevent you from purchasing this property, but if matched with a comparable property, some factors will edge one over the other. Perhaps this is one of them.
v.   Will the seller remove parts of the garden, such as storage boxes, sheds, pots, and shrubs?
vi. Will the garden take continued high efforts to maintain?
vii. Are there any large trees dominating the garden?
viii. Do neighbouring houses overlook the garden?
ix. Can you see into the neighbour's garden? If so, how are they living?
x.   Do hedges overhang pavements or roads, and are they the homeowner's responsibility to maintain?

While viewing the garden, keep an eye out for things like plants that can damage your property, damage to outbuildings or general signs of neglect. The work needed to rectify may be rather significant if previously left unattended. Issues like Japanese Knotweed, ivy, large cracks, or rotten structures could be indicators that the garden needs more work than you are willing to provide. Remember, this kind of work is classed as dead money. It might improve the garden, but it will not help you achieve a higher rent, and often, it will not add much worth to the property's overall value either.

This list is anything but exhaustive but rather a basic overview of a standard two or three-bedroom property. You should take the proper time to observe anything significant, noticeable, or unusual that jumps out at you during your viewing. Most importantly, are you equipped to buy this property? Does it fit your model, experience, and level of expertise, and are you capable of running, maintaining and potentially managing this property or its needs, even if you plan on using an agent?

Inspecting the property before committing to the purchase for obvious reasons is essential so that you have no regrets and can be confident that the property fits your requirements. Before committing to an offer, you must be sure this is the right property for your portfolio. You may initially feel like rushing your viewing or due diligence as you don't want to waste anyone's time and really want to get things going; it is entirely up to you how you proceed, but by now, you will no doubt know my feelings with that.

Warning signs during your viewing

Here, I have created a simple 'structural' house viewing checklist of the main issues to keep in mind when walking through a property ®. These are points to consider across the entire house, as many of the issues highlighted may be a sign of structural problems and require a property survey to dictate the extent of the damage. These include:

1. Are there any cracks or signs of subsidence? Major cracks could signify structural movement, which will mean hiring a structural expert to assess the issue. Major structural movement could result in costly damage control and constant monitoring. If the issues become too dangerous, it could mean underpinning is required, which is an invasive and expensive procedure. Understand that we are not talking about hairline cracks in

197

ceilings or walls. These are very common and are usually a result of the organic movement in a property or a poorly taped or secured joint on the plasterboard. When we talk about cracks, we are talking about cracks large enough to get a standard-thickness pencil into.

2. Is the roof in good condition? Does it dip at any points? Roofing is expensive to replace, and a poorly maintained roof can lead to structural and damp issues in the future. Furthermore, if the issue is the roof frame, replacing it becomes even more costly. Dipped or uneven rooflines are common on ex-council estates, often when secondary roofing has replaced older-style flat concrete roofs.

3. Is the roof flat? Though a cheaper option, flat roofs will not last as long as pitched roofs, so keep an eye out for signs of wear and tear as well as ingress on the ceilings below, and always have this inspected.

4. Is the property at risk of flooding? Speak to your estate agent about whether the property is on a flood plain, but also keep an eye out for any running water nearby. If in doubt, you can check www.gov.uk/check-long-term-flood-risk for clarification.

5. Are the drains and gutters modern and functioning? Avoid stagnant, pooling water by scrutinising the drainage and drainpipes and guttering during your viewing.

6. Can you see or smell dampness, mould, or mildew in the house? Keep a keen eye out for any signs of dampness, especially in older homes. In many cases, this is easily managed, but you'll want to arrange for a damp specialist survey to assess the situation if in doubt properly. Damp and timber reports can be obtained for a couple of hundred pounds. Damp proofing may prove costly and affect your choice to purchase, or it may help you negotiate an alternative offer on the property.

7. Do the windows and doors open and close easily? Warped frames can signify structural movement or, at the very least, mean replacing the windows and doors.

To go alongside these checklists, I have also created a few top tips on getting more information about the house and getting the absolute best out of your viewing experience.

Our top tips for viewing a house are:

1. View the property at different times of the day. If possible, arrange for a second viewing at a different time of day so you can get a feel for the property throughout a typical day.
2. Explore the area at different peak times. Walk around the area in the morning, during afternoon commuting hours, and evening. This will ensure that traffic and noise are manageable at all times.
3. Try to view the property with another. Always go with an agent and bring a partner, family member or friend along to the viewing. A second opinion is always helpful as they will spot things you did not.
4. Take your time. Don't feel rushed during a house viewing; take your time to really take in the property. Don't be afraid to split off from the estate agent for a walk around.
5. Take lots of photographs. You'll likely be viewing a range of houses, so keep everything fresh in your mind by taking photos throughout the viewing *(it is courteous to ask permission, of course).*
6. Drive around the area. Get a feel for the safety of the area by driving around the streets.
7. Put together a list of questions. Prepare a list of questions ahead of time to ask the seller or estate agent so you are fully prepared.

When viewing a flat

Although many questions will be relevant for both viewing a house and a flat, there are some differences to consider.

Here are a few additional questions to ask when viewing a flat:

1. Is it leasehold or freehold?
2. Is there ground rent or a service charge? How much will this cost?
3. Will you have to contribute to a sinking fund?
4. What's the name of the freeholder or managing agent?
5. How long is the lease?
6. Are there options to extend the lease, and if so, at what cost
7. Are there communal spaces?
8. How many residents live here?
9. Are there any restrictive covenants to be aware of?
10. Are there any outdoor areas?
11. What services will be shared between residents?
12. Is there a residents' committee?

So, there you have it, my **minimum**, which for those listening to the book is bold and underlined, viable checklist and several smaller lists to consider when viewing properties. Now, please note that an exhaustive checklist cannot be created here since your requirements and the type of houses you are looking for will present different scenarios and considerations. Therefore, it is down to you to do your due diligence and do it well. Hopefully, you have plenty of food for thought from the above to run with.

13 Finance

"There is always plenty of capital available for those who can create practical plans for using it"
                                        Napoleon Hill 1883-1970

Let me be clear from the very start of this chapter, 'money is not your inhibitor'. It may still remain **your excuse**, but no longer does it justify why you cannot begin to build your property business.
This may sound like an obvious statement to make, but the more money you have, the easier your journey will be, of course. But having no liquid investment capital should no longer prevent you from starting a property business.

The modern-day investor has multiple routes to finance their business. Equity release, using other people's money (OPM) and employing a no money down (NMD) approach to investing are all viable options and have been for many years now.

You may dismiss these avenues since you might be cash rich right now, but trust me, you will begin to run low on capital at some point on your journey. This is the point that you may want to leverage an angel investor or tap into the resources of a chosen or pre-empted stakeholder. Perhaps you find a deal that you deem financially out of reach until you explore joint venturing or the advantages of leveraging a bridging loan.

Contrary to this, it may be that your less-than-compelling finances mean your short-term goal is to seek advice and education on building your property business despite this current limitation.

Regardless of your chosen route, however, a firm understanding of each financial opportunity is essential when determining how to fund and progress a specific deal.

For the benefit of your progression and the development of your education, forget what you currently believe as to how you will invest; Remain open-minded and understand that the fastest route to success is to create fluidity in your approach. Explore different avenues, run multiple scenarios and consider adopting multiple routes to finance. At this stage of your research, you should carefully consider what options are available to you. Investigate each avenue to help identify what your potential is. This should include any option that allows you to profit from an investment. Being owned, leased, leveraged or other.

A quick example of how I continue to increase my portfolio and wealth exponentially year after year is that although my own capital has historically been used for around 60% of my portfolio, and remember that a large portion of this has come from the compounded capital generated by accruing rent. The rest of my portfolio has come from leveraging stakeholders' capital, approaching angel investors, and bridging companies. Further, I have tapped many times into my network to source rent-to-rent and lease option properties, meaning there was little to no capital injected to benefit from rental profits.

I have and still do benefit from the profits generated from managing other people's property portfolios and by historically overseeing extensive refurbishments and developments, though not so much recently since my focus is elsewhere, predominantly on my free time. Furthermore, I have reinvested profits generated from sourcing property for other investors. Although I do this rarely and by no means count on this as a revenue stream, that does not mean this is not a viable option for you should you want to capitalise on this opportunity.

Before we discuss some of the plethoras of financing options available to you, it is time to follow through with the promise I made earlier in the book and demonstrate what each of you should include when financing your deals.

Helping you to understand the mathematics more clearly will help you head into each venture with your eyes open. This will limit the damage that nasty surprises can do to your portfolio growth, emotional state and, arguably more crucially, your mindset.

Whether you are using your own money to fund the deal or leveraging someone else's is somewhat irrelevant here. All of the costs need to be accounted for and, of course, paid for, at least by someone and at some point. The main difference when leveraging finance is that there will likely be more costs involved, which will differ depending on whom you leverage it from. For example, the costs to borrow from a close friend or family member will undoubtedly be lower than that of an angel investor you meet at a networking event. These will likely be lower than when leveraging a standard bridging company.

Until now, most of the calculations we have demonstrated have been void of some or all of the taxes, penalties for early redemption, set-up fees and mortgage arrangement costs. Below I will demonstrate the full implications of the investments. To demonstrate these figures accurately, I need to discuss several options generalising into two principal categories. Those being:

1) A standard ready-to-let property. What I call a 'Turnkey.'
2) A 'Flip' or 'BRR' type property. Essentially profiting or recycling cash from the deal

Firstly, when purchasing the property, there is not much difference between the three. Regarding the financials, your spreadsheet does not care if you will immediately let the property, flip it, or convert it into a six-bedroom luxury HMO.
Side note, we are talking specifically about the financial side of the deal here. It is essential that you source the correct product for the deal, something I will highlight in depth in a short while.

Although lenders do have different products available for standard buy-to-lets, flips or HMOs, we can still demonstrate a standard mortgage product for a typical £100,000 property, regardless of our intended model. All fees include VAT which, incidentally, investors cannot claim back. However, this is to your benefit since there is also no VAT chargeable on the rent you accrue, so the pros of being VAT exempt far outweigh the cons. For the benefit of the audible audience, and since this is an especially heavy chapter concerning mathematics, the following demonstrations will form part of the free resource pack accompanying this book.

Deposit Capital @ the standard 75% loan to value	**£25,000**
Stamp Duty Land Tax @ 3% above current base rate	**£3,000**
Solicitors charges, including all searches and external fees *(Note that this will differ from deal to deal and firm to firm)*	**£1,000**
Personal Guarantor (PG) advice for LTD company purchases *(explained below)*	**£210**
Brooker Fees	**£350**
Mortgage Valuation Fee *(specific to the deal, sometimes free)*	**£350**
Mortgage Arrangement Fee *(differs with each deal)* *(Note that this is added to the loan of the mortgage, so it is not an up-front cost)*	**£1200**
Mortgage Application Fee *(specific to the deal, sometimes free)*	**£250**
Survey Fees, if applicable or required by the lender *(This is an anomaly in most cases; therefore, we have inputted zero since there are too many variables, and they are often not required)*	**£0**

The total 'upfront costs' for this property are **£30,160.** However, for clarity, this is not an exact figure but rather a generalisation of a typical product. The difference can be the exception of free mortgage fees, cheaper solicitor costs and leveraging a free broker service.

We could argue that should the Gods be working in our favour that day, the variable might be reduced to **£28,750.** This would be a very best-case and, if I am honest, an improbable scenario since it relies on me reducing the solicitor costs to £750 and removing the personal guarantor advice in the hope that your relationship with another solicitor is well established and leverageable, like mine is. The broker fees have been wholly removed by employing a free broker service or sourcing the mortgage yourself, which is an option. The mortgage application and valuation fees have been removed since they are often free, or some lenders offer cash back upon completion.

That said, the actual figure above, being £28,750 or £30,160, is irrelevant for this demonstration. What is essential is the understanding of what needs to be included in your calculations. The above will give you a firm understanding of what to look for when developing your own spreadsheet or working through your calculations.

There are some key points to discuss highlighted within the above table. Firstly, as I am sure you are aware, the stamp duty land tax (SDLT) that is due changes as the purchase price of the property changes. At the end of this rather lengthy chapter on finance, I will place a table demonstrating the current percentages which have changed recently and in favour of us investors.

For investors, SDLT is charged at 3% above domestic homeowners' standard land tax rate. However, if your first buy-to-let is your first owned property, i.e., you currently rent, live with friends or family, and do not own your own home, then there is no SDLT to pay on your first buy-to-let should you opt to purchase this through a personal avenue. This is because the rules surrounding SDLT for investors are levied as a 'Second Home' tax. Meaning that if this is your first home, there is no 'second home' SDLT due.

If this sounds like your current scenario, then you must seek professional advice since if you intend to buy a home for yourself or your family further down the line, you do not want to pay the SDLT or 'second home' tax on your personal home. Given the probability of the higher purchase price, it may result in a higher tax bill.

Should you decide to invest through a limited company, however, then the exemption on it being your first property is removed, despite your current ownership of property, being three properties or zero properties. Investing through a limited company means the second home SDLT comes into immediate effect.

As you will see from the table at the end of this finance chapter, second home SDLT does not come into effect until £40,000, regardless of how many properties you own or what investment vehicle you choose, being personal or a limited company avenue.

Secondly, it became standard practice for mortgage lenders to require a Personal Guarantee (PG) for limited company purchases around the time that this became typical, which was some time ago. Essentially, since the word limited in your limited company stands for limited liability, the amount of liability undertaken by the company's shareholders is, well, in short, limited. Consequently, most lenders want firm protection in place should the company become insolvent, hence the need for a 'Personal Guarantee'.

This personal guarantee offers that protection for the lender. You are required to seek legal advice and sign a declaration of understanding and intent in the presence of a solicitor. By signing this personal guarantor form, you guarantee that you will personally pay the loan should the company fail, be dissolved or other.

The main points to note are that regardless of how many individuals are in the business, each director must sign their own personal guarantee. This effectively means that the more directors there are, the more the cost will rise since each director will or rather, in the eyes of the law, should be dealt with and offered this advice independently. For example, suppose your property company has two directors. In that case, both directors will usually incur a separate or individual charge and be given independent advice even if the other director is your spouse, partner, parent, offspring or other.

Furthermore, it is essential to understand that you are effectively guaranteeing the other director or directors within the business, and they are you. In the case of insolvency or failure to adhere to the agreed mortgage payment plan, the lender can pursue either one of you for the total amount due.

Whether this is a calculated 'best chance' of redemption or a random 'short straw' decision by the lender is their call, and you must abide.

Word of caution here, to justify their absurd charges, solicitors will often keep you longer than they need to whilst putting the fear of God into you when offering this mandatory legal advice. Painting a picture of a doomsday scenario is not uncommon. It is crucial that you remain strong-minded here. Remember, by this point, you should be more than confident that the decision you have made is the correct one. This advice should take around 5-10 minutes, including completing the signatures, but it often lasts much longer. To reiterate and affirm my appal, this is to justify the stellar charges applied to this simple process.

Next, we need to talk about the mortgage fees. Firstly mortgage valuations and application fees are different on almost every deal. They range from being free of charge to around £200-£350 for either charge. Some lenders will offer cashback upon completion for the valuation fee. Mortgage valuations are often carried out by companies external to the lender, meaning they incur a cost when a valuation occurs. This cost is often passed on to you but reimbursed as cash upon completion. This avoids the 'out of pocket' scenario for the lender should the mortgage not continue through to completion. Your broker should detail these types of charges in their summary, and they can also be found on your agreement in principle.

Mortgage arrangement fees (MAF), however, are not a necessary or mandatory upfront cost. They are routinely added to the loan's value.

This, in most cases, is optional. However, I can confirm that I have never paid an arrangement fee upfront. A typical 75% loan-to-value mortgage product with a property purchase price of £100,000 would have a £75,000 leveraged loan amount as standard, plus the mortgage arrangement fee. If we use the MAF from the example above, we will have a minimum redemption of £76,200 rather than the 75%LTV or £75,000 we leveraged for the purchase.

Of course, this excludes any early redemption charge (ERC), something we will discuss as we continue demonstrating the numbers. The principal advantage of adding the mortgage arrangement fee to the loan cost is that we need less capital to progress with the deal. Furthermore, as demonstrated earlier in the book, the value of this fee, along with the loan itself, will be stripped through inflation.

The variables with your calculations will play out when considering the types and models of property you intend to pursue. The most significant will be the refurbishment or development costs of the project. For instance, a standard turnkey buy-to-let purchase might incur a somewhat surmountable remedial cost of between £500-£1,500, which will not alter your numbers too much. However, a BRR or flip project might have a more significant refurbishment cost of, say, £15,000, which will undoubtedly have a more significant effect. Should we continue through to a large HMO conversion that could potentially run into tens of thousands of pounds, our numbers will alter once again.

Aside from the fact that you will need to ensure these funds are readily available, whether from your own working capital or obtained through one of the avenues mentioned previously and which will be explained in greater depth shortly, it is paramount that you include these figures in your calculations. This is especially important when looking to refinance through the BRR model or selling through the flipping model. We have already discussed the importance of accurately assessing these costs since a slight misjudgement in your calculations can negatively impact your profits or ability to repay your angel investors.

Let us now look at what your figures might look like when inputted into your spreadsheet to ensure mistakes are not made. Early redemption charges (ERCs) must be considered when applying different property models, which will be explained below.

Firstly we will look at a standard turnkey buy-to-let property with a small further investment of £1,000. As explained, there is not much difference this will make to the numbers, but for edification, we will demonstrate.

Let us use the most recent example of a £100,000 property and include all the relevant costs highlighted in our table above. You may remember that we realistically require £30,160 to purchase this property. Adding our small £1,000 remedial costs takes this total to £31,160.

Since the turnkey model relies upon longevity, we will not be selling or revaluing, *otherwise expressed as redeeming the mortgage*, at any time through the fixed term of the product, in this case, five years. Therefore the early redemption fee is irrelevant. The only real difference the small further investment makes comes in the form of a slightly lower ROI.

Our ROI reduces from 14.42% should we not require the £1,000 remedial to 13.96% if we do as in our example. Here we are using a standard interest-only mortgage at 4.6%. It is a self-managed venture and renting for £650 per calendar month. Hardly noticeable concerning your return on investment or, indeed, the capital required to purchase the property.

If we move on from turnkey to look at a typical BRR or flip deal, you will begin to see some differences since we must redeem the mortgage before the end of the initial fixed term, be it a two or five-year deal.

Before I demonstrate the figure with the BRR model, I want to take a brief but relevant detour to clarify what I mean by the 'initial fixed term' and why mortgage companies apply early redemption charges.

As you probably know, a standard buy-to-let mortgage usually has a 25-year term. This product will run down to zero as the years pass by.

However, as it does, your lender will want to tie you into their product for what they call 'fixed periods' within this 25-year term. Typically, the fixed period starts from day one of your loan; therefore, the length of the initial fixed term needs to be established before you search for the product. Most commonly, this is a two or five-year fixed term, albeit as I write this, three-year terms are becoming more available than they were historically.

The fixed term means that you are tied into that particular product at that particular rate with those particular terms and conditions for the fixed term or period, be it two, three or five years. Should you want to exit from the liability of debt and redeem or 'pay back' the loan, you will be required to pay a penalty for this privilege. Enter the early redemption charge. Typical early redemption charges for a five-year fixed term are 5% of the loan in year one, 4% in year two, 3% in year three and so on.

Typical charges for a two-year fixed term are 2-2.5% In the first year to 1-1.5% in year two. Conversely, these can have fixed charges instead of percentages, for example, £1,250 at any point during the fixed term. I must stress that every lender and every deal is different, so consult your broker to clarify since mortgages do change continually.

Lenders apply these early redemption charges because their business objectives are long-term lending. They base their model on keeping you signed up for the entire 25-year term. They want the longevity of the contract rather than offering you a pay-as-you-go service. Mortgage lenders are often not specialists in short-term lending. We generally need to head to an angel investor or a bridging loan specialist for this. These early redemption charges are high partly due to the result of the popularity of the BRR model.

Before this model was commonly applied, lenders had much smaller redemption charges since most investors hardly redeemed their products, certainly not within the fixed period. However, since the use of the BRR model has grown considerably, lenders have increased their protection by applying higher charges to early redemptions since, as explained, short-term lending is not their objective.

Of course, other mortgage products are available, which can incur smaller costs like ERCs, thereby increasing your profits. The big two are 'Discounted Variable' and 'Tracker' mortgages, which will be explained later in this chapter under the mortgage sub-section. For now, we will continue to demonstrate an early redemption charge's impact on the mathematics of the deal.

The following table shows what considerations we need to calculate our profit or equity release from a particular deal, whether a BRR, flip or HMO development. Essentially these are the same thing in financial terms. We are buying a property, converting or refurbishing it and then using the equity created from our development as our profit. The common denominator is that you are redeeming the mortgage in full. The principal difference between a BRR and a flip is the costs that must be accounted for. The considerations are all included below. I will then highlight the difference between the BRR and the flip in a like-for-like deal.

Again, we will use £100,000 as our purchase price, using a typical 75% loan to value, interest-only mortgage at 4.6% with a five-year fixed term. We will purchase the property using a sole director, limited company as the vehicle.

Flip Model Numbers

Purchase Costs

Deposit Contribution	**£25,000**
SDLT	**£3,000**
Solicitor Fees	**£1,000**
Personal Guarantee	**£210**
Broker Fee	**£350**
Mortgage Valuation Fee	**£350**
Mortgage Arrangement Fee	**£1,200** *(added to the cost of the loan)*

Mortgage Application Fee	**£250**
Total Purchase Cost	**£30,160**

Post-Purchase Costs

Refurbishment	**£15,000**
Council Tax Payments	*To be added for the duration that the property is owned and/or not let (optional)*
Mortgage Payments	*To be added for the duration that the property is owned and/or not let (optional)*
Energy Costs	*To be added for the duration that the property is owned and/or not let (optional)*

Sale or Refinance Fees

Post Refurbishment Valuation	**£135,000**
New Leveraged Loan	This is 75% LTV on the done-up-value (*to be used when refinancing*)
Existing Loan Redemption	£75,000 + £1200 *MAF* = **£76,200**
Early Redemption charge	**5%** (year-1), 4% (year-2) etc.
Broker fees	To be applied when refinancing the property
New mortgage fees	To be applied when refinancing the property
Solicitor fees	**£750** to either sell or refinance
Sale fees	To be applied if flipping the property

If we apply the relevant fields from the above table to a property that we intend to flip, let us look at what can be made from the property:

Total Purchase Cost	**£30,160** *as above*

Post-Purchase Costs

Refurbishment	**£15,000** *as above*
Council Tax payments	**£600** *two months refurbishment, one month to sell, plus two months conveyancing (five months in total)*
Mortgage payments	**£1,725** *five months in total*
Energy costs	**£360** *including the usage to maintain the heating whilst the conveyancing* is progressing
Total running costs	**£17,397.50**

Sale Fees

Post refurbishment valuation	**£135,000**
New leveraged loan	*No new loan is being taken out since we are selling not refinancing.*
Existing loan redemption	£75,000 + £1200 = **£76,200**
Early redemption charges	**£3,750** *at 5%*
Broker fee	*No broker needed to sell the property*
New mortgage fees	*No new mortgage, so no fees to be added*
Solicitor fees	**£750** *to sell the property*
Sale fees	**£1,800** *(£1500+VAT)*
Total fees payable	**£82,500**

Now that we have united the relevant fields into our table, our calculations for profit are as follows:

Sale Price	£135,000
minus the running costs	- £17,397.50
minus fees	- £82,500
Original investment	- £30,160
Total taxable profit	**£4,942.50**

Hardly a sizable profit in this example especially considering this might have been a long and time-consuming project. However, the outcome is irrelevant here since all I am trying to demonstrate is the process for calculating your potential profit.

If we now apply this to a property that we intend to employ the BRR model, let us look at the difference in the costs we need to account for and what can be made of the deal:

BRR Model Numbers

Purchase Costs   **£30,160** *as above*

Post-Purchase Costs

Refurbishment   **£15,000** *as above*

Council Tax payments   **£600** *two months refurbishment, one month to let (three months in total)*

Mortgage payments   **£862.50** *three months in total*

Energy costs   **£216** *including the usage to maintain the heating whilst the property is marketed for rent*

Total running costs   **£16,678.50**

Refinance Fees

Post refurbishment valuation	**£135,000**
New leveraged loan @75% LTV	**£101,250**
Existing loan redemption	£75,000 + £1200 (MAF) = **£76,200**
Early redemption charges	**£3,750** *at 5%*
Broker fee	**£350**
New mortgage fees	**£600** *valuation and application fees combined*
Solicitor fees	**£750** *to refinance*
Sale fees	*No sale fees*
Total fees payable	**£81,650**

Therefore our calculations for profit are as follows:

Post refurbishment valuation	**£135,000**
Advancement from lender	**£101,250** *to be used in the subtotal calculation*
Minus the running costs	*these are not included at this stage for a*
BRR	
	calculation (see below with investment total)
Minus fees	**-£81,650**
Capital back from the lender	**£19,600** *this is the difference between the new leveraged loan minus paying back the original loan, fees, and charges*
Investment total	£30,160 *Purchase costs* + *£16,678.50 of our previously omitted running costs*
	= **£47,378.50**

We now calculate as follows:

Investment total	**£47,378.50**
Minus new mortgage capital	**-£19,600**
Total	**£27,778.50** *(this is the capital you have tied up in the deal after refinancing)*

This can otherwise be expressed as having 41.37% of your working capital back in your account after refinancing the deal.

I must clarify here that this is not the benchmark, nor is it intended to excite or, conversely, put you off the idea of a flip or a BRR. The calculations were demonstrated by pulling purchase and sale prices from thin air to run through the demonstration. Should we have used a purchase price of £80,000, the figures would have looked like this

Profits from a flip	**£26,000**
Cash back in the bank from the BRR model	**£35,350** *(84.61% of your cash back in account)*
Cash left in the deal from the BRR model	**£6,428.50**

My job as a responsible educator and the author of a property investing book is not to excite or deter you from any particular avenue within property investing. There are many books out there that will do that for you. I do not want to be responsible for any illusion or false premises within the industry, nor do I want to appear to be trying to convince or funnel you down any particular avenue or model within property investing. I merely want to offer you the tools to be able to calculate these decisions accurately and confidently for yourself. Showing the end user how to consider their options is my primary objective.

Note: BRRs usually take six months before you can apply for refinancing; therefore, your capital is usually back with you around month eight. However, you may note that our energy costs, council tax, and mortgage payments above were only demonstrated as three months. This is because these are no longer costs when the property is let. Yes, the mortgage still needs to be paid, except this time, someone else is paying this cost. The difference here is that you are in profit, not loss, with these payments. Whether you decide to add these running costs is entirely up to you.

I know many investors who view this as pedantic or overkill, and I agree that layering contingencies or costs can make deals look less attractive and have a counterproductive effect with respect to your mindset. However, suppose you are using an angel investor or stakeholder for 100% of the loan since you have no working capital because your investment model is other people's money (OPM). In that case, you must ensure that your costs stack up correctly.

Council tax, energy and repayments, especially higher repayments from an angel investor, can add up. An unwanted surprise might await if these numbers are not recorded or correctly considered. In many cases, you might have to find thousands of pounds that you simply did not account for with your naive calculations.

As you progress with these, however, or when you find deals that produce significant returns, you can be less vigilant regarding these minor variables.

The above tables can all be adjusted to include costs from your angel investor or bridging loan company. Mostly they will be almost identical to the examples above, with higher costs inputted. Should you want to add a specific row for anything, do so at your convenience; just ensure it falls within the correct section. For instance, if you wanted to add the interest paid to an angel investor, add a row in the fees section or simply add this cost to the repayments in the running costs. The calculation and system for calculating will remain the same.

Before we move forward and discuss the different types of finance available and how these work, I want to touch on something highlighted in the above table. Something which is very important when considering your mortgage for the BRR and flip model. You might have noticed that I input a 5% redemption charge and opted for a five-year fixed term with the examples above. The keen-eyed or experienced readers may have thought this a bit curious or even a rookie's error. I did, however, input this on purpose since this mistake is more common than you might suppose.

More often than not, when inexperienced investors search for mortgage products, they take the best interest rate or product with the lowest fees, as advised by their broker. In most cases, especially with long-term buy-to-let properties, this is the best option. However, when we know we will redeem the mortgage sooner rather than later, most likely within the first year of the fixed term, as is the case when carrying out a flip or BRR, we must communicate this intent to our broker. Your broker is not a mind reader. Their assumption will almost certainly be that of a long-term mortgage; we need to ensure they understand our intentions with the product they are about to find us. The following comment is vital when considering either a flip or the BRR model. **'The mortgage product leveraged must suit the deal'.**

There is no simpler way to explain this. If we invest for the long term without the need to redeem the mortgage inside the fixed term period, then the early redemption charge is irrelevant. However, if we know that we will redeem this product after several months, we must ensure our broker sources the correct mortgage product.

The way in which we do this is simple. We add all the costs or fees together for the entire duration that we will leverage the mortgage, and whichever yields the lowest total is the deal we go for. Does it matter if the product you chose has a 6% interest rate if the redemption charge is only 2% versus 5% if we intend to flip the property? We are only paying the mortgage for around five months, and then it will be redeemed. The difference on a £100,000 mortgage between a 6% and 4.6% interest payment over five months is £437.50. However, the difference between a 5% and a 2% early redemption charge is £2,250. The contra to this could very well be the mortgage fees, be it the arrangement fee, valuation fee or even application fee. With this in mind, let's look at a few different mortgages for the same deal ®.

We know we will be flipping this property, so the mortgage choice will need to represent this. This way, you will know how to calculate the entire costs of the mortgage to determine the best product for yourself. No clever tactic is employed below, and nothing is inputted to throw you off the scent. I will merely make the figures up as I type, not giving a second thought to the outcome so that we can work through the process of totalling the costs to analyse the difference.

Again, for ease of demonstration, the property we are buying is £100,000, and we will use an interest-only mortgage.

The three mortgage products presented to us by our broker are as follows

Mortgage one is a five-year fixed deal at 4.6%. It has a £1,500 Mortgage arrangement fee which, as you will recall from earlier, is added to the loan, so it bears no upfront cost. The valuation fee is £350, and it has a free application fee.

Mortgage two is a two-year fixed deal at 6%. It has a £2,500 mortgage arrangement fee added to the loan. The valuation fee is £350, the application fee is £250, and there is £500 cashback upon completion.

Mortgage three is a two-year fixed deal at 6.2%. It has a £2,500 mortgage arrangement fee which is simply added to the loan. The valuation fee is £350, and the application fee is £250.

Mortgage Product Option One

Mortgage interest rate	4.6% - **£287.59** per calendar month
Mortgage arrangement fee	**£1,500**
Mortgage valuation fee	**£350**
Mortgage application fee	**FREE**
Cashback on completion	**NONE**
Mortgage redemption	5% Year one - **£3,750**
Total mortgage charges	**£7037.95** Based on five months

Mortgage Product Option Two

Mortgage interest rate	6% - **£375** per calendar month
Mortgage arrangement fee	**£2,500**
Mortgage valuation fee	**£350**
Mortgage application fee	**£250**
Cashback on completion	**£500**
Mortgage redemption	2% Year one - **£1,500**
Total mortgage charges	**£5975** Based on five months

Mortgage Product Option Three

Mortgage interest rate	6.2% - **£387.50** per calendar month
Mortgage arrangement fee	**£2,500**
Mortgage valuation fee	**£350**
Mortgage application fee	**£250**
Cash back on completion	**NONE**
Mortgage redemption	**NONE**
Total mortgage charges	**£5,037.50** Based on five months

As you can see from the three presented mortgage examples, product three is the best mortgage to opt for, given our chosen model. At first glance, however, given the summary above, which would be a typical overview from your broker, mortgage one probably sounded like the best option. Your mortgage broker, if not up to speed with your intentions with the deal, would have most likely advised product one.

We will discuss mortgage products in more depth as we now progress through financing the deal.

Financing the Deal

"The most important word in the world of money is cash flow. The second most important word is leverage"

Robert Kiyosaki

"Raising money is not an accomplishment, it is an obligation"

Mark Cuban

Although the 90s gave us arguably, nay categorically, the best decade of music in modern times. Anyone who argues that any of the predeceasing decades equalled the 90s only needs to look at what this decade gave us. Agreed, the 60s gave us greats like Aretha Franklin, Jimmy Hendrix, The Stones, and Bill Withers, but the diversity of music in the 1990s was far superior on all fronts, from the rise or introduction of house music to the evolution of the hip-hop culture to the return of guitar music with its huge indie music scene. But let us not divert off-topic despite my inclination to prove my point with further examples.

Let us agree that the 90s gave us the greatest era of music in recent times. Still, with its mono property investment model, particularly its binary views of finance, be it you can if you have capital and you cannot if you do not, we might all agree it was well below par on that front. The concern is that it often still presents itself in the minds of the financially unaware as the only way to finance a property purchase.

As you will soon discover from the following 13,000 words or just over one hour and forty minutes of narration, there are far more avenues and options to finance a deal. In fact, the typical mortgage route, often the only route people are aware of, can be thrown into the mix and pulled apart as we break this down into the vast abyss of variable options.

Below I will detail some of the common as well as some of the more modern ways of financing your property investment deals.

A Cash Purchase

Cash is the term used for using your own money to fund the deal instead of the standard method of finance, essentially a mortgage. When an estate agent asks if you will be using a mortgage or paying cash for the property you have just placed an offer on, they do not assume you will drop by their office with a wheelbarrow full of used £20 notes. Funding the entire deal using cash is a unique purchasing model that should only really be considered for three primary reasons. The first is an abundance of capital to the point that you can achieve your goals and vision with that capital without the need to raise finance.

The second and more common reason is that your goals, objectives and vision are not as inspirational as the average investor. Not everyone working through this book aspires to grandeur. There will be a small but measurable portion of readers who only want to build a small retirement portfolio for themselves. Their goal is stability within their business; they are most likely more risk-averse than the average person. This is completely normal, and unless their thinking has changed as they have progressed through the book, they should continue with this mindset while completing their research. Again I am not trying to convince anyone to be someone other than who they are or who they want to become. Showing you the possibilities and gently encouraging you to alter your mindset is one of my objectives, but telling you what to do, no. I will leave those life-changing decisions to you.

The third reason we would purchase a property using cash alone will be revealed in a short while.

For the rest of you, whom I am assuming are a little more adventurous, I will be clear when I tell you not to fund 100% of your property purchase using your own cash. It is by far the slowest way to build anything like a sizable portfolio, except when funds are unlimited, of course. For every one property bought using cash, you can buy three with standard mortgage-type finance. Furthermore, you will have a sizable lump of capital left.

For example, an £85,000 property bought solely for cash would buy you three properties leveraging a standard buy-to-let mortgage with £8,500 change. This example includes all the associated fees and taxes. If we increase our purchase price to £150,000, then for every property we could buy using cash, we could buy three with a standard buy-to-let mortgage and have pocket change totalling £18,900. The cashflow on these two examples would be as follows. £85,000 rented for £525 per calendar month using cash to fund the purchase would give us an annual cashflow of £6,300. However, if we leveraged a standard buy-to-let mortgage, we would achieve just over £10,100. The respective cashflows at £150,000 with a monthly rent of £825 would be £9,900 per annum using cash and £14,175 when leveraging a standard buy-to-let mortgage. Remember we would have £18,900 change with this option too.

The crowning glory and deciding factor arises when we consider our most faithful friend, compounding. Should we continue to grow our portfolio and adopt our prechosen method of funding the deal, it would take us more than 14 years to purchase another property using cash alone. This is because our annual cashflow is only £6,300, yet we must wait until around £88,550 of rental profit is accrued to account for SDLT and the associated purchase fees.

Remember, too, this £6,300 is pre-tax profit. Therefore, after accounting for our tax liability, the repurchase timeframe leaps up to around 17 and a half years, whereby I am sure you can imagine that with inflation striping the value of our capital coupled with the capital growth on the bricks and mortar, we would struggle to secure a comparable property anywhere near £85,000 - Effectively rendering this process and model irreplicable. That said, rent increases over the years would reduce this damage negligibly; however, since we have not accounted for any maintenance in the £6,300 figure, which might well tip the scales back again. The point I am making here is that building a portfolio this way is far too time-consuming and a model that is unable to be scaled.

To offer a comparison for demonstrative purposes, if we leveraged a standard buy-to-let mortgage for our £85,000 properties, we would be able to purchase another in around 1.7 years. This is worked out as follows. To purchase an £85,000 property, we need around £25,500, including fees and taxes. We already had £8,500 in change by choosing to leverage finance in the form of a standard mortgage product. Therefore, £25,500 minus £8,500 leaves £17,000 to accrue. Our annual profit was £10,102.68. so if we divide £17,000 by £10,102.68 it leaves us with around 1.7 years. As explained, this excludes the tax due on our profit and maintenance fees to demonstrate the difference between cash purchases and leveraged purchases more simply. The exclusion was there for both avenues when I cited a repurchase timeframe of 14 years initially using cash, so the difference is relative. The fact that the cash route is irreplicable means that even taking the time to factor in the 19% tax due, as well as nominating a percentage of the profits to voids or maintenance, would have clearly demonstrated that the leverage option was far superior

There is, however, a few exceptions to this rule but they all centre around the same point. Contrary to what has just been explained, I have, in fact, funded 100% of the purchase costs using cash many times over the years. Let me explain why.

In my area of the Northeast of England, property has been notoriously cheap for many years, only increasing significantly over the past couple of years as it starts to level up with other areas in the North. The issue I have faced when looking at property deals, specifically BRR or flips, is that mortgage companies tend to have minimum thresholds for lending. Historically some lenders entered the market at £70,000, more at £75,000, then £80,000, and so on. For years, many properties in my area that were in need of refurbishment fell under what we call the minimum mortgage threshold. This means I was left with two obvious choices. One, forget about the property and search for an alternative deal, or two, purchase it for cash.

Because of the potential profits associated with some of these properties, I chose the latter to progress rather than seeking out alternatives.

There is a further bonus to your profits when purchasing these properties using cash. Your profit from a flip or your cash back from the deal is increased since there are no initial broker fees of C.£350. No mortgage valuation fees of C.£370 or any application fees of C.250. Furthermore, when you come to sell the property or refinance it, you have no mortgage arrangement fees of C.£1,200, nor do you have any redemption charges of C.2-5%. If this were a £60,000 property with a 2% early redemption charge, you would save around £3,100 combined, which would be credited to your profit or cash back in your account after refinancing.

Furthermore, you can use cash to your advantage when negotiating with a vendor. Should you view a property that you would like to make an offer on knowing that the area is good, the property looks solid, and you are confident it will be desirable to rent. There is a good chance that others have arrived at the same conclusion. Offering to purchase the property using that wheelbarrow full of cash might be the thing that puts you in pole position with your offer. Often vendors are willing to take slightly lower offers when cash is involved. Mortgage companies can be tricky to work with, and conveyancing often becomes messy.

Agents and vendors are aware of this and will seek to avoid this route if possible. In many cases, due to the speed of the sale when using cash, agents will use their negotiating prowess to funnel a vendor down a cash purchase for you. Remember, you can move the property across to finance after six months of ownership. This might incur slightly higher costs than using leverage in the first instance due to the use of solicitors. Once to purchase the property and again to leverage finance, but if it means you secure the property that you really wanted in your portfolio or the one you can see the potential with, then it simply goes down as a business expense. There is a good chance that the below-market value price you paid quickly compensates you for this. Furthermore, a leveraged loan may not have been an option with this hypothetical direct-to-vendor deal, where the speed of the sale was vital to securing the deal. In this case, the added costs will most likely again have been mitigated by the slightly lower below-market value offer on the property.

The underlining point with all these examples is that using cash to fund 100% of the property purchase is circumstantial but always short-term. In each example above, finance was raised at the first opportunity, except in the instance of a flip at which all your capital and profit is returned, again in the short term. This, by the way, was the third variant I alluded to a short while ago.

If the deal is dependent on a cash purchase or you have the funds readily available, and it will not inhibit your growth if you use it, i.e., you have a surplus to continue investing while this capital is tied up or it significantly increases your profits; then cash can be a viable option. But to reiterate, it is purely circumstantial and, more often than not, short-term.

Standard Mortgage Lenders

Despite all of the imaginative and wonderful ways to finance a property, leveraging a standard buy-to-let mortgage is still the most commonly used method to establish a property portfolio. That is why I am surprised how little people know of the finer details of this avenue. As previously discussed, leverage is one of the most effective tools in property investment. Not only can we leverage finance quickly and effectively, enabling us to grow our portfolio more quickly, but we are also able to leverage gained experience from professionals.

Speaking with your broker in depth at this stage of your research is paramount to your development. It may seem presumptuous to talk at this early stage, but it can help decide your control strategy for your business, be it investing through a personal avenue or a limited company. Furthermore, it may highlight any pitfalls within your current understanding or approach and even elevate any misconceptions you had about your position.

Contrary to popular belief, there are not that many stipulations when investing in buy-to-let properties. As a brief overview by an unqualified professional who relies heavily on their broker's experience and knowledge but does speak with her weekly for advice, here are some of my observations, specifically relating to mortgages in 2023 and, in some cases, historically.

Firstly, qualification is not as complicated as you might expect. Restrictions on products usually come in the form of experience rather than income. Not all lenders require a minimum income. Even some of the big high street lenders, such as NatWest, have no minimum requirement for income at the time of writing.

As part of their responsible lending programme, they will all ensure that you are equipped with contingency in the case of voids or unexpected maintenance, so the more you earn, the better chance you have of attaining a buy-to-let mortgage. Usually, earning around £25,000 opens you up to the entire market, meaning you can choose from a broader range of products resulting in better deals for you and your property.

Regardless of your control strategy, obtaining a buy-to-let mortgage as a first-time landlord (FTL), first-time buyer (FTB) will be more challenging. Owning a property you either live in or let out will dramatically increase your chances of qualification. However, should you hold both the FTL and FTB titles simultaneously, then you will need to seek more specific lenders, which are available but may come with a premium. An example of one of these lenders at the time of writing is Leek building society, which currently provides finance for first-time buyers, first-time landlords.

You must have lived in the UK for around 12 months or had a UK bank account to qualify with lenders. A handful of lenders will lend to ex-pats, but again, these are more specific than general and will most likely come at a premium too. Although the likes of The Mortgage Works (TMW) and

Fleet Mortgages will lend on purchase values of around £60,000 and the aforementioned 'Together' plus a handful of other lenders will drop to £50,000, The market and the choice of products really begin to become competitive at around of £75,000.

Defaults on your credit history are perhaps your biggest challenge when looking at your mortgage eligibility, especially the lower down in purchase value you go. If we rewind the clock a couple of years, companies like Precise Mortgages would usually lend despite defaults. Regulations tightened up in 2022, and now even they will usually reject your approach. There is some relief here, however. If your default is three years or older and it is satisfied, then some lenders are available, but yes, you guessed it, at a premium.

The final restriction I feel you should be aware of is specialist HMO mortgages. Most lenders want experience as their security when dishing out loans on HMOs. Typically, this only comes in the form of being a landlord owning just one property. However, they often require you to have owned this property for more than two years. The more property you own, the less this time restriction is applied, and the quicker you can obtain their specialist products, usually starting at around £100,000.

The most significant change of recent times must be how mortgage lenders stress-test their products. For a buy-to-let product to stack up with lending, it must pass specific stress tests applied by the lender. Let me explain how this works, so you can calculate this for yourself to avoid any disappointment [®].

Let us imagine a mortgage has been applied for requiring a £100,000 advancement. Historically the lenders stressed this at 5.5%, but now it is more like 6%. Therefore, the calculations they make are as follows.

£100,000 x 6% = £6,000 per annum
£6,000 / 12 = £500 per month
£500 + 125% 'stress test' = **£625** per month

This means the monthly rent needs to be £625 or higher to pass their tests. Should the expected rent be lower than this, your mortgage application will likely be denied. It is important to note that this calculation is for a personal avenue mortgage for basic rate taxpayers. Should you be a higher-rate taxpayer, the calculation is as follows:

£100,000 x 6% = £6,000 per annum
£6,000 / 12 = £500 per month
£500 + **145%** 'stress test' = **£725** per month

The difference is the rate at which they stress, rising from 25% to 45%. Limited companies are different. They only stress at 25% regardless of income.

Generally, a limited company calculation is the mortgage advancement times the rate you have secured (+2%) divided by 12 and then stressed at 25%. The example is as follows:

£100,000 x (rate of 4.6% + 2%) 6.6% = £6,600
£6,600 / 12 = £550 per month
£550 + 125% = **£687.50** per month

In this example, the rent obtained from the property would need to be £687.50 as a minimum to qualify for the mortgage. Remember, this is not based on a £100,000 property but rather a £100,000 advancement. At a 75% LTV, this would be a property secured at around £133,500.

As with everything I have outlined above, there are always lenders who will lend despite your circumstances; furthermore, there are always other options for lending which will be explained later in this chapter.

The 125% or 145% is termed the ICR or interest cover ratio. The following explanation is lifted straight from Google and may prove helpful in understanding the term.

'Affordability for buy-to-let mortgages is typically assessed by looking at the interest cover ratio or ICR. This is the ratio of gross rental income to

mortgage interest repayments. Lenders will typically look for a minimum ICR of 125% calculated using an appropriate stressed interest rate.'

Depending on various factors, the ICR can differ from 125% up to 145%. For example, tax status, a non-portfolio landlord (a landlord with less than four properties), portfolio landlord (four or more) or purchasing through a limited company vehicle.

Mortgage types

When we think of buy-to-let mortgages, there are three main types of mortgages available to us. These are fixed-rate mortgages, discounted variable-rate mortgages, and tracker mortgages. Generally, these are at a 75% loan-to-value. This means that the lender will allow you to leverage 75% of the property's value, provided you can contribute the other 25%.

A property purchase of £85,000 would come with an advancement from the lender of £63,750. The rest to make up the £85,000 purchase, £21,250, along with all fees and taxes payable, must come from your working capital. There are, of course, other loan-to-value ratios available from time to time and from product to product; most commonly in the buy-to-let world, these are 70% and 80% LTVs.

Fixed Rate Mortgage

Fixed-rate mortgages have been the most commonly used example as you have progressed through the book, so even though this heading could be far more expansive, this brief overview is by means of a refresher to your already established and increasing education. This is about as far as I feel I need to elaborate since this is the most common type of mortgage available and is somewhat self-explanatory.

In short, a fixed-term mortgage is a product that has the first portion of the mortgage fixed, meaning the interest rate given at the time of the mortgage 'offer in principle' is fixed until the fixed term is spent. Most commonly, the fixed term is two or five years. As explained previously, any attempt to release yourself from this term will result in an early redemption charge (ERC) being applied. At the end of the fixed term, the mortgage reverts to what is known as the 'Standard Variable Rate' (SVR) until you secure or switch to another product. Most of the time, we simply switch products with the lender to a new fixed rate, and the whole process of a fixed term begins again. Should the lender not have any products that attract you or other lenders have more favourable rates available, this would be the perfect time to switch lenders. Once we are free from the shackles of the fixed term, the liability of early redemption is no longer upon us.

It is often cheaper to stay with your chosen lender due to the added costs when switching. Remaining loyal to your lender can mean the new mortgage arrangement fee is far lower or, as often the case, non-existent. Furthermore, switching lenders will result in the new lender wanting to conduct a property valuation. In contrast, the existing lender may do what is known as a desktop valuation to switch the product.

As always, adopt leverage in this situation and speak with your broker. Adding the fees together in both instances and offsetting them against the difference in cashflow, we have the answer to the illustrious question, should I stay, or should I go? I can only assume this was joe strummer's predicament when writing the lyrics for his 1982 hit. Incidentally, it is the '70s which gave rise to bands like 'The Clash', which is the 3rd best decade for music. In case you were craving my opinion.

An example of this is if your existing lender is offering you a new fixed term of 5.2% for five years with a mortgage arrangement fee of £400. The other lender is offering 4.5%, again fixed for five years, but there will be a £370 valuation fee and a mortgage arrangement fee of £1,500. There will be a £350 broker fee to add to these costs. While we are on the subject, most brokers will not charge for a product switch with the same lender, so there is no added cost with that option.

The mathematics of this is as follows:

Let us assume that the monthly mortgage payments are £325 at 5.2% and £281 at 4.5%. Over the five years, we will pay back £19,500 and £16,860, respectively, in mortgage payments. When we add the costs associated with the mortgage arrangement, we have a total five-year payment of £19,900 and £19,095. That means in this instance, providing we have accounted for all the associated costs, which would be checked with our mortgage broker, it would be the better option to switch to another lender, financially, at least. It might be worth mentioning here that we have to weigh up the logistics of the move. The switch will be more time-consuming and will, in most cases, require a visit to the property by the new mortgage lenders' valuation team as well as the services of a solicitor. Although when switching a personal mortgage product, the fees associated with the valuation and the solicitor are usually free, they are generally applied if this is a limited company switch.

Visits to the property can spook existing tenants creating unrest and unnecessary time and effort trying to reassure your tenant that you are simply switching the mortgage product. Unfortunately, due to their nature of rarely taking out mortgage products, tenants do not understand mortgages and their intricacies, so they will most likely fear the worst and conclude that you intend to sell the property. This, along with the added paperwork, may swing the balance, especially if the difference is marginal, as in my example. Remember to divide the difference between the two routes by the number of months of the fixed term to see what the switch represents to you monthly.

For instance, in my above example, the difference was £805. However, when we divide that by the number of months of the five-year product, 60, we get £13.41 per month. This might be enough of a saving for you, but it might not. Only you can decide this. If you own 50 houses, it will represent a little over £8,000 per annum, so it is a decision you need to make based on your circumstances. Food for thought as and when the time comes, but now you are equipped to calculate this for yourself should you be required.

Variable Rate Mortgage

A variable rate or discounted variable rate mortgage is one that tracks the lender's specific standard variable rate (SVR), which should not be confused with the Bank of England's 'base rate'. However, the irony is, in essence, this often is one of the factors that determine the SVRs, just not directly or exclusively. Most variable-rate mortgages for buy-to-lets are discounted variable-rate mortgages, so rather than being linked to the Bank of England base rate; discounts are linked to the lender's standard variable rate (SVR). For example, if the SVR is 4.6% with a discount of 1%, the payable mortgage rate is 3.6%. If the standard variable rate rose to 5.5%, the pay rate would consequently rise to 4.5%. The 1% discount still applies for the duration of the term, regardless of any changes to the SVR. Unlike a fixed-term mortgage and fluctuation in the SVR would be applied to your mortgage payments.

The thing to remember is that the standard variable rate changes are at the lender's discretion. So, your mortgage payments could change even if there has been no alteration in the Bank of England base rate. But understand that this can be a decrease as well as an increase, of course. Moreover, if the standard variable rate changes following a move in the base rate, there is no guarantee that it will increase or decrease by the same amount.

As a result, trackers, which will be explained next, are usually seen as more transparent than discounted deals. When the base rate fell from 5% to 0.5% between October 2008 and March 2009, Lloyds TSB was the only top-20 lender to reduce its standard variable rate by the full 4.5%. All the others cut their rates by a lower amount.

At the time of writing, the standard discount on a variable rate for an average limited company purchasing a property around the £100,000 mark is 2.25%. This figure is obtained from 'The Nottingham Building Society'. Their standard variable rate (SVR) is currently 6.54%, meaning their current mortgage rate after the discount would be 4.29%. With interest rates being higher now than where they have been for the past 14 years, with no indication of where they will go over the next year or two, we now need to consider our options concerning mortgage products more than ever.

Historically there was no question with regard to mortgages. Most investors wanted to fix the lower rates for as long as possible. But over the last few months, mortgage interest rates on fixed products have risen to around 6.9%. Still, they have come down considerably as I edit this section. The average fixed rate today is around 4.8% as we close in on the end of April 2023. What they will be tomorrow remains unclear.

If we compare these two mortgages over the course of the fixed term on the discounted variable rate, which is two years, we will gain a clearer picture of how to decide between the two. To avoid getting into the many variables with these two mortgages, and so we are able to concentrate on the difference in types and rates, we will compare both products using the same associated fees. Therefore, the respective monthly payments are £268.13 and £343.75.

Should the Bank of England's base rate remain constant over the two years, opting for the discounted variable rate would save you £1,814.88. Of course, this is also reliant on The Nottingham Building Society keeping their SVR at 6.54%, which is no guarantee, but for us to consider this, we need to look at where we think the Bank of England base rate is heading. If we believe rates will rise beyond four or five per cent, we might assume that the SVR will rise at least marginally; therefore, 4% would mean an increase of around 0.5%, increasing the rate to 4.79%, and adjusting the monthly payment to £299.38. Rates heading to 5% may mean an increase of around 1.5%, increasing the rate to 5.79% and adjusting the monthly payment to £361.88. The consideration here is twofold.

Firstly, how likely do you think this is? And secondly, at what point over the next two years do you think this will increase? There is a better-than-average chance that even if this happens, the initial savings of the lower rate will outstrip the extra charge by the time the rate hits 5.79%. Remember, the SVR may not necessarily increase at exactly the same rate as in our example, and should the base rate lower, then there is a good chance that the SVR will lower too.

It is all a bit of a guessing game, unfortunately. However, for complete transparency, until the rates come back down, most of my new mortgages and those due for renewal at the end of their fixed terms are being placed on discounted variable rate mortgages, usually as a two-year product. That said, you should consider what your position is based on the time you take the mortgage out, the deal or investment model, your security desires, and of course, after speaking with your trusted broker.

Tracker Mortgages

As the name suggests, these products 'track' the Bank of England's base rate. They are, in one sense, fixed in the fact that they are at a fixed rate above the Bank of England's base rate. For example, if your tracker is fixed at 1.5% above the base rate, this will currently be, at the time of writing, 5%. Unlike the discounted variable rate, which can change at the lender's discretion, the tracker will only change with a base rate shift. Your job is once again to estimate the likelihood of this happening.

One of the principal values of a tracker rate mortgage is that there often a lower to no early redemption charge. Therefore, if we decide that a shorter-term mortgage may be required, as in the case of a BRR deal, and we are confident that the base rate will not change drastically, then a tracker mortgage can be a wise choice in this instance. To avoid confusion, reaffirm my opinion and cement my advice, as always, tap into your network and use leverage by consulting your broker for their expert opinion.

The obvious question that presents itself here is why you would choose a discounted variable rate over a tracker. The answer is forecasting and timing. If we rewind the clock a few months, no one knew what the interest rates would do and how high they would likely rise. In this case, a tracker is more of a gamble than a DVR since, as explained, discounted variable-rate mortgages do not always change when the base rate changes. Usually, the standard variable rate that determines the DVR is based on how expensive the capital was for the lender to borrow rather than the base rate.

Interest Only Mortgages Versus Repayment

Perhaps the thing that causes us the most conative dissonance when new to investing is the decision to invest using an interest-only mortgage. Here we will explain the difference between the two avenues and try to demonstrate the benefits of adopting the widely used interest-only route. So, for the complete novice, in layperson terms and by no means wishing to patronise or attempt to teach anyone how to suck the proverbial egg, the difference is as follows.

A repayment mortgage pays the total value of the loan down over the term of the mortgage, including the agreed interest on the loan. Typically this is over 25 years; depending on your age and circumstances, shorter or even longer terms are available. They are sometimes the only option available, but this is generally circumstantial and most commonly relates to age, more the golden years rather than the earlier ones. On the last day of the mortgage, you will make your last monthly payment to the lender, subsequently relieving you of any financial liability of debt with the property. The lender will release the first charge held on the property, and you are now free to consider your next move, whether that is to reap the benefits of a higher monthly income from the property, sell it for your payday or, in some cases, to remortgage once again.

Side note: A first charge is something that your solicitor will place on the property for the lender during the conveyancing. The idea of this charge is to protect the leveraged capital. In the case of the property being sold, the amount of charge placed on the property, usually the 75% mortgage contribution, must be paid to the lender before any capital is paid across to the individual. If the sale cannot satisfy the charge, the solicitor usually will not begin the conveyancing until the deficit is received.

An interest-only mortgage pays the agreed 'interest' on the mortgage monthly, with no reduction of the original loan. When the term of the mortgage is spent after 25 years, the lender will request the total amount that was initially borrowed plus any fees that have been added to the loan over the years, typically mortgage arrangement fees.

Both avenues come with attractions and an equal measure of downsides. Depending on your individual strategy, you may decide to go one way or the other or even hold a mixture of both mortgage types throughout your portfolio, but before you decide, let me shed some light and give you my opinion.

As you might appreciate, a repayment mortgage is usually the choice of the more cautious investor. Generally speaking, investors that are buying property as a retirement pot or a little boost of income in line with their current job employ this product option. In the same sense as using cash to fund the deal, unless funds are limitless, it is a far slower way to build a sizeable portfolio. However, I fully appreciate that building a portfolio slow and steady for longer-term gains on a more solid foundation is a model that some will adopt, and if this is your choice, then you absolutely can be successful in doing so. It is deemed a more cautious approach, but that does not mean you cannot make a significant sum of money by adopting this option.

I want to recap a story from my previous book since it holds significate weight with this example and is such a pivotal moment in the history of my financial education.

It may surprise you to hear that I started my portfolio in precisely this way and still to this day hold some properties on a repayment basis, albeit only a few circumstantial ones.

When I started investing many years ago, being from a typical working-class northeastern family, it had been ingrained in me throughout my youth to work hard, save for the future, do not buy or spend unless you can afford to, or more accurately, really need to. Definitely, under no circumstances do you get into debt. You were to save up for what you wanted and delay that gratification until you could easily afford to indulge, at which point the interest in what you craved would have likely subsided.

With this in mind, my first few mortgages were all taken out on a repayment term. I even overpaid the repayments at the maximum permissible rate without any redemption charges being applied to my account.
I did all the repairs, renovations and improvements myself on a weekend or an evening after work. I only bought more property when my working capital was saved enough to cover the new purchase holding back a contingency of around 10% for any unforeseen events.

This approach was a long and slow process for someone who, at that time, had a higher-than-average income. Before I continue with my story, it is worth mentioning that I do not look back and regret this approach; after all, my upbringing governed the way I invested. I nearly dismissed the idea of investing through my cautious attitude, and again I do not begrudge my upbringing. Both factors contributed in their own way to the modern-day me.

My upbringing gave me great financial sense and respect for the value of money, and my initial approach to buying property gave me an arguably more solid foundation enabling future, more stable exponential growth possible. I might argue that it gave me a better foundation for rapid growth.

That aside, if I knew what I know now about the industry, I would have been a lot further on than I am, even now or at least I would have reached these heights much sooner. Hindsight is beautiful, but the beauty of education is that I can pass my hindsight on so that you can benefit from it directly. Significantly reducing your own learning curve.

A couple of years into my slow and part-time, makeshift property journey, I had the opportunity to purchase two direct-to-vendor properties simultaneously from an existing and retiring client of mine from my gas business. The only way I was able to purchase both properties was due to the fact that I purchased them with a good friend at the time, who is now one of my very successful business partners.

Steven, his real name, was at the time and still is all about cashflow. Build the pot quickly and aggressively, and worry about the future later. Take the rewards while they are on the table and cross the proverbial bridge when or even if you ever come to it was and still is his mantra.

This mindset back in the day worried me greatly, as I'm sure it will currently worry a great deal of you, but Steven had convinced me to put these properties on an interest-only mortgage to increase our cashflow. Should I have been able to purchase these properties without the need for his half of the capital, I would have. However, there was no way to split these purchases. My client was retiring, and she wanted to sell them both at once.

After purchasing these two properties, I returned to my old way of investing with repayment mortgages and making small penalty-free overpayments when and where I could. I now had some balance within my expanding portfolio. A couple of cash-generating properties and the others on a repayment basis. A lower loan to value than that of an interest-only portfolio and some cashflow to bolster the accrued rent. This was and still is today a fantastic lower-risk strategy that I am sure some of you will adopt and will do very well by doing so.

Several years later, after reaping the cash from these two interest-only properties, the penny finally dropped whilst talking with a colleague at one of the few networking events I attended in early 2009. I had recently bought a repossession for the modest sum of £35,000 and had to pay cash to get this deal through since no mortgages were available for that purchase value. I remember his exact words, "wow, I remember how much £35,000 was when I was 29 years old; it doesn't seem that much these days, huh?"

It took me a minute of quiet contemplation, but I asked him his age. He told me he was 49 years old. His comment resonated with me concerning the money I had just invested and the differences in amounts from one generation to the next due to increases in inflation. Later when I returned home, I researched to gauge property prices 20-25 years ago and how much I would have to pay back in, say, 25 years. Yes, you guessed it, the term of a mortgage.

I had to buy this property for cash initially but believe me that six months later when I applied for a mortgage, it went on an interest-only product. And every single mortgage since then has too. You see, what I had realised, finally and most likely well after everyone else, is that, as explained earlier in the book, inflation pays down the cost of the loan. It erodes the value of the debt over time.

I often think that given my time again with a more privileged start to investing whereby I had more capital to invest immediately in property without having to accrue further funds, I would still like to remain a little cautious and spread the eggs by having a percentage of my mortgages split between interest only and repayment products. Then my real-life investing cap gets thrown back on, bringing me back down to the reality of why I am a professional investor, which is to buy property as fast as is reasonably participle, without being foolish, whilst adopting a sound, well, thought out strategy, of course.

The reality is, given my time again with the knowledge I have gained so far; I would always opt for an interest-only product, no question. Obviously, everyone is different, and it takes a particular person to reach certain heights, and if you know in your heart that this is not you, then I would urge a more cautious approach initially. You can continually educate, and later on in your journey, you might change your thinking, as I did. Remember, education opens the boundaries of our belief systems and helps us to view the world in a different light.

The concern for the more modern-day investor who is considering using a repayment product is that the monthly mortgage payments are much higher due to the repayment element of the loan.
This means your cash flow each month is subsequently lower, which in turn means it will take longer to accrue funds to repeat the process. Albeit, the solid counter-argument for this is that someone else is paying your mortgage down over the term. However, should you have any void periods, this will have a higher impact on your capital until the property is re-let. This means there may be increased pressure throughout the term to meet payment demands from the lender, or your profit will erode faster during these void periods.

The interest-only route is a faster, more aggressive, and **slightly** higher-risk avenue, which, as I've just mentioned, would leave you with a lump sum to pay at the end of the mortgage term. However, it does have some significant benefits to boot. Firstly, since the monthly payments are far lower, your cash accrues faster, building your working capital back up at a faster rate which compounds the more property you own. The faster you can buy subsequent property, the better for your business regarding cashflow and repetition. This compounding is exciting news for investors, especially us professional investors who aim to run our portfolios like a business or hope for the property industry to give them the flexibility and freedom within their life that no job can offer. Remember, cash is king.

Buying property this way not only enables you to build your portfolio at a faster rate, but you can have a better short-term lifestyle, if that is your preference, since the returns are far more attractive.

This is an opportunity to show an example of an interest-only product versus a repayment product.

Let us say once again that the purchase price is £100,000 with a 75% loan to value. For ease of demonstration and since I have just discussed these in-depth earlier in this chapter, I will omit the associated costs and fees attached to each mortgage option. Therefore, interest-only and repayment products require you to use £25,000 of your working capital. Consequently, the leveraged loan amount is £75,000 for both. Again this is demonstrated using an interest rate of 4.6%.

After performing a quick Google search, I can see that the monthly payment on a repayment-type mortgage would be £421, but an interest-only mortgage payment would significantly reduce to £287 per calendar month. This is, of course, only for the fixed term specified within the mortgage offer. Whether that is a two or five-year fixed deal is irrelevant to this demonstration.

You can see from the example above that the difference in your monthly payments between the two mortgage types would be £134, equating to £1,608 per annum. Remember that this is the extra amount you will receive between the two payment methods, not the amount you make. This figure demonstrates a noticeable difference in profit that reflects well in your account even when you only own a single property. However, as you begin to acquire multiple properties, this figure becomes far more significant. For instance, when we hit the arbitrary milestone of ten owned properties, the difference here is £16,080

Let us suppose you have this £100,000 property on an interest-only mortgage over a 25-year term, with the rent being £700 per calendar month. For demonstration purposes, this is based on an idyllic scenario of full occupancy and no significant repairs beyond your remit. You can hope to achieve around £5,000 in pre-tax profits each year from this property. If we couple that figure with the second or subsequent property of equivalent standing, you can see that it will not take long to accrue the funds needed to either buy another rental, have a more lavish lifestyle or even replace your current employed income. All of which are measurable milestones within your life.

It is clear for most people that the primary concern of the interest-only route is the lump repayment sum in 25 years, but I feel we have indisputably mitigated that with the erosion of your loan through inflation coupled with the inevitable capital growth of the property.

To decide which route to finance you would choose to leverage, you need to determine your overall goals, vision, objectives, aims, and risk-to-reward feelings on the matter. This is another reason why this chapter is placed after so many of my other laws of investing.

You must bear in mind your current financial position and talk to as many professional investors as possible. Not your parents, cautious friends or work colleagues unless, of course, they are both professional and successful investors. Always seek advice from the people you are trying to emulate or that have qualities you do not currently have but do desire for yourself.

Equity Release

As people's financial education increases, they become more comfortable with the concept of funding their portfolio growth through equity release. This can be equity within your current portfolio, but more commonly, this is within your home. The idea of releasing equity from your home needs careful consideration and a lengthy conversation with your broker, your partner, or anyone else directly connected to the financial side of your life. In some cases, it would be wise to contact an independent financial advisor or accountant to further this decision.

I want to be clear when I tell you that I am not qualified to give you specific advice regarding equity release from your mortgage. What I intend to do here is to highlight the principles and offer you the knowledge needed to begin to calculate whether this is a possible avenue to increase your working capital ®.

To calculate this correctly, we need information from various sources. We need to speak with our current mortgage provider, a local estate agent and check out some information online, principally Zoopla. Finally, we need to contact a good reputable 'whole of market' mortgage broker ®. Your first port of call should be to contact your current mortgage provider to enquire about how much you currently owe on your mortgage. It would be wise to get the full redemption figure at this point, including the original mortgage application fees and any early redemption charges (ERC).

The primary reason we need the ERC at this point is that one is applicable but only, say one or two thousand pounds, yet we have the potential to release several hundred thousand pounds, then it may be that we deem this charge surmountable. However, if we are releasing a more modest sum of, say, forty to fifty thousand pounds and the ERC is, for example, £5,000, we might have a different view altogether. With this in mind, you should find out whilst on the call when your current fixed rate ends. Let us say it is in four years, yet our ERC is only £2,000; then, we may consider using this money despite that charge regardless of the equity release amount. Conversely, if it ends in three or four months, you may hold off and save the ERC.

The final information needed regarding your current mortgage is the current mortgage payments. This will be used to calculate the deficit between the old and the new payments to see how much your equity release needs to earn you to at least break even.
Of course, breaking even is not the point of equity release, but at least this would give you an initial benchmark. This essentially is all that is needed at this point since we are only considering this option for now.

The next part of the puzzle is the current valuation of your property. To do this, we need to contact our local estate agent for an estimate or, even better, a physical valuation. As I discussed earlier, we can corroborate this by heading across to the Zoopla website, selecting 'house prices', adding in your postcode, selecting your property from the list, and checking their current valuation. You must take note of the confidence rating underneath this valuation, remember. You are only really concerned if the valuation has a 'high confidence' rating.

The final questions are for your mortgage broker. It is essential that your broker is 'whole of market', meaning they can access every lender and their respective products rather than being tied to a specific pool of lenders. The question you need to broach is, what is your mortgage eligibility? This is generally based on your earnings. You need to understand the maximum loan you would be able to obtain from a chosen lender. Do not let the word maximum scare you at this stage. Remember, you can mitigate fear through education, but more so, you might not necessarily choose to leverage the full amount. However, it is better to have all the information needed to calculate the potential at this point than to revisit it later.

You will need to know your new mortgage payments on the new leveraged amount based on your eligibility and the higher loan amount from your property. For instance, if the property is worth £500,000 having £300,000 of equity since you currently owe £200,000 on your existing mortgage, but your maximum eligibility is only £300,000, then you are only able to raise £100,000 rather than the entire equity amount. Conversely, if your eligibility is £800,000, you can only raise a maximum of £300,000, which is the total equity available. This is, broadly speaking and not considering LTV, which incidentally is usually a maximum of 85% when releasing equity to use as investment funds. The eligibility is based on this being calculated and taken into consideration by your broker.

Once you have all the information required, your job is easy. Simply pull all the information together and calculate whether equity release is the best option for you at this stage. Let me explain how ®

Just like your information-gathering process, you calculate this in stages. Firstly, calculate how much equity you can release by taking the full redemption figure for your current mortgage away from the new loan amount. Assuming the redemption figure from your current mortgage was, let us say, £240,000, and the new loan amount was £370,000, based on an 85% loan to value. This means our equity release in this instance is £130,000.

Next, calculate the difference in your mortgage payments, essentially taking the old payments on your existing mortgage away from what the new payments would be should you decide to go ahead and release the equity. Assuming that your existing monthly mortgage payments are £540, and the new payments would be £1,200. We simply take the £540 existing payment away from the £1,200 new payment. This leaves you with a monthly deficit of £660 of increased mortgage payments. Now hold that thought while the palpitations settle and allow me to continue.

I am fully aware of your concern that in this fictitious scenario of semi-fabricated figures, we have more than doubled your mortgage payments for you. I am also aware that this goes against everything you have been told and consequently worked towards for many years.

Before you press stop or throw the idea of equity release out the window, presumably along with this book, you need to consider the possibilities of this newly established working capital, specifically in terms of property purchases and subsequent cashflow.

A basic example would be as follows:

You now have £130,000 to take full advantage of. This capital would buy, conservatively, two or three turnkey single-let properties and an up-and-running HMO. As a rough guide, these prudent acquisitions would give you a gross monthly cashflow of around £1,800. From that figure, we take away the deficit between the two mortgage payments. So that is £1,800 in rent minus the £660 deficit, which leaves us with just over £1,100 each month of profit.

To be clear, you are now only liable for the same mortgage payment as before since your portfolio makes up the deficit and gives you £13,200 per year of profit. That is £132,000 profit if you have ten years left on your mortgage. £198,000 if you have fifteen years left.

Should you decide to use the £1,800 in accrued profit to pay the entire mortgage payments, it would look this:

£1,800 minus our new mortgage payments of £1,200 leaves us with £600 cashflow every single month. This is a little over £7,000 per year of pre-tax profits.

I feel congratulations are now in order because you have just achieved precisely what you've been working towards for many years and presumably were still a long way from achieving.

Effectively you are now mortgage free.

By releasing the equity in your home to buy cash-generating assets, these assets are now possibly paying your entire mortgage down for you. Moreover, they are leaving you with a tidy profit to boot. Interesting right? But remember, the point of equity release is not to pay your mortgage down. It is to grow your property business. That example was inputted for comfort and to offer perspective. You are welcome, by the way. Nothing gives me greater pleasure than the sound of the penny dropping.

The last thing you need to determine is if the figure that you are left with, either in full, by paying the deficit between your two mortgage payments or the entire mortgage for you, is measurable enough. And if you feel it is going to support and further your journey in the correct manner. At this point, you will have the answers you seek regarding equity release, or at the very least, you will have the information needed to help make your decision.

All that remains is for you to block out the noise from any negative outside influence, educate your partner or anyone else connected with you financially and decide when to pull the trigger to get your adventure going. Just remember to consider this carefully and always seek professional advice before committing to anything.

I am aware the above section on mortgages was hefty and will have no doubt left a great deal of you feeling overwhelmed with the number of calculations and figures involved. However, since the vast majority of readers will be leveraging finance primarily via this avenue, I feel it is important to have demonstrated it in such depth.

The following avenues of bridging loans, angel funding and joint venturing can work in infinite ways. The research into these avenues of finance remains with you and should form part of your working schedule.

For this book, I will broadly summarise the inner workings so you can understand the logic of the avenues and look for their advantages. Not everything needs to be determined at this stage. How you will finance a deal absolutely should be before you offer on a property, but an understanding of the options is all you need to be able to research further. The finer workings of finance will be deal-specific and can be determined closer to the point of considering a property.

Bridging loans

Generally, bridging loans are short-term loans designed to 'bridge' a period between two situations; usually, this is the purchase and then the revaluation or mortgage of a property. The interim is the refurbishment or development. This does not always have to be a new deal, however. Investors often use bridging finance to bridge gaps in their existing deals.

Bridging loans can be employed to secure auction properties or direct-to-vendor purchases where time is of the essence. Since some auction houses typically require buyers to complete within 28 days, standard mortgage company-type loans will not suffice, so sometimes a bridging loan may be your only viable route.

Speed is the key here. You may have found a property where the vendor needs a quick sale but is prepared to offer the property at a discount in exchange. In this case, a bridging loan could be leveraged until you align the more standard mortgage route. Often this is in six months, but as I explained earlier in the book and by means of a refresher, and at the time of writing, Paragon mortgages have a day-one refinance option

This means the bridging loan would be used to purchase the property at the speed the above examples require, but then the mortgage lender could be approached soon after completion rather than having to wait the more typical six-month period. This has obvious advantages regarding payments and cashflow, since bridging loan payments are often far higher than standard mortgage company payments. Meaning the quicker you switch, the quicker your profits can increase.

In the case of the BRR model, an investor would want to buy, renovate, and then let the property to a tenant. But in some cases, when buying a run-down property, it may be deemed un-mortgageable by a typical lender. *This is usually the case when the kitchen and bathroom are not present at the property. The actual specifics are basic living comforts such as cooking and washing facilities;* therefore, if you do look to buy a property and there are none of the above, a bridging loan may be the best choice.

Recently we bought a property for £30,000 cash as part of a bigger deal. We did not particularly want this property, but we did want another that the vendor owned since it was next door to another HMO we own. The unwanted property had been empty for the past few years. We knew of this property since we had looked at it several years ago after posting a note through the vendor's door trying to purchase the one next to our HMO. He declined that approach back then but offered to show us this one. Initially, we did not offer on the property since we deemed the refurbishment to be too exhaustive of funds to make a decent profit.

However, many years later, the market had risen significantly, but his asking price had not. To stop the property we actually sought from hitting Rightmove, we offered to ease his troubles and purchase both properties simultaneously. We leveraged a bridging loan to fund the deals, and our goal was to make a few thousand pounds, maybe £10,000, on the cheaper property to cover the bridging loan costs etc. The reality was somewhat different.

We stripped the property of all flooring, doors, and most of the kitchen, then swept right through to present the property better. This was then placed back on the market within a few days of our completion, and one week from then, we had three offers, all over £60,000.

The reason for the story is two-fold. One to highlight that this may not have been possible without employing a bridging loan, and two to note that we intentionally left the cooker, the kitchen sink and the bathroom in situ when we stripped out. This was intentional for the instance that a potential buyer might look to leverage a standard mortgage product. Should we not have done this, their only option would have been a bridging loan, since the property would have been deemed unmortgageable and, therefore, may have proved too costly for a small single-let purchase, especially at the price they paid.

Incidentally, we accepted the middle offer of £61,500 due to it being a cash buyer. Therefore, no mortgage valuation was to be carried out on the property. As I have explained previously, sales or purchases using wheelbarrows full of cash are often far quicker as a byproduct of not involving a mortgage lender.

Because of this, six weeks later, the £30,000 profit was in our account. That is £61,500 Minus our £30,000 purchase costs; *remember, there is no SDLT to pay under £40,000.* Minus £750 estate agent's fees, £500 solicitor fees and £250 for the removal and disposal of the above items as well as the general cleanup. The reality is that this acquisition paid for all the bridging fees and the entire refurbishment of the newly acquired HMO. Job done.

In this case, if we were not able to leverage the bridging company to help us purchase at speed, the vendor may have approached an agent who might have put this property on Rightmove, which would have had its obvious disadvantages for us, not least with potentially missing out on the HMO conversion.

Bridging loans can be used to purchase the property and, in some cases, fund the entire renovation providing there is further equity somewhere to bridge over. The lender will do their due diligence to ensure enough profit or scope within the deal, of course, so be sure the deal stacks up. Essentially you would get a typical loan from the bridging company, and it is worth pointing out that the lower LTV you go to, the better the rates, usually. So, say you had opted for a 65% LTV; you can then bridge the remaining amount across a property in which you had equity. Either from your portfolio or your home, in some cases. Effectively meaning the entire capital is coming from the bridging company.

You can then remortgage the property once it is renovated or improved in some way, creating the equity you desire and repay the bridging lender while profiting from any surplus funds accrued in creating this equity.

Bridging loans really come to stand out when considering developing or converting a large property. For instance, a developer may have secured planning permission to build multiple dwellings. But with the cost of buying land on which to build and the forthcoming cost of labourers and builders, the developer may look at bridging finance to leverage the development cost. Once the development is complete, the developer could either remortgage, move to a commercial mortgage, or sell or rent the development and repay the bridging lender.

The beauty of bridging loans, in this instance, is their flexibility. In some cases, you can delay repayments until a later date. For instance, In the case of development, this could be until you can raise finance from an alternative lender, sell part of the development as it completes or, in the case of letting when the revenue starts to come in from the tenants as you complete the development in various stages.

We are discussing specialist lending here, so offering generic information can be challenging. Although it is usually quick to acquire, lending is mainly leveraged for the short term, with the exception of specific requirements, like developments. However, even in this instance, any developer would likely want the bridging loan settled at their first available opportunity. The principal points are that bridging is flexible but short-term in most cases. Bridging companies opens you to a new world of fun and opportunity. Anything is possible when we consider bridging loans.

Side note: The Financial Conduct Authority (FCA) does not offer protection for bridging loans used to secure an investment property, buy-to-let investment, or commercial property. This means all bridging loans, including commercial and residential are unregulated. However, this does not mean that their conduct and professionalism are compromised. When explaining the bridging process to someone, I was asked if this means they are usually back street crooks. Far from it was my answer. Bridging companies are lenders for big boys and girls; they lend on small properties and multi-million-pound developments equally. The latter of which is where a typical high street lender would back away.

Furthermore, your bridging lender will generally belong to one of the following esteemed bodies: The National Association of Commercial Finance Brokers (NACFB). The Financial Intermediary and Broker Association (FIBA). Or The Association of Short-Term Lenders (ASTL).

Angel Investors

Let me start by expressing my dislike of this term and its inaccuracy which can often lead to confusion. In the true sense of the term, an angel investor would be a joint venture partner or a joint venture between two parties. The term angel investor in the business world is an individual willing to invest a sizable amount of capital into your business, usually in exchange for equity within that business. Think 'Dragons Den', and you are thinking of angel investment. I can only surmise that the term angel investor has come to light because these individuals are coming to your aid much like an angel is deemed to do so.

That said, to aid continuation and not to confuse you from the mass usage of the term online, I will refer to it as an angel investment despite my reluctance.

Angel investment is similar to bridging lending in the way that it is set up regarding speed, fees and usage, but where bridging companies are often big commercial-type lenders, an angel investor is usually a sole individual or small business. They come in all shapes and sizes, from the guy down the pub who has just inherited a fortune. Your accountant who has been successful in business for the past 30 years, to someone you have just met at a networking event or in a property group online. The latter being the most common route to connecting with an angel investor.

Given the fact that you are effectively borrowing a specific sum of money from an individual, these loans can work in an infinite number of ways. It will depend on your relationship with your angel investor regarding how the lending is established. For instance, if your angel investor is your great uncle Bob, he will no doubt have a more relaxed attitude to the contractual obligations, repayment terms, fees, and overall set-up than that of Mrs Trunchbull. Who, incidentally, you have just met for the first time at a local networking event. She looks pretty authoritative, and on first impressions, you think she is a stickler for doing things the right way. Plenty of I's to dot and T's to cross with her.

Fees such as set-up costs, exit fees, early redemption charges, and interest paid will vary from deal to deal and from angel to angel. Historically, though, interest rates have ranged between 0.5% to around 1% per month for a standard angel loan. On top of these charges, there may have been small set-up or exit fees, as well as any solicitors' costs to be covered for contractual agreements. In the instance where the angel investor required a first or second charge on the property for their protection, this would almost certainly come from your end. The benefit of leveraging an angel investor is that it is not uncommon to hear of 100% loans.

An angel investor, should they deem the deal presented to them to be profitable enough, will often lend the entire purchase and refurbishment costs for the deal. This means that should you be fortuitous enough to come by a flip or a BRR deal, either direct-to-vendor or through a sourcing company that enables 100% of the capital back, including expenses; then you can genuinely fund the deal using someone else's money. Just be sure to calculate the mathematics correctly. Ensuring that all the numbers relating to the interest payments and fees are accounted for is essential.

Remember, these loans can work in a number of ways. However, an example of a 100% leveraged option would be as follows:

Let us say we have found a genuine 100% cash-back BRR deal, but we need to fund the purchase using someone else's money. Enter Trunchbull and her non-negotiable stipulations.

Firstly she will require the contract to be witnessed by a solicitor and a first charge to be placed on the property for added protection. There is a small set-up fee to cover her time, and the monthly interest rate payable is set at 1% for the term of the loan.

The property is for sale for £80,000 but requires a further investment of £25,000 through a refurbishment. Including the solicitor costs to purchase and the SDLT charge, the amount leveraged from the angel investor is £108,400.

After your expert refurbishment is complete, the property is valued at £145,000, meaning, at a 75% LTV you release £108,750. This is a true example of a 100% cash-out BRR should you find the deal yourself. However, when leveraging an angel investor, this does not demonstrate the entire story. The interest payments on the £108,400 were £1,084 per month, and since the revaluation started at month six due to the lender's ownership requirement and the conveyancing taking a further two months, we need to multiply the interest paid by eight. Therefore, our interest payments equate to £8,672. The setup fees plus the legal charges for dealing with the contract and 1st charge were a further £750 meaning our total angel costs were £9,422.

This effectively means we are leaving £9,072 of our own money in the deal once we subtract the £350 accrued from the deficit between the new leveraged amount versus the initial angel loan.

Should we not be able to cover this with our own working capital, we should not have taken the loan in the first instance since we should have included these fees in our initial calculations. If we can cover this from our own capital and remember by this time, we should have had a few months' rent accruing profits to reduce the deficit; then the deal is on.

It may be worth mentioning that if we flipped this property, we would have made somewhere in the region of £25,000, depending on the agent's sale costs, even after the fees and interest payments are applied. In this instance, it may have been worth considering the flip option, especially if there was an inability to cover the £9,422 angel costs. The last thing we want to do is upset Trunchbull. We don't want to end up in the chokey, do we?

Maybe 50% of you will get that joke.

We have only discussed 100% angel loans, but there are, of course, many other options. For a start, some people who can fund the purchase via a standard mortgage product may want to angel the cost of the refurbishment. Releasing the equity in the property gained through the refurbishment, paying back the angel and their costs with the profit made is a widespread technique for leveraging angel investors.

What you most certainly cannot do is use angel investment to fund your deposit when using a mortgage to fund the purchase. Mortgage companies want their clients to have 'skin in the game', but more so, do not want to spend time carrying out due diligence on third parties. So although this used to be an avenue many years ago, it is not the case now.

The good news is that the above-mentioned bridging companies will often allow this.

They may want to see the build-up of funds in the angel investor's bank account to satisfy their anti-money laundering regulation checks, but you can proceed if your angel investor is on board with this.

Again this is specialist advice and should be sought from a specialist advisor. My aim in highlighting it here is to offer you some insight. Enough that you are aware of the options available. Should capital be your weakness in the big three, then at least you have areas of research to pursue, and as these areas start to develop, you will realise that these self-imposed inhibitors are falsely weighted. Within a few hours of researching angel investors and joining some property groups on LinkedIn and Facebook, you will see how widespread this lending method is. Further to this, you will see how easily accessible and readily available it is.

Joint Venturing or JV Partners

In the simplest sense, a JV is where two or more parties come together to work jointly on a project. The key to a successful JV is finding the proper marriage of skills and resources to make the project work for both or all concerned. With this in mind, not all JVs work as a 50/50 monetary exchange. It is not uncommon for one JV partner to fund a higher portion of the capital. Even funding 100% is not uncommon if the other partner involved is the 'man on the ground' with the sourcing ability, the building skills or connections and is prepared to manage the project to ensure its success.

The JV relationship can look similar to the angel investor in this case, except the cost of borrowing the capital is not measured by fees but rather in joint ownership. For instance, if someone approached me with the above deal mentioned in my angel investor demonstration with the 100% BRR property or flip, I would, in most cases, return to the person and suggest a JV collaboration rather than a straight-up angel loan. It may be that they seek alternative lending, but it may be that they choose my approach, given my expertise. Regardless of this scenario, the point I want to make is that just like angel investing, this can work in infinite ways and is often determined by relationships, skillsets or what each individual can bring to the table with their involvement.

A joint venture partner can be anyone you are connected with. Be it your grandfather, who would most likely be a partner for capital, your builder, who would likely be a partner for their skillset or another property investor who would likely be a partner to align commercial interests.

For example, you wish to pursue more extensive or advanced property deals. Of course, each of the above can bring more to the table than suggested. Your grandfather may be an ex-tradesman, and your builder may have some capital to invest, as well as bringing on board his knowledge and skillset. The options are endless for Joint venturing. Just be sure to manage expectations right from the start of the relationship to avoid disruption further down the line. Who is bringing what to the table, and who is responsible for what aspects of the project need to be established early in the relationship.

Since this law centres around finance and I truly could write an entire book on JVs, my focus should switch to accessing JVs to help your business financially and not manually, as in the case of a builder. Most importantly, you need to know how to access financial JV partners. Most commonly, we access partnerships from what is known as our stakeholders.

A stakeholder is anyone in your network but, more typically, friends, family, work colleagues and professional connections. The biggest inhibitor placed on securing a JV partnership from your stakeholders is usually the phrase, and I repeatedly hear this. "Oh, I would not like to ask so and so to lend me money". Firstly, let me tell you; they are not 'lending you money'. You are forming a partnership in the most literal sense. You are bringing them an opportunity and a way to increase their wealth.

Let us rewind the clock a few hours to when we were talking about inflation and my demonstration of what someone's capital will look like in 12 months due to the detrimental effect inflation has on their capital. When approaching them with this business proposition, what you are really doing is a favour. This piece of information is your loaded gun. How inflation strips the value of your capital is something you should lead with. As I write this in early 2023, this has increased leverage due to the astronomical inflation rate, but even when this returns to the average rate, it should be your ammo.

Approaching a stakeholder to leverage capital in a JV scenario is an opportunity for them to join you on your wealth creation journey. Remember that when you approach anyone. Trust me when I tell you that anyone with money is always looking to make more. And anyone with a skillset, without money, is looking to make some.

Property Sourcing

We have already discussed property sourcing several times throughout the book; therefore, to avoid sounding like a broken record, I will summarise as follows:

For me, personally, the jury is out on whether you should use property sourcing to fund your portfolio growth. On the one hand, should you have experience as an investor or builder. Or you have expertise in your local area and have spent significant time increasing your property knowledge to the point that you genuinely feel that you have a keen eye for quality property, then I am all for using this medium to increase your working capital.

The concern is raised when underqualified and inexperienced investors are trained to find deals for other naive investors based on mathematical returns. Although this book is heavy on maths, property investing is far more than mathematics, as I have repeatedly explained. Buying a property just because the maths stack up can have dire ramifications.

At £3,000 a deal, it might be hard for you to ignore. My only advice is to ensure that you are at a point whereby you can honestly and truthfully say that, given the capital, you would buy this property for your own portfolio.

Property sourcing can be a fantastic way to increase your working capital or grow a business from scratch without much start-up cost. You will, however, need to know how to conduct your ethical sourcing business from the outset.

Since you will effectively be acting on behalf of the buyer in sourcing the property, you will be governed by the Estate Agents Act 1979.

You will also need to do the following:

1. Be registered with a property ombudsman, such as The Property Ombudsman (TPO)
2. Be registered with the Information Commissioner's Office (ICO)
3. Be registered with a professional body, such as the National Residential Landlords Association (NRLA)
4. Have professional indemnity insurance in place

Sourcing property requires an ethical approach. Get well-educated on what you are doing, and you can stand out from the crowd.

Peer to Peer lending or P2P

Peer-to-peer lending (P2P) is effectively brokerage in a marketplace. Typically online sites. P2P lending platforms take your details and requirements and then match them with lenders that can fill your requirements. For instance, if you would like to borrow £25,000 at a fixed rate of 1% per month, you have a credit score of 654, you want to borrow the capital for 12 months, you are happy with an early redemption charge, and your dog's name is uninspiringly Fido then their algorithm will yield results that synchronise to you and the lender. Choosing which lender you want to use is all that remains. Since I have never used P2P lending nor know anyone who has, and I do not feel it is a very efficient or effective route to raising finance to purchase property, this is about the extent of my knowledge. Therefore, I cannot honestly tell you more. If this avenue interests you even slightly, another entry should be made to your to-do list.

Credit Cards and Bank Loans

Finally, credit cards and bank loans. This is a truly excellent medium for pursuing property and, in fact, one that I encourage people to look at before leveraging anything else.

I started my journey with £150,000 worth of credit card debt, and within six months, I was a gazillionaire with 10,000 properties, a villa in Monte Carlo and a fleet of Lamborghinis.

Sorry, that is not how I intended to start this section. Let me rephrase those last paragraphs to suit my tone.

Credit cards. Bank loans. Seriously? Come on, people, get with it.

Should you be considering leveraging a credit card or a bank loan to start your property journey, then my advice would be to stop, rethink your position, shake your head with vigour, go and take a cold shower and then work on getting yourself into a more stable financial position before you even consider this industry.

Please do not let the dramatised, exaggerated, and glorified stories you hear about being in debt with loans convince you that it is the way to start or even that, in 2023, it is a viable way to start a property business. It may have been a route a few lucky people managed to adopt many years ago but not anymore.

Money regulations are tighter, due diligence is carried out far more thoroughly, and there is less money in the average property deal now with the increased costs and regulations than there was back in the good old days. If that is where you are right now, and you are considering this as an option, then use other people's money (OPM), R2R, or Lease option.

Tap your stakeholders, but DO NOT use bank loans or credit cards despite the rounded-off and glorified 'success' stories.

Maybe it worked for half a per cent of the people who tried it many years ago. But do you like those odds?

Just stay well clear. Learn the lessons from this book and apply some patience. This book's entire premise is building solid foundations and creating a stable business, not rolling the dice. When you gamble with finance or property requiring finance, you are gambling with people's lives.

Remember, we often over-calculate what can be achieved in a year but under-calculate what can be achieved long term. You can absolutely create a property investment business if you currently have no capital, but not with credit cards or bank loans.

To sum up, finance is far more readily available than you might think. There are many options other than the standard high-street mortgage lender, and your broker, as well as your research and network, will be able to open your world with these options.

....

As promised earlier in the chapter, here is the current SDLT table. This is correct at the time of inserting and recording in March 2023

Purchase Value	SDLT (std Rate)	SDLT (Investors)
Under £40,000	0%	0%
Up to £250,000	0%	3%
Over £250,000 to £925,000.	5%	8%
Over £925,000 to £1,500,000.	10%	13%
Over £1,500,000	12%	15%

14. Network

"The richest people in the world look for and build networks, everyone else just looks for work"

Robert Kiyosaki

Networking brings leverage, compounding and exponential growth to your business.

The past few days have been very interesting for me. I have been searching through various spreadsheets, purchase files, and desktop folders to attempt to compile some kind of overview that would help me to articulate the enormous power your network can have on your business. The result of my research is not surprising, yet it is pleasing as I view it in black and white.

Over the past three years alone, my network has been wholly or partly responsible for 78 properties for myself and my close network.

These have come in the form of 26 direct-to-vendor purchases via friends, family, and social media following. 19 direct-to-vendor purchases via word of mouth, landlord associations, contractors or friends of people we have purchased from. The remaining 33 purchases have come via the agents we work with. However, these properties never made it to Rightmove. We were one of the agent's first port of calls, and we acted quicker than anyone else.

These properties comprise 'Turnkeys', 'BRR' deals, 'Flips', and 'Conversions' – Principally HMOs and deals we sold on to our extended network, either circumstantial mentees or long-standing management company clients.

If I loosely calculate the profit made by these network purchases alone. Remember that these do not include open market deals that we have secured. The total profit generated from these would be in the region of £1,730,000. And can be broken down loosely as follows:

Around £650k in profit was generated from flips and BRR equity released. £850k in equity was created through capital growth and BRR equity but not released for one reason or another. Lastly, around £230k in fees were generated from sourcing property and the profit from controlling renovations and refurbishments.

I might mention here that the above does not include extra ongoing revenue created by managing the properties bought through my joint venture companies and the sourced properties for our clients. Incidentally, this totals around £30-40k per year of passive income from the above list alone. At least, it is passive to me since I am seldom involved with the management company running and growth these days.

Although this overview is pleasing for me to write, and I am sure for most of you, it is to read since it offers encouragement and, hopefully, inspiration, it is not an ego trip but rather an example of the power of your network. However, it is only part of the story.

My network extends far beyond direct revenue. Over the past 12 months, whilst writing this book, I have tapped into my accountant on many occasions to help clarify rules and regulations, tax queries, or to help with specific mathematical scenarios, least of all to corroborate the accuracy of my workings. My mortgage broker has been used frequently regarding mortgage rates and has helped edit sections of the book referring to mortgages and their respective products, as well as to offer an opinion on the current state of the market.

Furthermore, my solicitor has occasionally been used to help keep the legal aspects on point. I may be the so-called property expert, but you are way off the mark if you think this book's content has been written by sitting down and spilling my knowledge exclusively from what is encased within my mind. When I attack legalities, mortgages, finance and other such complexities, I am in constant contact with my network of professionals to ensure my advice is unquestionable and reliable.

Remember that this industry is built on leverage; as I stated earlier in the book, there would be no property industry without it.

You do not need to be the finished product, the expert in the industry that has all of the answers all of the time to be successful with property investing. You merely need to follow a disciplined approach to your business and understand where to find the answers you seek.

The difference between you and me at this stage of your journey is that If I am stuck with anything, any information I need or help with any scenario, I know precisely who to speak with to get answers. Whether that is my broker, accountant, solicitor, architect, property mastermind group, builder or even someone like UKALA, who is the 'UK Association of Letting Agents'. A professional membership body that supports our management company to stay legally compliant and can help with any tenancy-related issue that may arise.

It is a bold statement, but no single problem could arise within my business or portfolio that could not be sorted by making a couple of quick calls to my network. The power of anyone's network is the power of their business. Essentially you have an extended family of staff at your disposal should you choose to leverage it. This does not get established on day-one ready to spring you into action; instead, it grows with you. How fast it grows, however, is entirely down to you.

Some people use the 'I have made every mistake there is, learn from my mistakes so you don't need to make them for yourself' claim to their material. I will never do this because despite what you learn, you will always make mistakes in your journey. Hopefully, the more methodical you are and the more educated you become, the lesser the severity of these mistakes. That said, perhaps the biggest mistake I made in my early career as a property investor or business owner, since I did this in my gas career, too, was not actively increasing my network. If I could rewind the clock and approach one thing differently, this would be it.

New investors often overlook networking, but it can have just as much power for the newly enrolled as it can for the big-time, big-deal investor.

With the rise of social media and, might I now mention, my soon-to-be live or, depending on when you read this book, firmly established investor network platform and application, networking is far easier than you might suppose. ®

The social media aspect of the above comment may seem slightly contradictory since I am rarely active on social media. Still, the reason for this is that I have built my network outside of this platform, nor do I need to grow my business any longer by using this platform, therefore rendering my social media presence almost redundant. Social proof is all we use social media for. However, for your business, this is something that seriously needs consideration. The power of networking through social media is instantaneous and exponential. You do, of course, again need to consider the big three of 'time, capital and education' when concluding this for yourself.

For example, should you have a plethora of time but not much capital or education, networking, especially via social media platforms, is almost a necessity. However, should capital and education not be a concern, we may consider sticking to professionals for networking, at least as a more focused approach to social media presence. There are many variations of why you may primarily use social media to build your network. Still, just like everything else in property, this will depend on your specific set of circumstances.

This medium for building your network is not the only way to proceed, of course, it is simply a tool for your Arsenal. It just so happens that in the 21st century, it is en-vouge and free; further, it can be done in your spare time.

To offer insight into how your network can help resolve obstacles on your journey, I can demonstrate a few examples I have encountered over the past few days. I have been approached on separate occasions by people who have added me to their network and are leveraging me or my network as an extension of their own. On each occasion, the solution to their problem was, in fact, a network problem.

These are not your typical rounded-off, overexaggerated, hugely inspirational examples you would usually find in a book like this, but rather, real-life, everyday genuine cases that occurred within the last week of my writing this chapter. Only the names of the individuals have been changed. Stuart, an ex-mentee, approached me for a copy of a joint venture agreement. He wants a basic agreement to use for his latest JV deal. Since my joint ventures come in the form of friends and family where no JV agreement exists, or they are via a limited company. As such, the joint venture agreement is covered in the form of a shareholder's agreement within the limited company. The solution was to advise Stuart to join a specific networking group I was aware of and then request one within the group. As I understand it, he was given an agreement within a few short hours of posting his request, and that agreement was used for his venture. A straightforward problem for some, maybe, but for Stuart, this was a blockade. A simple question to a small part of his network, AKA me, and he had some direction. One more step, and he had his solution. His problem was solved because he has a network. His network has now further extended and grown exponentially since he joined the group and has made subsequent connections.

Steve and Andria are at the start of their journey and are in the process of setting up their company and corresponding bank account. Due to their circumstances, Andria being a non-British citizen, the only bank they have been able to operate through is Starling. Starling requires them to present a basic business plan and obtain a decision in principle to activate the account. Steve and Andria currently have no network with regard to white-collar professionals, so they approached me as I am part of their growing network. I sent two emails to my broker and accountant, respectively and within 24 hours, they had an AIP or 'agreement in principle' and a basic editable business plan template. When they approached me, their problem was presented as insurmountable, and to them, it seemed to prevent them from beginning their journey, but the reality was that the solution was a simple network tap.

A long-established friend and fellow landlord I met through my network many years ago called me to see what I would do in his scenario. Pete was attending a property that had just been purchased and discovered a file with birth, death and marriage certificates, insurance documents and other sensitive documents enclosed. Using these documents, we immediately took out a line of credit and bought a super yacht. I do hope you enjoyed the book, but I need to go now; THE END!

In all honesty, "Shall we buy a boat" was my initial reply to Pete, but the real help came when he informed me that his emails to the national agency, one which I will not divulge, had not yielded a satisfactory result. I immediately picked up the phone and called the local representative, Charlotte, her real name, who resolved the issue. She contacted the vendor, who was ecstatic with the discovery and, as I understand it, equally upset with her husband for not clearing out the loft properly.

You can see now why I mitigated the magnitude of these three examples. The point I wanted to make is not how a network can massively alter your company's direction and growth, although this is precisely the point and the direct consequence of networking. But instead, offer some simple examples of real-life everyday challenges that may act as an inhibitor, leaving you feeling lost and alone when in fact, there is a simple solution.

Understand that your network will help your business on every level, from its conception to its growth and then help you to hit the heights you strive for. It can help orchestrate huge life-changing events but is equally useful for the everyday challenges you may face.

Recently, I have been involved in opening a multi-director limited company for the sole purpose of student let accommodation. This was a business concept and a sizeable ready-to-go deal that someone in my network presented me with, incidentally rendering my sourcing of this and the many associated challenges redundant. Just like Steve and Andria, we were required to open a bank account for the company. When I approached Barclays, I was informed that they were, as a company, not allowing any new business accounts to be opened except for single director, small businesses or sole proprietor-type accounts. Of course, my next port of call was my Barclays business manager since she forms part of my network. She only served to corroborate what the new accounts team informed me. Not wanting to inconvenience of separate logins for my business accounts, I called my accountant who put me in touch with a more senior manager at Barclays. Within 24 hours, I spoke with this manager, and our application was started the same day. This bank account is now open and in use.

Like the above issues, my network was the solution to my problem. Furthermore, the regional Barclays manager now forms part of my growing network. Agreeably it is maybe five or so years too late, but then previously, I have had no call to include him, and I knew that he was only ever one step removed and, as a result, readily available through my direct network.

These are simple examples of how your network can help you overcome the challenges a professional investor may face at the start or as they continue with their journey. There are far more variants that we could discuss, but the outcome will always be the same regardless of the complexity. Your network can help you solve almost any problem or challenge you may face.

Twenty-first-century networking

We might argue that building your network is the simplest thing you can do within your business that will unquestionably carry the most weight as a ratio to the effort required.

Today more than ever, networking is one of the simplest things you can do. With the rise, power and reach of social media, it has become, as stated, a stay-at-home task. Of course, nothing will replace face-to-face contact with your relationships, but not all relationships need to be so deeply rooted. The idea of tapping into a social media network is not always to establish long-standing relationships. It can be, of course, but that is something that will come with time. The real power of the social media network is speed and diversity.

Can anyone recommend a broker, an accountant, or a lender that deals with first-time landlords, first-time buyers? Does anyone know this area of the country well enough to offer insight? Can anyone help with a shareholders agreement or an angel investor agreement? I am considering investing in HMOs, can anyone recommend a good YouTube channel or property course? I have a problem with a tenant. Can anyone help? I am investing in this town or city, does anyone know of any local Facebook, LinkedIn or landlord association groups in this area?

These are the types of questions that get answered instantly over messaging and can often solve what might be a tedious and time-consuming research task.

This is before we get into the more significant questions like, does anyone know of a good sourcing company based in, *insert area here*! Or can anyone put me in touch with someone who can help finance this BRR project?

Today the power of networking and, in particular, the speed of social media networking can be the sole thing that will help someone who has very little property knowledge and experience get going with their journey. Its gravity cannot be ignored. Networking opens doors that you are unable to open yourself. What is more, when one door opens via your network, it leads to several others, growing exponentially as you progress.

I have witnessed this on many occasions with past and present clients. A single post results in several answers, perhaps a few phone calls, one or two meetings, and the upshot is a long-established and successful partnership or relationship. The mentees that progress the most under my wing are the ones that tap into me the most, the ones that message and have calls with me continually, not the ones that remain on the peripheral using me sporadically.

This is not only because they tap into and can funnel my knowledge more but more so because they understand that I am just another part of their network. The reality is that these individuals are the individuals that network the most. If they tap into me, it creates momentum, which is transferred across the board to increasing their network with brokers, accountants, solicitors, estate agents, lettings teams, other local investors, and social media groups, which all help them to grow far beyond the investor who limits the growth of their network.

A large part of property investing is finding the deals and benefiting from the better, more profitable deals. Those of you who network will increase your chances of finding these deals tenfold, directly correlating to your networking.

The laws of 'Networking' and, as you will soon discover, 'Strategy' should be the ones that offer enormous confidence in your decision to become a property investor; since when we understand these two laws, we can identify a solution. Almost every problem we might encounter now and, in the future, from 'I do not know what to do next', to 'Can anyone help with finance' can be mitigated through these two laws, either exclusively or combined. If we strategise or tap into our network or both, we should be able to solve any problem.

For what you need at this research stage, networking is about one thing: get going and watch it grow. In the short time we have discussed networking, I have demonstrated its elemental powers and highlighted some favourable outcomes. I have indicated ways in which to get started through social media to local landlord groups. You will find local networking events held throughout the country via various organisations, and should you want more information on this, then, well, increase your network.

I could list a few national ones here, with local or regional meetings, but your experience and benefit will come from enquiring for yourself.

If you are unsure how to do this or where to find them, fire up Facebook and join a property group, post a message, and begin to build your own network.

"Your network is your net worth. How do you value your network? Well, if you don't value it, cultivate it and nurture it, it becomes worthless. If you do value it, it becomes priceless"

Robert G Allen

15 Strategy – Your DNA

"People should not be unfamiliar with strategy, those who understand it will survive, those who do not will perish"

Sun Tzu

"Hope is not strategy, hope fits with vision, but we must have a strategy and a process to make our vision become a reality"

John C Maxwell

In 2003 the Harvard Business Review published an article detailing their findings in what was known as the 'Evergreen Project'. This study followed 160 companies over a ten-year period and was perhaps the most comprehensive study of business management ever conducted. In summary, it concluded that the strongest predictor of success was to devise and maintain a clearly stated focused strategy.

Setting a goal without a solid process may lead to future frustration. Whereas following a process accompanied by the final vision gives meaning to the small things we do on a regular basis, meaning we are far more likely to achieve our goals and visions.

So how important is strategy in property investing? Well, I would speculate that since this book is aimed or written for people entering the industry as a beginner, most of you will have little to no property investing experience or at least any measured experience; therefore, strategy is merely fundamental. Unfortunately, there are currently no apprenticeships available within the industry. You cannot simply go out and get a job as a property investor or take an open university course in property investment. Not yet, anyway.

Therefore, to sum up the gravity of creating a strategy, I would decree that developing a coherent strategy within your property business is the single most consequential thing you can do to help your business grow from where you are now and succeed with it long-term.

As I have repeatedly stated, anyone can teach you to do what they do. Anyone who wants to invest in property can quickly do so and with relative ease. You do not need to be an expert, and you do not need experts' guidance. You do not need to follow the exact principles of this book in a disciplined fashion. Any existing investor can show you how they did it; they can highlight their failures and successes. Most experienced investors will be able to advise on cash flow, return on investment and what to look out for in their experience when seeking to purchase a property. Essentially all that is required is a firm grasp of the mathematics coupled with a basic understanding of an individual property's current and future needs.

The bad news, however, for those of you who intend to skip on your continued education at this crossroad is that, in this case, you will likely form part of the overpopulated and less profitable 95% investor pool. To reaffirm my point, this is because it takes one kind of person to show someone else how to do it and another to show someone how to be successful with what they do. Further, it takes a special kind of person to then go on and take action on what they have been taught and apply it to their own journey.

Just like anyone can set up shop in almost any industry and begin to work for themselves, not everyone can run a successful business. Strategy can, and in most cases, will be the difference. However, strategy is not what you have been led to believe it is.

Talk with any property investor and ask what their strategy is, and you will undoubtedly time and again hear one of the following terms. "I buy single-let property". "My strategy is BRR", or "I invest in high-yielding properties such as HMOs". "My strategy is to achieve a minimum of 12% ROI".

The truth is that none of these are strategic and certainly do not come close to forming any type of strategy.

A strategy is not a model or a type of investment; it does not have a monetary value or a percentage of return attached to it, and it is far from an idea for future growth. Often, we confuse goals, objectives and visions as a strategy, but the reality is that creating a strategy is far more focused than this. Goals, visions and objectives are vague terms that individually do not form your strategic approach.

A strategy needs to have a clear vision, an honest diagnosis as well as achievable goals and well thought out objectives. Above all else, though, it needs to adopt a coherent plan of action, or as Richard Rumelt calls it in his book 'Good Strategy, Bad Strategy', a guiding policy.

Strategy in property investing does not need to be an extensive overview of your entire journey, assessing where you are now and where you will go, precisely detailing and scrutinising every step of how you will get there. That would be an almost impossible task. There are too many variants to consider and too many branches of your journey to detail in one overriding magnum opus.

Okay, Impossible may be the wrong word to use. I suppose I would prefer to say that it would be too time-consuming and perhaps more comforting to hear after hearing the magnitude of this book; it would be major overkill. I doubt there would be a single reader or investor who would be able to, let alone want to detail such an enormous undertaking. If we allow developing a strategy to overwhelm us, there is little chance of its creation. The failure to create would then be disastrous to your business since perhaps as much as 50% of the power of any strategy comes from its very creation.

If we examine where many of you will be on your journey right now and collectively bundle you into one category, what you will have in common will most likely be your confusion about what to do next. This is where strategy comes in.

Strategy is used to create our action plan. If you strategically analyse your problems, you can break them down systematically and create a strategy to solve them. Its strength lies in keeping these strategies relatively simple but crucially localised to specific problems rather than macro events.

Before I explain how I want to make something profoundly clear. I discussed this earlier in the book, but I feel it is important to reiterate it at this stage to further cement it into your subconscious.

I understand and sympathise that most of you are looking for that giant leap forward, which takes you directly from a fumbling beginner to an accomplished property investor. But that route does not exist; you cannot bypass what is necessary.
Let me be clear when I say that if you use your energy trying to accomplish that giant leap forward, you will waste your time and money or worse, you may end up in deep water with your investments. By far, the best route to success is small action-oriented steps that, when combined, collectively move you towards your goal. Rome was not built in a day, nor is your property business.

Just take a second to consider where you are now. What industry do you work in? Are you someone who works with computers, a tradesperson, an engineer or a lawyer? At what point on that journey would you have been able to bypass your training and education? In the first few weeks of your employment or training, would you have been able to design a large sales brochure for a corporate event, build a house from scratch on your limited knowledge, design an exhaust system for a cruise ship or argue employment law in front of a judge?

The answer, I am guessing, would likely be no. Like it or not, contrary to what some might have you believe through their hyped-up dream selling, property investing is no different from any other business. And why would it be? This industry creates significant wealth. One that compounds and can grow exponentially, contra to your time and future input. Once established, it has a largely passive nature that can offer you the holy grail of time and control within your life. Yet we all want to bypass its fundamental laws as if the above draws are insufficient enough for us to apply effort and discipline. In the instance of building a property business, we can have our cake and eat it, but we need to spend focused time and energy baking it first.

The effort in building this kind of business is front-loaded. Unlike many other businesses, however, once it is established, we can take our foot off the gas and watch it grow from a distance. This is precisely why we cannot bypass this stage of our journey with that giant leap forward. Cementing these smaller steps ensures that the finer details are understood and solidified, creating stronger foundations for our business to grow.

Let me offer you some clarity; the reason you may be confused and unclear on what your next steps are is simple. You are inexperienced in this sector. This is normal and to be expected, as with my examples above from builders to lawyers. Things start to clear as we advance. The longer we are submerged in the industry, the more educated we become as a result.

Suppose we cut out the smaller, less tangible, less respected, less attractive, but arguably more valuable tasks. In that case, we are cutting out the experience and necessary gained knowledge we need to succeed within this field.

In his book atomic habits, James Clear details a story of a humble ice cube. The intended goal is to melt an ice cube that readily awaits its destiny, sitting motionless in its solid state on a table in the centre of a room. The temperature in the room is set to minus 17 degrees Celsius; therefore, the ice cube remains intact at this temperature. There is a periodic one-degree rise in temperature over the next few hours. At minus 16 degrees, there is no change to the physical state of the ice cube, nor at minus 15, 14 or 13. This pattern maintains until the room temperature reaches zero degrees Celsius. The intended goal is achieved around this point, and the ice cube begins to melt.

We can draw a parallel between melting the ice cube and your goal of becoming a property investor. At minus 17 degrees Celsius, the ice cube is a long way from melting. This is where you might be on your journey as you work through this book. At minus 17, you are set solid in your mind and in your actions, far from a fluid state of movement and progression. Remember though, the premise of his book is to create small changes that compound over time to give desired outcomes.

Periodically increasing the temperature by one degree are your smaller action-oriented steps. The cumulative effect of these smaller steps leads to the accomplishment of the larger goal. In this case, melting the ice cube represents your tangible vision of becoming a property investor.

The final change from minus one degree to zero degrees that initiated the change in the state of the ice cube to commence with its melting was nothing more significant than its 17 predecessors. It may have been the straw that broke the camel's back, but the action of turning the dial on the thermostat was no more significant than any of the changes that came before it. There was no giant leap, just another simple one-degree rise in temperature. In fact, you will agree that without the other 16 changes on the thermostat, it would have had no impact at all. On its own, it is meaningless; it is only when it is grouped together with the other small incremental steps that it creates the desired outcome.

Should you spend a few weeks implementing some of the plans identified when creating your strategy and then briefly glance back over your shoulder, it would become evident that what you achieved in such a short time is actually a giant leap forward, only this is incrementally made up of these smaller steps.

Your starting point becomes further away at each glace back until it is a mere dot on the horizon. The key to this is consistency, not how far you can make each step carry you. To this day, I still attack every project, big or small, one step at a time. Most deals have a systematic or specific timeline of events anyway, so small steps are all we can take. We need X before proceeding to Y in almost every deal, so we get used to making smaller steps.

Just consider what you may have learned so far from this book. I think you would agree that you are now further ahead on your journey than you were before you started it. All in a few short hours. You may find out today what you did not know yesterday and again tomorrow. This is how our education develops, and our understanding of a subject grows.

As you develop, your path becomes more apparent; it simply takes action to create the path. This, to repeat, is where strategy comes in.

D is for Diagnosis

A coherent strategy is the DNA of your property business; it will give you a clear idea of what you need to do to achieve any goal that is inputted into its simple formula.

To understand and clearly map out a course of coherent action to overcome any problem, we need to understand where we are going. This is your vision but is not to be confused with the vision from Law 6. That was an overriding vision or the first measurable impact within your life. When using strategy as a tool for property investment, we break components into bite-sized pieces, effectively chunking down a macro task into micro parts. We are not looking for the holy grail of strategic approaches; we are identifying what we are currently stuck with and then working through a plan or formula to rectify this problem. The D in your DNA reflects this. It is the '**D**iagnostics' of two things.

Firstly what problem or challenge do we intend to solve? This is our vision within our micro strategy. And secondly, where are we now with this? What is our starting point? We must honestly assess our current situation. How well are we equipped to solve this problem or challenge?

Remember to always consider the big three of time, education and capital and apply what is relevant. If you can identify the challenges, you can consider options to overcome them. As you have come to expect, I intend to break this down further by exemplifying it in a short while. But for now, let us move on to the N in our DNA abbreviation.

N is for Navigation

To help chunk our task down and to make it easier to navigate, we must lay out clear goals and objectives. These are the essential details of the plan of attack. This should comprise the most significant part of your strategy and be split into short, medium, and perhaps long-term goals. Bear in mind that there may be several of one and sometimes none of the other.

For instance, some strategies will have only short-term goals as it is a more minor, more timebound task that needs completing over the next week or so, and some will have a mix between all three, short, medium and long-term goals.

Next, we take each goal and detail how we will achieve that goal with objectives. This, in effect, is your to-do list, your guiding policy, and details precisely what you need to do to achieve your goal. The detailed objectives should be split further or filtered down to a micro level until explicit action is specified. If, however, the objective is apparent and gives definitive action, it can remain whole without further consideration. Again, do not worry if you do not follow me entirely here; I will give you an example shortly.

A is for Action

Once we have identified our vision, assessed how equipped we are to work through the challenge, laid out our primary goals and then structured these with objectives, all that is left is to take action. As with everything else, should we fail to take action, we will never accomplish what we set out to achieve. But when will you do this? The simple answer is when you schedule it. The final piece of our DNA coding is to set well-defined and structured actions. Essentially, we diarise what we have laid out with our objectives to ensure we are scheduled to complete them. And that essentially is it. There is nothing complicated about strategy. It is a simple but effective plan that will prevent procrastination and offer you guidance and direction, bringing clarity to your thinking and much-needed confidence through its very creation. But most of all, it will enable action and momentum.

Pause for a second and consider those terms. Procrastination; we all procrastinate and often wish to avoid it, right? Countless books have been written on the subject. Perhaps my favourite being Brian Tracy's 'Eat that Frog'. Furthermore, we have guidance, direction, confidence and, perhaps most importantly, clarity for you at this stage of your journey. Something we all seek. If these words do not encourage you to take a short time to develop a strategy to overcome your challenge, then nothing will. Remember, we are creating a strategy to overcome a specific problem or to help achieve a specific goal. Not creating an A to Z of property success.

Using the DNA approach to build a 'Coherent Strategy'

Over the years, I have employed many variants of a strategy and created many strategies to achieve many different things. To this day, I still use the following plan to determine my strategy for any challenge, problem or opportunity I face within my business. After reading Richard Rumelt's book Good Strategy, Bad Strategy' several years back, I developed the following quick and simple 5-step plan for building a coherent strategy. ®

In my humble opinion, he truly missed a trick by not using DNA for his three stages of development. Remember, though, you heard that here first.

Step 1. Determine your specific vision to build your strategy around
Step 2. Diagnose where you are now and why you've not already achieved this *(consider time, education & capital)*
Step 3. Set manageable goals (short, medium and maybe long-term)
Step 4. Detail definitive objectives for each goal set
Step 5. Diarise and action your objectives after weighting their importance

To keep things simple and effective, we keep strategy simple and assign it to individual challenges rather than multifaceted problems.

I learned many years ago from a close friend that should we want our change to be sustainable, we must not create obstacles to our feats. Instead, to create significant and sustained change within our life, we must find the simplest thing that enables the most significant effect on helping us with that change. Essentially, we should look for the easiest thing that creates the biggest change for us and run with that.

This is precisely the reason why we need to keep strategy simple, so that it is used as a sustainable tool that will help us continually advance and not be dismissed as corporate mumbo jumbo.

If we think back to earlier in the book, we have already strategically broken down finding our gold mine area. This model or principle needs to be applied going forward to whatever it is at that time we are strategising.

To highlight how simple yet effective a strategy can be, let me give you an example of a common problem.

Melanie is at a crossroads on her journey; she wants to become a property investor but only has a small amount of capital saved. She has a few friends who are investors, so after speaking with them, she listened to a few property books and watched some YouTube videos. The idea of property investment has sparked her interest, something she now wants to pursue. However, as explained, she only has a small amount of investment capital saved. For edification, we will attribute the figure of £12,000.

Let me exemplify how she could use strategy to help with her vision. To reiterate, we are not creating a guiding policy or an entire property investment plan, but instead using the newly discovered 5-part strategic approach to overcome a specific problem.

Step 1 intended vision or outcome of this specific problem. Melanie's vision is to become a property investor despite her lack of readily available funds; therefore, obtaining funds for her venture is the challenge.

Step 2 Diagnostics. Melanie has been unable to move to the next level of her journey since her funds have restricted any progress. She considers the big three at this stage after being convinced of a strategic approach since reading the highly rated '15 Laws of Successful Property Investment'. Considering her time availability, it quickly becomes apparent that she does not realistically know how much time she can dedicate to this business. She self-confesses that her education is in its infancy, and we already know that she considers her capital a restrictor. Although the outcome of this initial diagnostics exercise seems a touch melancholy, this is, in fact, excellent news for Melanie. We have two choices here. We can accept the apparent disadvantages and conclude a sorrowful outcome, or we can flip them on their head and offer a growth-based view of the challenge.

Essentially, we now have a basis for action. From here, Melanie can formulate goals and objectives. Steps 3 & 4, respectively.

Step 3 Goals. In this instance, understanding that strategy is fluid and specific to the individual, she only wants to assign short-term goals to move her to the next stage of her journey. She will set out a new course or assign some medium-term goals if the outcome is favourable.

Short-term goals

a. Assess availability of time
b. Look at improving property education
c. Look at finance and its options on a deeper level

Step 4 Objectives. Melanie's job now is to assign tangible objectives to her goals.

a. Time availability
   i. Take a deeper look at what commitments I have

    ii. Assign work, sleep, family, social, gym, and downtime to ascertain what available time I would have to work on my property business

   iii. Look at what is mandatory, what is beneficial and what can be put on hold to work on my property business

b. Look at improving property education

    i. Speak with my friends again about their investments and try to get some clarity to my questions.

    ii. Formulate a list of ongoing questions I have to enable me to discover answers

   iii. Download some of the best-rated property investment books on audible

   iv. Research what free and paid-for property training courses are available to me

    v. Allocate time to researching property investment via Google

   vi. Look at attending some local networking events to speak with other investors

  vii. Join networking groups on the social media platforms I use and consider signing up with others

c. Look at finance and its options on a deeper level

    i. Speak with a local broker about my intentions and situation

    ii. Speak with a local accountant

   iii. Research finance options surrounding property investing

   iv. Look at equity release within my home

    v. Speak with other investors (friends and networking) about finance

   vi. Speak with friends, family and colleagues I know who have excess capital and broach the Joint Venturing or Angel investment subject

This is a simple demonstration, but the further Melanie breaks these objectives down, the more definitive the action and the clearer she will become about her next steps. For example, if we take Point C, step 1, which was 'Speak with a local broker', we could micro this further to make a list of three brokers. Carrying this on, we might detail, speak with investor friends about whom they use, or to look on Google for brokers who deal with buy-to-let financing and have the best ratings. If you filter each objective to the point where it cannot be filtered further, then we have the very definition of a tangible action. Let us assume Melanie applies this logic to the above list. At this point, she would have clear and specific bulletproof actions. The only thing that would remain would be step 5.

Step 5 Diarise and action your objectives after weighting their importance. Melanie's job now is to apply weighting to each objective. Assigning each objective to a level one, two or three category helps her decide which one to pursue first. Level one is essential, level two is beneficial, and level three is awareness. Once these are assigned, Melanie can diarise these tasks, meaning she is far more likely to begin working through them.

The result of this strategic approach is that Melanie has gained some clarity on what her next steps are. Furthermore, simply by creating her strategy, her confidence has increased immeasurably since she now realises that any problem she encounters can be broken down in this manner. Melanie firmly understands that these, at this stage, are mere baby steps. Still, instead of restricting her growth and plateauing with her development, she is enabling it by actively seeking out basic answers to her questions. I might add questions that seemed vast and impenetrable before she applied a simple strategy to break them down. Now they seem minor and solvable.

Should she decide to look back over her shoulder in a few weeks, she will discover that she has progressed far from the starting line. All she sees now is Dan. Dan is stuck in the gates, frantically searching for a shortcut or the giant leap forward. Looking around for someone else to give him answers to the fundamental question of 'What do I do next'? If only he asked himself the simple question, 'What is it that I want to know'. He could then apply a strategic approach to discovering the answer for himself.

The silver lining to Melanie's decision to activate a strategic approach is that she soon realises as she works through her objectives that there are, in fact, many ways in which she can access finance. Discovering the many ways available to build a property business and realising that her capital is not her restrictor; instead, her time is her advantage has excited her and given her a new sense of belief. If we then couple that with her new burning desire to educate, we have a person who has exponentially grown her desire to achieve her vision.

What do you think is the next thing Melanie decides to do as she waves over her shoulder toward Dan? Yes, you guessed it, she decided to formulate another strategy. This time it may centre around equity release or no money-down investment models. Rent to serviced accommodation or to secure a joint venture partner or an angel investor. Perhaps she is looking for BRR and flip opportunities in and around the country or possibly any of the many other options that her initial strategic objectives uncovered.

Melanie now fully comprehends all the fifteen fundamental laws of property investing and accepts that the smaller steps are what carry you the furthest.

The example used above for Melanie's problem was, as I indicated, a simplified version of what can be a far more complex undertaking should it be required. In essence, you will all produce personalised variants. However deep you decide to go will be determined by your personality and your desire to achieve the goals, and how complex the problem you are trying to solve is. However, if you follow the principles of the DNA approach and work through this 5-step plan until you feel you have clear objectives, you can precisely detail in your weekly calendar what you need to do. In that case, you will all move closer to your goal despite the complexity of your plan. And remember, I cited earlier, that up to 50% of the power of any strategy comes through its creation. This is due to the confidence gained as you work through it. Working through your strategy creates clarity of approach. This, in turn, gives immeasurable confidence and develops your education simultaneously.

All of this propels you further on your journey to the point it did for Melanie. It is what led Melanie to become a property investor, and despite her initial understanding and less than favourable starting position, a successful one in her own right. Melanie is not a real example, but she or any other variant imaginable could very well be you, should a strategic approach be adopted with your development.

All things considered

As we approach the end of this book, I want to briefly summarise, reiterate and offer further insight into some of the essential points mentioned throughout the book. Further, I will use the opportunity to offer some closing thoughts and statements to help further solidify my opinions on this industry and what it potentially means for you.

It is important to understand that this book was written to offer sound advice on creating a successful business and not for the purpose of general or generic property education. The plenitude of information available to us now via Google, YouTube and social media has not brought clarity to the industry but rather a counterproductive foggy outlook. This is brought on by salespeople offering Utopian visions of success or lifestyle through unsustainable or irresponsible methods.

If this book has overwhelmed you even at all, do not worry. Remember, I have tried to cover an entire industry whilst appealing to a broader audience than just you. You are but an incidental cog in this vast machine. You only need to take the relevant parts of this book to formulate your own plan.

It is the formula, not the inputs

The numbers used for my demonstrations throughout this book, regarding purchase prices, rental charges, profit margins, and crucially those relating to interest rates, are irrelevant, especially if you are reading this at some point in the book's future, where rates have presumably altered. What is important are the calculations and the process used to determine the results you need to make your own decisions. Simply follow the formulas and logic demonstrated throughout the book but input the variable numbers that relate to you and your property during the analysis.

As part of this book's resource pack, I have put together some spreadsheets that will help you with these calculations. Additionally, I have developed a quick 15-laws worksheet for you to follow.

This is a simple form that offers consideration and tasks to complete. The idea of working through my laws is to establish solid foundations in both your education and your business. Moreover, it will help create action and maintain momentum. This will be compounded as your network expands, opening multiple doors to each of the doors you open. As with this, your actions do this similarly.

Momentum is created when you begin working on your property business, and your to-do list will fill organically. This is when you will begin to increase your education one step at a time while you grow in confidence exponentially as many things begin to clarify making the whole journey feel less daunting.

Now is the 'Time'

Calculating the reality of your available time, no matter the outcome, can be energising. For a start, you will come to terms with the fact that you may not have time to do everything you want to do within your life and business, not at first anyway. But then, how many of us do? Show me someone who has mastered this, and I'll show you an illusionist.
It means you can stop beating yourself up for not doing what you could never manage. This has significant ramifications for your mindset.
You can now focus on what truly matters, what is essential and what needs to be done to progress your journey. This is efficiency; it forces us to strategise to formulate a coherent plan and, crucially, to carry out that plan in the most time-effective way, not watch generic property investing videos but rather ones specific to your investments or ideas.

This time calculation will help manage your expectations at the start of your journey like no other task. Once more, the consequence is your mindset. Feelings of productivity and clarity prevail, which in turn will lead to confidence. The byproduct of this stark realisation that you may not have 'as much as it needs' like you initially thought you did at this point in your development carries enormous weight. The contra to this and to maintain the positive spin is that you may realise that you do, in fact, have more than enough time to begin building the property business you currently desire. In essence, until we calculate this, we will never know for sure either way. Remember, we have a resource that can help you with this.

Understand Compounding

Somebody recently asked me if I could choose one thing in life outside of family, friends and hobbies; what is the thing you love the most? I considered this question for about ten seconds and swiftly replied, compounding!

Compounding has many faces; not only is it mathematically proven, but it reverberates throughout your entire working and personal life. There is a quote on the back of Darran Hardy's book 'The Compound Effect' that states that 'the compound effect is based on the principle that decisions shape your destiny. Little, everyday decisions will take you to either the life you desire or to disaster by default'.

Take time to understand how compounding helps your business grow far beyond your expectations, and you will understand why property investing is the obvious choice. Compounding works best if left undisturbed, or as Charlie Munger put it, 'the first rule of compounding is to never interrupt it unnecessarily'.

If you are in this industry for ego and to get rich quickly, then I'm sorry to be the one to tell you this, but you've got a long way to go with your education. This industry creates wealth, not riches; you will never be wealthy if you can't suppress your ego. Investing your capital and benefiting from the laws of compounding is the thing that makes all the difference to your growth. No matter how much you make from a deal or earn from your rental income initially, you will never be truly wealthy if you do not reinvest that money and allow the compound effect to grow your business exponentially.

Delay what you can spend today, and you will be rewarded with far more exciting options in the future.

Things are never as bad as they seem

Avoid the pessimistic views of the newspapers & articles. Our ears are pricked when presented with bad news. Suppose a well-respected figure assures you things are fine; we generally smile and nod in agreement, but when someone we have never met tells us that catastrophes are imminent, we clear our diary, sit up and take notes, fearing the worst. We are pre-programmed to think like this; it is a defence mechanism. It is not you; it is your system one brain, the one responsible for intuitive automatic responses being dominant over your more logical system two brain. If you learn to adopt the system two thinking more of the time, you have more chance of being rational when you are influenced negatively by outside sources®

Get to grips with luck and risk

You will have a better chance of understanding your investments if you do. Luck helps you identify what is possible in the property world, and risk will force you to do due diligence. Remember, all risk is mitigated and lessened through education, but risk is what pays off over time. If you do not risk anything, then do not expect to grow. Provided, of course, the risks you take are calculated correctly.

Luck and risk are intrinsically linked; they are, after all, as Morgan Housal puts it, siblings.

Counting sheep

Manage your investments, at least in the early days, in a way that helps you sleep well at night. That doesn't mean you need to start small or be extra cautious with your capital. Some people will want to grow as fast as possible, and providing their foundations are set, this is perfectly acceptable for that individual. However, others may want to build up a little slower, incrementally increasing their stakes in their business as they grow in confidence, which is perfectly acceptable for that individual too. Remember, this is your journey, and if you invest in a way that makes you uncomfortable, you have a lesser chance of it becoming a sustainable lifestyle.

The grey zone

Become okay with a few things going wrong. Remember, property is not a binary right or wrong do or do not industry. It is fluid and adapts to you and your desires. Often you will need to live in the grey zone whereby we need to adopt more directional thinking. This is understanding that we will never truly know, but we have enough information to make the best decision possible to advance. If you become okay with a few things going wrong, you can make decisions that help us sleep far easier than you would if you expect everything you do to turn to gold. Consider that what goes wrong today and seems like such a big deal will most likely feel insignificant as time passes.

Not all education comes through books & training

There is no replacement for experience; experience only comes from continued action over time. Remember Earl Nightingale's comments regarding working on your education daily. Little and often creates momentum and helps us gain experience and knowledge. But some knowledge only comes from experience, not via the books we read or the courses we attend. This is applied knowledge, not learned knowledge. You must accept that without certain experiences, you will never know certain things.

"Live as if you were to die tomorrow. Learn as if you were to live forever"

Mahatma Gandhi 1869 - 1948

The Jones' have the plague - Avoid them at all costs

This is your journey, no one else's. Property investing is unique to you; there are no two ways about that. We all invest for differing reasons, be it financial security for you and your family. The freedom of a job or a boss. The freedom of choice, to live life how you see fit. For capital growth or asset appreciation. To build wealth from your riches. To earn money from a merely passive income. For a pension fund or retirement pot. for cashflow or an income boost to your current employment. As a hedge against inflation. To exponentially grow a business contra to input. This is before we look at factors such as your purchase pricing, location, and control strategy. Different cashflowing models or types of investments and the availability of your time. Your knowledge and skills reflective of your approach. Your overall vision as well as your short, medium and long-term goals. Your threshold to risk and reward or hassle factors of your investments and models. This list extends far beyond this, yet with each point above, there are unlimited variations.

You have your own journey to conclude, and your approach needs to reflect you and your personality and desires. No one else's.

Block out the hype and concentrate on your own journey. We all play a different game with our property investments, so it's imperative that you are not influenced by someone who is playing an entirely different game from you.

Failure and your fear of it

"Failure is essential to invention and progress"

James Dyson

According to a New York Times article, failure has been changed from an action of *'I failed'* to an identity *'I am a failure'*. But we must conclude that failure is merely the path to discovering something great. All scientists understand this since they look at failure as evidence on their way to understanding how things work. Not acknowledging this will prevent you from learning from your mistakes. Understand that any mistake is a standard human function that happens on our way to improvement.

Fear keeps us from greatness. It keeps us from learning simple and practical lessons. There is no magic wand, no secret, just education. Fear blocks our reception with some forms of education, and allowing it to hang around creates cognitive dissonance. We've been brainwashed to believe that we must not get into debt; we must pay our mortgage down. Our property is our biggest asset, and we should work hard and save for the things we need. Suddenly the idea comes our way that this is erroneous, and there is, in fact, another way, but we can't handle this, so fear steps in and this uncomfortable feeling is resolved. Normal service can be resumed, and the brain's cognitive ease prevails.

You do not have to have limitless confidence or vast experience to get going. These are simple things you can work on as you advance. Just take two minutes and pause to think of something in your life that you had no confidence in or were not very good at initially. Perhaps this was driving a car, playing a musical instrument, your current profession or being a parent. You got better, right? Your confidence grew as you progressed through the journey. Now you are a great driver, an accomplished musician or an understanding parent. You may have been promoted, made a partner or even set up your own business. If the latter is the case, you may have been an excellent employee or technician, but does that make you a good business person? No, you had to work on that, too; it was just the next step in an ever-expanding world of education and experience.

Let us consider driving, a musician, a job or a business. You passed your test, learned the instrument got the promotion decided to open your business because your why was strong enough. You beat the challenge, ignored the dissonance and overcame the fear to the point that confidence prevailed because the outcome was worth it. Well, trust me on this, property investing is worth it, too.

Some fear the journey, but the irony is that the common or pushed belief that we do not need much effort to succeed robs us of the very thing we need to achieve it.

But what if the market crashes? That is my biggest fear

Okay, what if it does? Are you selling your property in this scenario? If not, what does it matter? Rental demand does not crash in tandem with a market crash. Demand and rental charges remain constant. And If you are selling, there is a better than average chance your property has increased significantly since you bought the property. This means that any crash would only have minimal impact. Perhaps the profit you stood to make has been eroded slightly. Most properties more than double in value over a 25-year mortgage, meaning that a market crash of 15% would merely reduce your profit by a surmountable amount.

The last time the property market crashed was after the financial crisis in 2008. Then the average house price in England fell from £188,657 to £159,340, according to Land Registry figures - a drop of 15% in a year.

But a little over a year later, average prices had recovered to £174,765, about 7% lower than two years earlier, which, as you can see, eases negative equity worries for most investors or homeowners.

Final thoughts

Action might have been the 16th law of this book and was considered on many occasions. However, action is something that reverberates through each of my 15 laws. It is a fundamental trait to create and maintain any change within your life and is not mutually exclusive to property investing. It is, however, simply an essential trait.

Action surrounds everything we do; it is not one law but engrained in every law. Without action, you will never succeed. With my hand on my heart, I can honestly say that if I can achieve what I have achieved in my time with property, so can each of you.

I have, or instead, had nothing to offer to get me and keep me going except my ability to take definitive action.

What will you see as you glance back over your shoulder in the next few months? Will you see the starting line some way back on the horizon, or will you be standing next to Dan with your hands in the air, waiting for the solution to fall from the sky?

In twenty years, will you regret your decision to invest, or will you regret never giving it a go?

Only you can decide what your future looks like, and only you can go and get the future you want. It will never fall from the sky, and it will never happen unless you take action. Words, books, training, intent and knowledge are all useless without action. Remember thinking about something or talking about something doesn't make it happen. Only the action makes it happen; this is precisely the reason I have not got a six-pack regardless of the YouTube videos I watched, the fancy abb roller I bought and the flavoured protein powder that now both sit in the garage gathering dust.

Your dream or idea of becoming a property investor can categorically happen from whatever starting position you are in currently, but you must be prepared for the journey. The only thing that will make this a reality is you!

Use what you have learned throughout this book to create momentum. Your property business is there waiting for you, waiting to happen, lying dormant in your future for you to grab it and take action to make it happen. So what is stopping you? Will you make it happen, or will you move straight on to the next self-help masterpiece without viewing the resources that accompany this book?

Get your mindset on point

Before I leave you to reflect on what you have learned and how you will proceed with your subsequent journey, I want you to know that we are all a product of our environment, an outcome of the stories we have told or the narratives we have given ourselves over the years. Some of these may have been the result of unwanted social heredity or be an accumulation of how you have reacted to your past experiences. But remember, you are in full control of how you let this affect your future. Fear and confidence are directly linked to mindset and education, so adopting a growth-based outlook is something you may need to focus heavily on as you advance.

If I can leave you with two statements, it would be these.

Firstly, for every potential investor I have spoken with over the past 17 years who struggled at the beginning of their property journey, the one common denominator was exclusively their mindset. The good news is that you know that now, so you have no excuse. Work on developing your mindset in tandem as you work on developing your concepts and strategies.

Finally, I can honestly say that this industry is open and readily accessible to every one of you. It does not discriminate against levels of academia nor a lack of capital or time; instead, it rewards you handsomely with wealth and freedom, and all it asks for in exchange is respect, applied effort and patience.

•••

I genuinely hope this book was insightful and has helped you to further understand this wonderful industry on a deeper level. If you want it, it is there for you. You simply need to go out and make it happen.

Thank you for reading my thoughts, David Tarn...

Might I ask of you, one small favour. If this book has been of use to you, it would be a huge help and massively appreciated if you were to leave me a positive review.

....

The **resource page** for this book includes over 50 different resources. All resources mentioned in this book, plus more recently added material and helpful links, and further reading and education.

This can be accessed by heading over to the following address:

www.wiseowlpropertytraining.co.uk/15laws

....

If you would like to stay updated with some of the things that go on in my world, as well as receive news, guides and regulation changes, then you can find us on Facebook

'Wise Owl Property' are on Facebook

Your notes

Printed in Great Britain
by Amazon

61670984R00167